SPY!

ALSO BY RICHARD DEACON

The Private Life of Mr Gladstone

Madoc and the Discovery of America

John Dee

William Caxton: The First English Editor

Matthew Hopkins: Witchfinder-General

A History of the British Secret Service

A History of the Russian Secret Service

A History of the Chinese Secret Service

The Israeli Secret Service

The Silent War:
A History of Western Naval Intelligence

The British Connection:
Russia's Manipulation of British Individuals and Institutions

RICHARD DEACON
with Nigel West

SPY!

Additional research by
Bernard Adamczewski
and Linda McCarthy

BRITISH BROADCASTING CORPORATION

This book is published in conjunction with the BBC television series SPY! devised by Allan Prior, produced by Frank Cox; the television scripts were written by Ruth Carter, Hugh Connor, John Elliot and Allan Prior.

Published by the
British Broadcasting Corporation
35 Marylebone High Street
London W1M 4AA

ISBN 0 563 17729 2

First Published 1980

Printed in England
by W & J Mackay Limited, Chatham

Contents

Preface

It is not without some significance that in the jargon of the world of espionage a spy, Intelligence agent, or even a spy-catcher, is referred to as a 'spook'. It is an apt nickname because spies do in many ways resemble ghosts.

Their lives are to some extent ghost-like. Even if they themselves can be seen, their real purpose must remain unseen. And, like ghosts, they often inhabit a kind of twilight world of their own.

In this book we take a look at seven 'spooks', six men and one woman. Each of them has been a central figure of the BBC Television series called 'Spy!'. These dramatised documentary films, most carefully researched for detailed background, provided an admirable combination of entertainment, thrills and accurate reportage. The purpose of this book is to try to fill in some of the inevitable gaps between the programmes and the often lengthy stories that lie behind them. Those who have seen the programmes will almost certainly have questions to pose about why so-and-so did this, or somebody else said that.

So here is an attempt to explore the background to these stories of espionage and to take a closer look at the leading characters, at the same time examining the impact they made on events and people and seeking some clues to their psychological motivation.

All the characters are markedly different from one another – so different that one wonders what they have in common. For my own part I see one vital common factor: though they were not all caught, they all made mistakes. Sorge made a simple yet incredible mistake for a professional: he failed to get rid of written evidence properly. The two British agents at Venlo failed to realise they were being deceived and took no adequate precautions against this. 'Cynthia' once allowed herself to be seduced before she had obtained the Intelligence she wanted from her seducer. 'Tate's' error was that he bathed his foot at a village pump after he parachuted into Britain. Stashinsky's error was to allow himself to be trapped into the role of an assassin, while John Vassall succumbed to blackmail.

All these mistakes differ both in degree and in kind. 'Tate' is perhaps the one man who could possibly argue that he was hardly responsible for his own mistake, as he had been betrayed to the British. After that he served as a double-agent and never made a single false move either with the British or the Germans. But a point worthy of serious consideration is that only those spies who make mistakes are either caught or ever heard of. It poses the question of whether the best spies are those who have never been heard of.

This may seem an academic question and not related to this subject, yet in many respects it is. Undoubtedly throughout history there have been many spies who have neither been caught nor heard of. But the probability is that they were also the dullest of spies whose caution was so great that, even when they retired from the game, either they had nothing exciting to tell, or they shrank from telling it.

'Cynthia' comes very close to being the perfect spy in every respect in this septet, but her daring exploits were such that somebody was almost bound to learn of them in due course. She became a legend in the Service and sooner or later it was inevitable that someone would write about her. Usually, too, the successful spy cannot resist telling his or her story, which was what happened with Cynthia.

In these stories are all types of spy: the superbly professional Sorge, the brilliant amateur who was Cynthia, the double-agent 'Tate', the blackmailed spy Vassall, and the assassin-spy Stashinsky. Three are English, two German, and one each from the USA and Russia. Each depended entirely on the spymasters and controllers behind them, and therefore had a second factor in common, all being manoeuvred like puppets on a string with the possible slight exception of Richard Sorge who seemed, despite the rigidity of the Soviet system, to enjoy something akin to a freelance status. But even he had to have his major plans approved personally by Stalin.

Otherwise the one characteristic one can detect in all of them is that, living dangerously in one way or another all the time, they tended to thrive on excitement. Thrills of all kinds – sexual as well as purely adventurous – were like a drug to all of them. Even John Vassall, who is certainly not a communist, said wistfully when he came out of prison, 'I suppose I do not really want to catch "the last train to Moscow", but at least there would be some guaranteed excitement there. I just know that something would be going on.'

RICHARD DEACON

SPY!

I

Sorge: The Tokyo Ring

'A careful man is a dull man . . . I hate dullness'

RICHARD SORGE

Richard Sorge was, in many respects, a man who delighted in being perverse and frequently contradicting his own precepts. It was not so much that he was all things to all people, but that he delighted in breaking his own rules of conduct.

Undoubtedly he was one of the outstanding spies of modern history. He might even have been a greater spy, or a brilliant spy-master, if all the Intelligence he provided had been believed by his Soviet directors during his lifetime. Efficient, resourceful, imaginative and hard-working, insisting on the strictest discipline from his agents, he eventually came to grief simply by ignoring one of the elementary rules of espionage. A serious intellectual and dedicated communist, he was at the same time a playboy who revelled in parties, hard-drinking and womanising.

'Sorge is all of a piece,' said one of his Russian colleagues, Nagi, an oriental specialist in the secret service world. 'Once he sees his way clear, he goes ahead. For him there is only black and white, there are no shades in between.' This was absolutely true: it was a characteristic in which lay both his strengths and weaknesses. It also explains why the Sorge story has everything – colour, melodrama, love interest, espionage on a vast scale, the exotic East as well as the strife-torn West of the thirties and forties, the game of the double-agent and the appeal of a likeable, if rumbustious character.

Sorge was born in 1895 at Baku, the Caucasian port on the Caspian Sea, the son of a German father and a Russian mother. His parents later moved to Berlin where Sorge was brought up in a prosperous middle-class German household. His father had been an engineer working for a German oil firm in the Caucasus. It is said – but this is purely from Sorge's Soviet biographer, Mayevsky – that Sorge's grandfather had been active in the abortive German revolution of 1848 and was a friend of Marx and Engels. In World War I Sorge joined up as a private in the German Army and was wounded on the Western Front. He had a lengthy spell in hospital and was eventually discharged. It says much for his pertinacity that he re-enlisted in 1916, by which time the authorities were not so particular about disabilities in recruits, and served on the Eastern Front. He was wounded a second time and that was the end of his military career.

Much of the following evidence about the earlier period of Sorge's life comes from his own confession to the Japanese when he was arrested as a spy. As a boy, though relatively popular with his contemporaries and happy at home, he had been nervous and sensitive, even to the extent of having a light burning in his bedroom all night. It was not until he was wounded for the second time that he started to study in real earnest, recalling that many of his fellow soldiers had been doubtful about the whole purpose of the war. Gradually, Sorge began to see war as something debased and futile; the product of a capitalist philosophy. And, of course, in 1914–16, with huge private profits being made out of the sale of death-dealing weapons, it largely was.

While in hospital during the war Sorge had become friendly with a Jewish nurse who was a Marxist intellectual and a member of the German Social Democrat Party. It was this girl who encouraged him to remember his Russian as well as his German roots and to study philosophy as a guide to Marxism. At university after the war he pursued this plan of study resolutely, at Berlin, Kiel and Hamburg. Not only was he won over to Marxism, but he started to win converts among other students. He put this into action by going down to the docks to talk to the workers.

Germany, at the end of World War I, contrasted markedly from her position at the end of World War II. In 1945 Germany suffered total defeat and was wholly occupied by the invading armies of the Allies, and yet, on the other hand, largely through generous American aid, she was able to recover her prosperity much more quickly. But in 1918 one had the paradox of a war that ended in armistice, not in the total defeat of the German armies. It is true that there were signs of revolution which precipitated that armistice, but, despite all the harsh decrees of the Treaty of Versailles, Germany could still claim she had not been defeated in the field. This thought rankled for years and was a factor leading up to World War II; the other factor was that after the armistice in 1918 impossible demands in the way of reparations were made of the German nation. These things caused resentment on the Right and the Left, seeking their expression in the twin cults of fascism and communism. A normally disciplined, hard-working nation was split into rival camps, with a tolerant but far too apathetic body of middle-ground opinion.

By 1919 Sorge had joined the German Communist Party and about the same time he moved from Kiel to Hamburg to complete the final part of his doctoral thesis in political science. He had every chance of being employed as an assistant to a professor of economics at the College of Technology at

Aachen, but Sorge hesitated before accepting because of his commitment to the conspiratorial activities of the Communist Party. Only when the Central Committee of the Party insisted on his taking this post as a cover for illegal work, did he agree to take it on.

Sorge had been tremendously influenced by his mother and, despite the fact that he was educated in Germany, spoke Russian fluently from childhood. He was, in fact, a natural linguist and later learned new languages within a matter of months, including English, French, Japanese and Chinese. No doubt he had already been marked down as a possible recruit for Soviet espionage, as the German Communist Party was closely linked to that of the Soviet Union through the Comintern, the newly-created international organisation which at that time controlled the various communist parties of the world.

While Sorge's own story is certainly confirmable up to the time of his leaving university, from then on it becomes rather more of a cover story. There is, for example, his statement that he wanted to find out more about the conditions of the average worker and that for a period he became a coal miner. It would seem that he worked in the Ruhr mines in 1920 and possibly in mines in the Dutch province of Limburg. The suggestion was that he organised communist cells among the mineworkers.

What is, however, certain is that Sorge was brought into the Soviet espionage network sometime in 1920. One who confirmed this was Ignace Reiss, then one of the chiefs of Russian Intelligence in Europe, who was later liquidated on the orders of Stalin. Reiss was operating in Germany and came into contact with Sorge in the course of his work. Police records of the years 1919–20 show that Sorge had already achieved a reputation for being an agitator among the miners, as well as contributing to a left-wing newspaper, *The Voice of the Mineworkers*, which emanated from the Ruhr town of Solingen. Yet there is still no trace of his having been a member of the German Communist Party in Hamburg, where all such registrations of CP membership were then made.

In May, 1921, Sorge married Christiane, the divorced wife of his former professor at Aachen University. At that time it was apparently the women who made the running rather than Sorge himself. Years later in her book, *My Husband, Richard Sorge*, Christiane stated that Richard was 'never importunate; he did not need to pay court to people. They flocked to him – men and women.' This portrait of the man is also largely confirmed by Ignace Reiss's wife, Elisabeth Poretsky, who was one of his closest friends. She said of him, 'Accounts of Sorge's later activities in the Far East picture this "formidable" secret agent as a hard drinker and a woman chaser, with a wife in Russia, another one, "a schoolteacher", in the United States, and some twenty women around him in Japan. I do not know how many women he knew in Japan, or anything about a Russian wife, unless that was a girl in Moscow who attached herself to him and whom he suspected of having been sent by the NKVD [*Narodnyi Komissariat Vnutrennikh Del*, the People's Commissariat of Internal Affairs, but in effect the Soviet secret police and predecessor of the modern KGB] to watch him. But the "schoolteacher" in the United States was his real wife, Christiane, a distinguished-looking, reddish-blonde German girl whom Sorge met when they were both at university.'

For the next few years Sorge was on probation, being tested out in his varying skills as agitator, recruiter for the Communist Party and gatherer of Intelligence. Having satisfied his superiors in all these things, he was recruited into the Russian Intelligence organisation in 1924–5. First of all he was ordered to resign from the German Communist Party (this would explain a possible erasure of membership in the records). Then he enrolled as an agent of the Comintern and was summoned to Moscow for training.

Christiane had a career of her own and she never seems to have been dragged into her husband's political or other activities. Indeed, she soon faded from his life. Perhaps it was Richard's new job which inevitably threw them apart, but she did not accompany him on many of his missions to other countries. When he moved to the Far East, Christiane was in Britain; when World War II broke out she went to the USA. The only strange thing about their association was how and why Sorge came to marry her. Perhaps it was just another instance of his irresistible itch to escape from dullness.

Sorge's training was thorough, so thorough that it would almost seem that someone in the Soviet hierarchy had regarded him as a man of destiny. He was on probation for three years. Not until 1928 was he admitted as a fully-fledged operative ready for work in foreign territory. The official Bulgarian news agency, BTA, revealed on 30 January, 1971, that the spy instructor who taught Sorge the art of espionage was 'engineer Nikolai Yablin, who lived in a quiet street in the Lozenets district of Sofia and who was publicly known only as a former director of the Bulgarian Radio'. Yablin, who survived his pupil and is still alive, was a Soviet Intelligence officer of high standing prior to and during World War II. He trained many intelligence radio operators from the Soviet Union and other countries, including Max Klausen, who became Sorge's radio operator in Tokyo. Yablin was born in Bulgaria and emigrated to the Soviet Union in 1923. He later became a member of the scientific and technical council of the Red Army Signal Corps.

In many respects Sorge was the first of the few – the very few dedicated communist agents who were assigned to the Comintern and specially chosen because of their background. In Sorge's case the combination of German and Russian backgrounds was of paramount importance because Germany was still the number one target for Soviet infiltration. What impressed the Russians most about their new recruit was his talent for learning languages speedily. On account of this he was given a trial run in Los Angeles, ostensibly to make a report on the Hollywood film industry under the cover of being a German magazine reporter. Russia, one of the first nations of the world to realise the potentials of the film for propaganda purposes, was intent on infiltrating Hollywood.

But this was also a chance for the USSR to set up contacts inside the American film industry. Sorge did all they could wish, linking up with the California branch of the American Communists. All this time he used his own name of Dr Richard Sorge, a German graduate of political science. During the next few years Sorge was posted to Scandinavia, Holland and Britain. In 1929 he stayed at a Bloomsbury boarding house in London. Despite the fact that at this very time the hierarchy of the Soviet Secret Service was insisting that professional agents should keep their contacts with foreign Communist Parties down to a minimum, Sorge was actually given a dual role, carrying out the work of a spy and at the same time establishing contacts with such parties and giving them advice.

Sorge disliked the implications of the dual role, feeling that the risks he ran could easily jeopardise his reputation as a professional agent. He feared that someone who might have remembered him as an openly-avowed communist in Hamburg would eventually recognise him. This was what actually happened in London where he was visited and questioned by Special Branch officers; someone in London had obviously found out his antecedents and the officers demanded to know whether he had ever lived in Hamburg. MI 5 did not believe his denials, so eventually his visit was terminated, more or less by a mutual, tacit understanding. 'England knows more about spies than any other country,' Sorge reported back to Moscow.

When he returned to Moscow Sorge reiterated his warning, stressing that espionage and Party activities were just not compatible with efficiency and that the combination of the two roles was courting disaster. It is probable that, though Sorge's talents were much appreciated in Moscow, some of his superior officers were suspicious of his German ancestry and that the plan to send him to Britain and Scandinavia was an attempt to test his loyalty. Sorge had always been independently minded, though well-disciplined, and he had also been the friend of many agents who were soon to be liquidated under Stalin's purges. Possibly, too, Sorge had scented the dangers to himself if he remained tied to the much-criticised Comintern, for he made an immediate request to be transferred to the Fourth Bureau of the Red Army Staff.

This was a remarkably sagacious move on Sorge's part, as his friend, Ignace Reiss, was already marked down to be killed in Switzerland, and he must have known that under Stalin's purges key agents in Hungary, Austria and other Eastern European countries were already being liquidated by the NKVD. Suddenly, the Comintern and its agents were regarded with suspicion in the Kremlin, partly because of indiscretions and inefficiency, especially in espionage, but also through Stalin's xenophobia. The Fourth Bureau was the Intelligence organisation of the Red Army, primarily concerned with Military Intelligence, but also collecting a great deal of political and economic information. It was an extremely powerful and thoroughly professional organisation, quite independent of the NKVD and the Comintern, and having direct access to the Communist Party leadership in Moscow.

Sorge's request was granted and he later declared: 'The shifting of the leadership of the revolutionary labour movement from the Comintern to the Russian Communist Party can be traced in my own career. All of my activity at first was connected with the Comintern. Later I came to work directly under the Soviet Union. All of my orders came from the Fourth Bureau of the Red Army. The Comintern gave me no orders.'

Had Sorge not joined the Fourth Bureau it is possible that the man who was to become Russia's ablest agent overseas would have been eliminated in the purges of the thirties. His independence of mind, his forthrightness in expressing an opinion would have made it very difficult for him to survive alongside the 'yes-men' of the thirties and forties. But here again one comes up against the extraordinary 'black and white' attitude of Sorge which enabled him to persuade himself to come to heel even in the face of something with which he disagreed.

Sorge's friend, Ignace Reiss, could tolerate Stalinism no longer. He was outraged and revolted by the purges of thousands of Soviet citizens and by the atmosphere of mistrust which permeated the ranks of officialdom whether in the Army or the NKVD, in the Comintern or Stalin's own entourage. So Reiss wrote his letter of protest and paid the penalty by being gunned down in an ambush in Switzerland. But Sorge had the supremely important gift of being able to be totally detached. He shared his friends' doubts about the way the USSR was developing, but he took the view that the preservation of the communist system was what mattered above all else. It was this belief which enabled Sorge to be a professional in every respect.

He was, of course, fortunate to be employed by the Fourth Bureau of the Red Army which had retained something of founder Trotsky's cosmopolitan approach to problems of Intelligence. When he was sent out to the Far East on the instructions of General Berzin, the Red Army's Chief of Intelligence, in 1930, Sorge was delighted with his brief. To a very large extent he was being given a completely free hand, and while his headquarters were based in Shanghai, his instructions were not restrictive. He was allowed to choose his own agents in setting up a spy network which was called 'The China Unit'. His original brief was simply to organise the collection of information on Chiang Kai-shek's growing Nationalist Army, but he went far beyond this, arguing with great prescience that the greatest menace to Russia in the Far East was Japan, due to her preoccupation with military adventures and expansionism.

Immediately after the Russian revolution the Soviet Union, through the Comintern, had concentrated its attention in the Far East almost solely on

China where, it was felt, the situation was ripe for a gradual revolutionary take-over. A great sensation had been caused in September, 1922, when it was reported from Hong Kong that plans for the conclusion of a Sino-Russian-German alliance had been discovered. Dr Sun Yat-sen, then the Chinese leader, established relations with a Soviet diplomatic agent in 1923 after his attempts to reach an understanding with Western capitalists had failed. The link with Russia meant, of course, recognition of the Chinese Communist Party. The USSR's first Comintern delegate to China was Mikhail Borodin, who had previously been in London. It was largely through his efforts that Sun Yat-sen agreed to admit Communists into the ranks of his own Nationalist Party and to accept Soviet aid. The ageing Chinese president had no illusions about the Russian experiment, however, summing up his own attitude by saying: 'The Republic is my child . . . I call for help to England and America. They stand on the bank and jeer at me. There comes a Russian straw. Drowning, I clutch at it. England and America on the bank shout at me on no account to clutch that Russian straw. But they do not help me. . . . I know it is a straw, but better than nothing.'

When Chiang Kai-shek succeeded Sun Yat-sen as head of the Kuomintang, he began to take a tougher line with the Russian 'advisers' to China such as Borodin and Blyukher. In December, 1928, there had been an attempt by the Chinese Communists, inspired by the Russians, to take over Canton. The Nationalist Chinese counter-attacked and not only killed three-quarters of the Russian Embassy staff, but seized documents from the Embassy. By that time Borodin had left China and it could then be said that the progress of communism of the Russian type had been halted in China, Chiang being firmly in command with his Nationalist forces and even Mao Tse-tung's Communist Party being wary of Moscow.

This was the situation into which Sorge was precipitated and he found it a depressing one from the Soviet viewpoint. Given a list of existing agents in the Far East, he discarded most of the names on it when he set up his headquarters in Shanghai. He also laid it down that the primary task of The Unit was to obtain Intelligence on Japan and that espionage concerning China was of secondary importance. This was a remarkably bold step for any Soviet agent to take in that particular period when Japanese expansionist plans were not fully appreciated.

While Sorge, with his forward-looking mind, detected Japan as the real target, the USSR had good reason to be worried about China at this time. For, as Madame Chiang Kai-shek herself put it, in 1926, 'the revolutionary [Chinese] Nationalist movement under the Kuomintang formally broke away from the talons of Soviet Russia in her aim to vassalise China'.

In Shanghai Sorge's cover was that of correspondent for *Soziologische Magazin* (The Sociological Magazine) and he immediately set about building up an extensive network covering Canton, Nanking, Hangchow, Peking and even Manchuria. Meanwhile he not only began mastering both the Chinese and Japanese languages, but spent long hours studying the politics and literature of each country. The last point is of special interest: Sorge always took the view that one could best understand any country and be able to talk to any of its natives with ease and confidence, if one knew its art and literature. He was not merely a conscientious agent, but a good director of Intelligence with a flair for selecting the right type of contact. He seems to have avoided using Russians, but to have employed a number of Americans, Germans, Japanese and Chinese. His radio operator was a German named Weingart and some of his most trusted agents were Americans, of whom there were a number in China at this time. Many of them had strong pro-Soviet views, largely created out of their dislike of what they had seen of the imperialism of the big European powers in China.

Sorge had been fortunate in that the man who recruited him into the Fourth Bureau had been the redoubtable General Jan Berzin, not only a competent and imaginative Intelligence officer who had had personal experience of clandestine missions abroad, but whose military experience enabled him to grasp what was essential in the field of Intelligence. For these reasons he allowed Sorge considerable latitude. But the truth was that in the Far East, Soviet intelligence had broken down: both in China and Japan it had been largely conducted by incompetent operators. Berzin had begun to realise this and Sorge confirmed it. But it was Sorge who survived and improved Far Eastern intelligence, while the able but luckless Berzin paid the penalty for failure by being executed on Stalin's orders.

When he arrived in China (he and Weingart had both travelled on German passports in their own names), Sorge used the prefix 'Doctor' in making contacts. Part of his cover story was that he wanted to write a series of articles on agricultural conditions in China. What better method of ascertaining the progress of and motives behind Mao Tse-tung's agrarian revolution plans? At this time he took no precautions to conceal his left-wing opinions. Indeed, in order to seek out the right kind of agent, he needed to win left-wing sympathies among his contacts. Perhaps he still had the feeling that the NKVD were shadowing him and that he must remove all reservations about his Comintern past at a time when all their agents were mistrusted in Moscow. But he decided early on that, with the China Unit entirely in his hands, he would eliminate the Russians already working there. This was one way to ensure that no Russian in China would be sending back reports on him to Moscow. Six months after he went to Shanghai his Russian chief in China was recalled at Sorge's request and from then onwards he was to all intents and purposes Resident Director in the Far East.

One of the Americans who worked closely with him over a long period was Miss Agnes Smedley, a communist sympathiser who arranged for her apartment to be used as a base for the network's secret radio. Agnes

Smedley, whose writings on China had attracted wide sympathy in liberal circles, also supplied Sorge with a number of Chinese and Japanese contacts, of whom perhaps the most notable was Ozaki Hozumi, a graduate of Tokyo University, who came from a wealthy family, and later became Sorge's most trusted assistant. Ozaki Hozumi worked as a journalist after he left university and, though he never joined the Communist Party, his sympathies in that direction were discernible in his early twenties. In 1927 he went to Shanghai as correspondent of the celebrated Tokyo newspaper, *Asahi Shimbun*. He only spent three years in that city, but during this time maintained close links with Sorge.

About this time Sorge changed his name for a short period and adopted the identity of William Johnson, an American journalist. It was not until six years later that Ozaki Hozumi discovered who 'William Johnson' really was, despite the fact that they had been working closely together. While in Shanghai he never knew for certain whether Agnes Smedley or 'Johnson' was the head of the network.

So well organised was Sorge's China Unit that even the most diligent inquiries by the Americans and others after the war failed to find out the names of all its members. Major-General Charles A. Willoughby, General MacArthur's chief of intelligence, stated in his book *Shanghai Conspiracy*, 'Sorge became head of the ring whose headquarters were at Shanghai but which covered most of China, being especially active in Hangchow, Nanking, Canton, Hankow, Kaifeng, Hsian, Peiping, and Manchuria . . . we know the names of sixteen of them, but probably there were more. Three principles which guided them are noteworthy: (1) while the group was highly cosmopolitan there seems not to have been a Russian among them; (2) while every member of the group was either a Communist Party member or a strong sympathiser, they avoided association with the Chinese Communist Party; (3) they did not function as a group and few of the members knew who the others were, or were even aware of their precise mission.'

The last precept was the most important of all. Sometimes it was important that an agent did not know exactly who he was working for – the Soviet Union, the Americans, undercover Japanese Liberals, Chinese Communists or even Nationalists. Thus Agnes Smedley, for example, went to great lengths to pretend that Chinese communism had nothing whatsoever in common with Soviet communism, even though she was working for the Russians.

In 1932 Ozaki Hozumi returned to Japan to set about extending the Soviet network in that country, closely following Sorge's instructions that any communist who was recruited into the ring must give up active membership of the party. One thing saddened him: on Sorge's orders he was told he must not see or correspond with Agnes Smedley again. If the Japanese secret police became aware of their friendship, warned Sorge, the whole network inside Japan might be endangered.

By the latter end of the thirties, Soviet Russia had by far the most efficient secret service of any of the powers in the Far East. The Americans lacked experienced operators and men knowledgeable about the politics of the area, and this was not rectified until after Pearl Harbor. Even their Intelligence officers, although they had heard all about Mao Tse-tung's celebrated 'Long March' two thousand miles into the remote fastness of Shenshi province, tended to believe the Chinese Communist Party was simply an agrarian organisation aiming to give the peasants a square deal. British Intelligence, which had at one time been good in the Far East, was now not much better. Ex-British Army officers who had had first-hand experience of the Japanese Army, had frequently sent back to London reports warning the authorities not to underrate Japanese military ability. These were completely ignored and Whitehall continued to employ fifth-rate spies in Japan.

Yet the Russian success was due almost entirely to Richard Sorge and his cosmopolitan mind. Before he arrived on the scene Russia had relied to some extent on the Tass (the official Russian news agency) correspondents in Japan. Captain Malcolm D. Kennedy, a British resident in Japan at that time, referring to three successive Tass correspondents in Tokyo, has this to say: 'Unlike his predecessor Slapec, whom he had succeeded as Tass correspondent a year or so previously, Romm was a well-trained and highly intelligent journalist. It seemed extraordinary therefore that, when Soviet hopes and wishes conflicted with rational reasoning, he always tended to give priority to the former in his assessment of any particular situation by believing what he wished to believe. During my years as a foreign correspondent in Japan, I came to know him and Nagi, his successor, well, and I developed a real liking for both of them. But time and again I was struck by the curious dichotomy in the reasoning of these two extremely intelligent, well-informed and likeable men. Slapec, Romm's predecessor, on the other hand, was a very different type, a slimy, shifty little creature who seemed more fitted for the role of a communist agitator than that of a foreign correspondent.'

Both Romm and Nagi were liquidated during the Soviet purges of the thirties. No doubt they paid the penalty for supplying the kind of Intelligence which Moscow wished to hear rather than what it needed to know. Colonel Rink, the Soviet military attaché in Tokyo, had taken the view that the Japanese military standards were far lower than had previously been imagined, and Golkovich, the local NKVD agent, took the view that Japan posed no real threat to the USSR. It must have come as a shock to Russia to learn that the Japanese military machine was very efficient indeed, when Sorge started sending in his own independent bulletins. He must have put in some extremely critical reports on Rink and Golkovich, who were also liquidated in the purges of 1937. The international situation was now changing rapidly and it was clear to such a cosmopolitan as Sorge that

Germany was turning from her traditional friendship with China in favour of an alliance with Japan. This posed a danger to Russia on two fronts – the east and the west.

From various sources – records captured by the Americans, Sorge's own confession and statement to the Japanese, and from German friends of Sorge who knew of his involvement with the USSR – it is possible to build up a picture of the reports he made to the Russians at this time. He warned that Japan would attack wherever the great powers were weakest and that Russia needed to build up her defences in the east. He also forecast that sooner or later Japan would strike a blow against the British Empire and that the British were far too complacent about their defences in the Far East. 'Singapore,' reported Sorge to Gunter Stein, one of his informants, 'is a symbol of British unpreparedness. It is not a citadel, but an open invitation to an adventurous invader and can be taken with comparatively small casualties in less than three days.'

On the strength of these reports Sorge was recalled to Moscow for urgent talks. Both the Fourth Bureau and the NKVD took joint action to improve still further their Far Eastern Intelligence system. From Sorge's point of view the important factor was that the direction of this Intelligence continued to come under the Red Army.

'The struggle against fascism, against a second world war, became the purpose of Sorge's life,' wrote his Russian biographer, Mayevsky. Though this is an official Soviet view, it is also the truth. Those who knew him best (and few could claim to know Sorge well) always felt that he was more anti-fascist than a communist fanatic. Even though he possessed a typically German obedience to authority – i.e. the Party – he was by temperament something of a rebel and certainly critical of many aspects of Stalinism. What saved him from being purged along with Ignace Reiss and his other dissident friends was not simply his excellent relationship with the Fourth Bureau, but his audacity. Stalin admired audacity when it was a question of someone else risking his life for the Soviet Union.

And Sorge had just such a plan. Having been highly praised for his work in China, he had been urged by the Fourth Bureau to devote all his efforts to obtaining intelligence from inside Japan. 'It is not merely incidental intelligence we want,' he was told, 'but top secret information. Russia must not merely know what Japan is doing now, but what she plans to do in three years time.' There was a belated realisation in the Kremlin that Japan's expansionist dreams might extend to Russia herself. Sorge's answer to this was a proposal that was almost the quintessence of madness at a time when Stalin was seeing traitors in every corner of the USSR. He suggested that he should return to Germany and establish contacts with the leading Nazis. Then he would aim to join the ranks of the Gestapo, or some other powerful German agency and, in this guise, go to Japan as a Soviet spy inside the German camp.

If Sorge's scheme failed, he ran the risk of being tortured and executed by the Nazis; if he succeeded, there was always the chance of his being dubbed a traitorous double-agent by someone in the Politburo hierarchy. Even the chiefs of the Fourth Bureau were so alarmed at the possible consequences to them if anything went wrong with the Sorge project that it was considered unwise to agree to it without consulting Stalin first. The Soviet leader is said to have nodded silent approval and so in May, 1933, Sorge set out for Berlin.

Elisabeth Poretsky gives an interesting commentary on Sorge in this period: she has said that he 'could not be bothered with safety and the little details that were essential to such work' and that 'his joining the Nazi Party in his own country where he had a well-documented police record was hazardous, to say the least, even if, as some people think, he had protection from high up in the Party itself. And his staying in the very lion's den in Berlin, while his application for membership was being processed, was indeed flirting with death. Such actions were typical of . . . his superb self-assurance.'

Possibly Sorge got away with his dangerous charade because of his strong personality and extrovert behaviour. He was outgoing in every sense of the word and his purposeful, somewhat cynical and quizzical face blended naturally into the beer garden atmosphere of Berlin. 'He looked one straight in the eye,' said Franz Hoffman, a German who knew him in this period. 'He made *you* feel guilty. One did not entertain suspicions about him. His was very much a questioning face, almost that of a Gestapo man.'

Yet even this statement only gives a picture of one side of Sorge. He was not a quick-change artist in espionage such as Sir Paul Dukes who used as many as half a dozen disguises when spying inside Russia during the Civil War of 1918–20. In many respects Sorge was more careful to protect his own agents than himself, thus inspiring great confidence in his leadership. Left to himself he would sometimes take incredible risks that were totally alien to one of his profession. He was sad when he guessed correctly that his recruiter, Berzin, had been liquidated, but he never allowed the deaths of his friends or the outrages perpetuated in the name of Stalin to sway him from his belief in the ultimate triumph of 'the system' and the survival of the Soviet Union. He had complete faith in Stalin as the one man able to control and direct the juggernaut that was the Russian people. A brilliant agent, he was more of an ardent patriot than a professional spy, a lover of life who still had about him something of the aura of the martyr. But he was modest enough to confide in his closest agents that 'I only survive in this game because I can out-drink all the others and hold my tongue when they are loosening theirs. It is my strong stomach not my brain which keeps me alive.'

Once he acquired membership of the Nazi Party Sorge was relatively safe from further German probes into his background. Perhaps it was his charm which misled the Nazis, but it is astonishing that the Gestapo failed to find anything wrong in his faked documents and did not discover that he had been a member of the German Communist Party years before. Soon he was not only on the staff of the *Frankfurter Zeitung*, a German newspaper with a world-wide reputation, but attending parties at which the top executives of the Nazi Party were present. It was even whispered that he was a friend of Heinrich Himmler, chief of the Gestapo.

The next stage in Sorge's plan was to go to Tokyo as a foreign correspondent and there to ingratiate himself with the German Embassy personnel and Japanese Army officers. Just before he left Berlin, the Nazi Press Club gave a dinner in his honour, attended by Goebbels himself. Once in the Japanese capital he lost little time in building up an espionage ring which was perhaps even more effective than his China Unit. The key people in this ring, apart from Ozaki Hozumi, already mentioned (his code-name was 'Otto'), were Max Klausen, the former German communist and radio operator whose cover was that of a German businessman accepting orders from Japan (code-name 'Fritz'); Branko de Voukelitch ('Gigolo'), a former Yugoslav Army officer who was Tokyo correspondent for the French *La Vue*; and Miyagi Yotoku ('Joe'), who had spent some time in the USA and Okinawa, and whose pose was that of a Japanese artist who was earning a modest living in his native country. So thorough was Sorge in trying to protect his network that he made a point of regularly scrutinising the 'cover' stories of all members of his ring and ascertaining that they were living up to them in every detail and not creating any discrepancies in their mode of living. He swiftly discovered that the ubiquitous Japanese secret military police, the Kempeitai, lost no time in unobtrusively investigating every foreign newcomer to Tokyo. His training had enabled him to detect that his luggage had been searched in his hotel room shortly after he arrived in Japan.

Sorge (code-name 'Ramsey') confined his role to general supervision of the ring and maintaining his official German and Japanese contacts. Ozaki was responsible for top-level Japanese reports, while Voukelitch concentrated on American, British and French official circles. Miyagi kept a watch on Japanese Army and Navy programmes as well as armaments and industrial production, while Klausen, as well as being radio operator, was also encouraged to report on Japanese external trade.

Though he made no secret of his close links with both the German Embassy and Japanese Army circles, Sorge never overplayed his role as a member of the Nazi Party. Just as his charm had misled the Nazis in Berlin so in Tokyo he was still able to make friendly contacts with resident Britons. Captain Malcolm Kennedy found him 'a pleasantly quiet, intelligent sort of chap. I little suspected his true role.' Richard Hughes, the London *Sunday Times* correspondent in the Far East for many years, met Sorge when he was head of the Australian Consolidated Press Bureau in Tokyo in 1940 and recalls that he was always good company and something of a charmer. At their very first meeting Sorge intervened to protect Hughes from a punch-up in a bar patronised by Nazis. 'He steered clear of the foreign press as a general rule,' says Hughes, 'and we all accepted him as almost a caricature of the true Nazi believer.'

His closest confidant in the German ranks was Lieutenant-Colonel Eugen Ott, an artillery expert attached to the Japanese Army. Ott and Sorge had one special bond: they had served in the same regiment in the First World War in which the latter had been awarded the Iron Cross (second class). It was on this kind of basis of friendship that Ott, when he was military attaché in Tokyo, would sometimes give Sorge a coded despatch from Berlin and ask for his help in decoding. As this type of Intelligence came his way with increasing frequency, Sorge had greater need of using radio communication with Russia via the Soviet station at Vladivostok. Later Ott became a major-general and succeeded Dr Herbert von Dirksen as German ambassador in Japan. Ott had such trust in Sorge that he sometimes showed him copies of secret reports he sent to Berlin, details of which Sorge passed back to Russia.

At the same time Sorge joined the German Club in Tokyo and generally conducted himself as a fervent believer in the Third Reich, but with sufficient good manners and lack of arrogance to make himself agreeable to a wide range of acquaintances. He was even careful to choose a house which would correspond with the kind of salary he would have as a journalist. It was unostentatious, a two-storey wooden house in a middle-class neighbourhood, Number 30, Nagasakimachi, Azabu-ku, Tokyo. Here Sorge started to give parties: his domain was a Bohemian island in an ocean of respectability.

This undoubtedly drew attention to Sorge, but it suited his tactics. He worked on the principle that there are two types of top-level efficient spies: the first is the quiet, unobtrusive, meek and mild agent who will go unnoticed (admirable for a long-term spy who has been planted in a key ministry, say); the second is the flamboyant, noisy spy who attracts so much attention that nobody can believe he is a spy. In fact, over a very long period Sorge was a combination of both these types, which probably made him exceptional. In the early days he urgently needed to keep in constant touch with the network, partly for reasons of ensuring security and checking on their methods, but also because Russia was demanding quick results. So his method of cover was to stage large and noisy parties at his home. Whenever he wanted to see his chief agents, men like Ozaki, Voukelitch and Klausen, he gave a party in the most flamboyant manner, inviting geisha girls along to entertain the guests as well as many people who were totally ignorant of Sorge's real activities. The noise of these goings-on was alone guaranteed to attract the attention of the secret police, but they would naturally never believe that anything of a clandestine nature could be carried on at so blatantly orgiastic a gathering. What the Kempeitai agents failed to notice was that long after the geishas and other guests had gone, Sorge's key agents remained behind until dawn. It was in the early hours of the morning that plans were discussed and information exchanged.

Drink and women were Sorge's methods of baffling the Japanese secret police. He realised that what he appeared to do in his spare time was what they would be most interested in. And if they merely reported that he indulged in drinking bouts and wild parties and that he changed mistresses like another man changed his suits, nobody would begin to suspect he was a spy. And, of course, his links with the German Embassy gave the impression that he was pro-Japanese.

These bold tactics of Sorge were largely justified by the fact that, with war approaching, quick results of top Intelligence were needed. But the more demanding Intelligence chiefs are for top secret information the graver the risks for the spy. And so, while Sorge's deception of noisy parties proved effective for a long time, it ceased to be valid when the Kempeitai stepped up their watch on him. A counter-espionage organisation will concentrate on a man's weaknesses and it was for this reason that the secret police eventually planted a female spy on Sorge. What is puzzling is whether ultimately Sorge had a kind of death wish and adopted a totally fatalistic attitude, or whether he became too confident that he could baffle the Japanese. The latter attitude seems unlikely because Sorge had a talent for self-criticism and also he was aware that he had been constantly watched by the Japanese secret police despite all his pro-German links. His maid and laundryman were often questioned by the police and his house was searched while he was away on a visit to China. It required a strong nerve to operate under these conditions and the only clue one has is that Sorge told some of his confederates that the Japanese police were too interested in little things and not sufficiently alert to the more important aspects of counter-espionage.

Eventually Sorge's friendship with Ott secured for him the post of press attaché in the German Embassy. Each morning at breakfast Sorge would regale the German Ambassador with gossip and information about Japanese affairs and in return the latter would tell him all manner of things about his own relations with the Japanese. Often, almost under the nose of the Gestapo agent in the Embassy, Colonel Meissinger, Sorge would photograph documents with his pocket camera.

When he was ultimately captured by the Japanese, Sorge listed in his confession those subjects on which the Fourth Bureau had asked him to concentrate. They were: (1) Japan's policy towards Russia following the invasion of Manchuria. To ascertain whether Japan intended to attack the Soviet Union; (2) the battle order of the Japanese Army and Air Force and organisational details of both services (much less attention was paid to the Japanese Navy); (3) Japan's policy towards China and her activity there; (4)

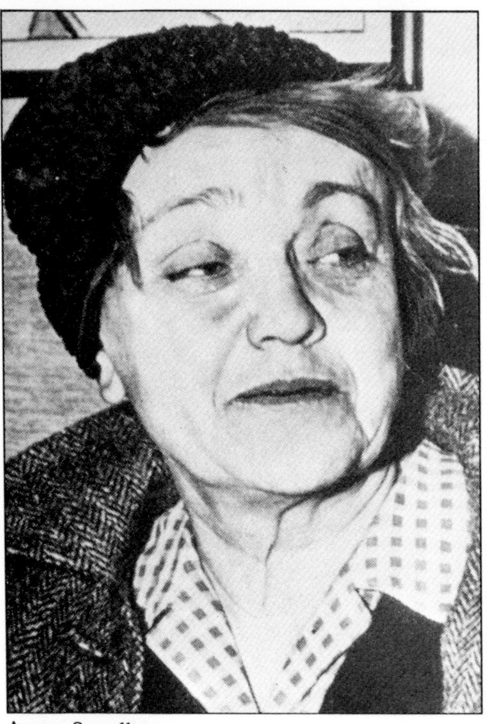

Agnes Smedley

Sorge, in the garden of his bungalow

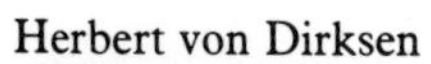

Herbert von Dirksen

Prince Konoye

Hirohito, Emperor of Japan

Major-General Ott in adopted Japanese dress

Miyake Hanako with a bust of Sorge

Miyake Hanako at Sorge's grave

Japan's relations with the USA and Britain and the possibility of her waging war on either; (5) the influence of the Japanese war lords on the purely political front; (6) all intelligence and details of operations and movements in Manchuria.

It can be seen from this that Sorge was not merely a collector of information, but an analyser and an evaluator as well. It was his duty to assess the evidence, to sum it up and to make the correct deductions as well. Although he avoided close contact with most of the other foreign correspondents in Tokyo, he kept his lines open to include contacts with Britons, Americans, Dutch and French, often giving away some titbit of information in order to get a reaction to it. Sometimes the reactions enabled him to change his assessments and even to rewrite his reports. Some of these were sent by radio, some by microfilm to Shanghai.

Sorge always maintained that his job as a writer for newspapers and magazines helped him enormously in his quest for intelligence. 'A shrewd spy,' he declared in a confessional statement, 'will not spend all his time on the collection of military and political secrets and classified documents. Also, I may add, reliable information cannot be procured by effort alone; espionage work entails the accumulation of information, often fragmentary, covering a broad field, and the drawing of conclusions based thereon. This means that a spy in Japan, for example, must study Japanese history and the racial characteristics of the people and orient himself thoroughly on Japan's politics, society, economics and culture. . . . Similarly, contacts with foreigners are essential.'

That he practised what he preached was evident from the discovery by the Japanese secret police of something approaching two thousand books on all aspects of Japanese life found at his home after his arrest.

Curiously enough, Sorge, the reputedly great womaniser, considered that women generally were unfit for espionage work and even went so far as to assert that he 'never received satisfactory information from any of them'. This may have been true as regards Japan, but even Sorge had to make one exception – Agnes Smedley. He said of her that she had 'a good educational background and a brilliant mind, but as a wife her value was nil. In short, she was like a man. I might add that cultivation of intimate relations with married women for purposes of espionage will arouse the jealousy of their husbands and hence react to the detriment of the cause.'

Sorge's first major coup was obtained for him by Ozaki, the principal and most valuable of all his informants. A special report on Japan's economic problems and political plans for 1936 was prepared by the Japanese Foreign Minister, and Ozaki, who was a counsellor of the Japanese Government, was shown the papers and asked to give his opinion on those sections that related to China. Ozaki, regarded as an authority on Chinese affairs, was trusted absolutely by the Japanese Cabinet. He photographed the whole report and, as a result, Sorge was able to radio back to Moscow that Japan had no plans

OPPOSITE Japanese troops enter Manchuria

for an attack on Russia in the immediate future and that the invasion of South China depended on how soon the Japanese could get their factories in Manchuria into full production.

When Japan's drive into China was slowed down, Ozaki was made unofficial adviser on China to the Japanese Cabinet. He held this post until the fall of the Prince Konoye Cabinet in 1939 and was then made adviser to the South Manchurian Railway, a post which enabled him to retain links with the new Cabinet as well as putting him in an excellent position to furnish further Intelligence to Sorge. But the really vital work carried out by Sorge and Ozaki was during the Konoye Cabinet period when it seems possible that through contacts with the Prince and his entourage they may even have influenced the slowing down of the China campaign and the decision not to attack in Siberia.

In 1939 Sorge warned Moscow that the German invasion of Poland was scheduled for 1 September. Again in April, 1941, he reported that 150 German divisions were being concentrated on the Soviet border and gave a general résumé of Hitler's war plans. In a subsequent message he even spelt out the exact date of the invasion – 22 June. Mayevsky states: 'Analogous information reached Moscow through other channels. But Stalin disregarded it. How many thousands and millions of lives might have been saved had the information from Richard Sorge and others not been sealed up in a safe! Alas, we paid in full for this mistrust and disregard of people which was an inseparable part of the personality cult.' One must remember that Mayevsky wrote this in 1964 when de-Stalinisation was still in fashion, but the validity of what he asserts is evident when one recalls the British Secret Service warnings which were passed on to Moscow at the same time and equally ignored.

Throughout the summer of 1941 Russia was desperately fighting for survival as the Nazi armies poured across the steppes, drawing ever closer to Moscow. It was vital for Sorge to ascertain what Japan would do and how many troops from the eastern front the Soviet Union could safely withdraw and switch to meet the threat in the west. His information was that the Japanese would honour their 1940 neutrality pact with the USSR while they planned for an attack against the Philippines: this certainly helped the Russians to deploy more troops in the west even though Stalin's naturally doubting mind was suspicious of the original intelligence.

There seems to be no doubt that Moscow was now pressing Sorge for harder information and that he had to take greater risks than he would have done normally. In peacetime it is possible for a spy to be ultra-cautious and to wait for results, keeping a low profile and occasionally seeing his contacts as unobtrusively as possible. In wartime not only is frequent contact essential, but with speed of communication being critical, greater risks have to be taken. Communications had always been a problem, as Sorge realised full well that Japan had made astonishing progress both in developing new methods of secret transmission and in deciphering other nations' hush-hush traffic. For this reason he insisted on Klausen moving his radio set after each transmission. Klausen had built a radio transmitter and receiver which could operate over a range of approximately three thousand miles, but compact enough to be easily portable. The code employed was changed monthly, but Sorge insisted that only the most urgent information was to be radioed to Moscow; the rest of their material was to be passed by couriers. The Fourth Bureau arranged the courier system, which was usually very much of a slow process, via Shanghai or Hong Kong. By the summer of 1941 Inspector Osashi, of the secret police, as well as officers of the Kempeitai, became certain that a major foreign spy ring was operating in Tokyo. At this stage they were not sure whether it was an American, a British or a Soviet network. Japanese radio-detectors reported that they had suspected the presence of an illegal radio transmitter somewhere in the Tokyo area, but that they had been unable to trace transmissions to an area of less than two kilometres. Klausen noticed about this time that a radio detector van was parked near his apartment and he had to report to Sorge about inexplicable casual visits from an 'electrician' and a man who said he must have been given the wrong address. It was soon obvious that Sorge himself was being investigated and watched.

Knowing that a surprise search of the apartments of any one of the ring might reveal something, Sorge urged a further precaution apart from moving the transmitter set frequently. He hired a fishing-boat and ordered the set to be placed there when transmissions to Russia were necessary. Japanese counter-intelligence was always very alert and the Kempeitai were ready to follow up the slenderest clues with enthusiasm. Sorge knew in his heart that the ring had achieved great things, but that its luck could not hold much longer. Common sense might have decreed that the wisest plan would have been to close down the ring, allowing an interval of inactivity before starting up again with new personnel, and for Sorge to have left the country.

But luck is something which tends to destroy those it blesses. It is remarkable how many people to whom the nickname 'Lucky' has been given have suddenly been faced with disaster, when it is least expected. Sorge may have been too confident, for he was certainly lucky over a long period. Not long after he arrived in Tokyo he foolishly employed a Japanese woman who had been a cook at the Soviet Embassy there. This could have been a fatal error. Then in 1938 he was involved in a motor-cycling accident. He had driven his motor cycle much too fast, an error a professional spy should never have committed. Taken to hospital without losing consciousness, he had the presence of mind to send a message to Klausen to come to him immediately.

Klausen had no doubt why he had been summoned to the hospital. He was shown into the room where Sorge was lying and, without any exchange of pleasantries, he just asked, 'Where is it?' With an effort, Sorge gestured towards his coat. Max Klausen swiftly ran his hands through the pockets, found an envelope containing secret messages and American dollars (strictly forbidden currency in Japan). He pocketed this and hastily left the hospital. He said afterwards that 'as if he was relieved to know that his one great fear was removed, Sorge fainted. I went straight to his house to remove all papers relating to our work, even taking his diary.'

Within a few minutes of Klausen's departure from the hospital two uniformed Kempeitai officers arrived to make inquiries.

Sorge was extremely fortunate, too, in his relationship with the Otts. True, he had to handle Frau Ott, whom he laughingly called 'Auntie', rather tactfully. She would sometimes chide him on his drinking and womanising. It should be stressed that Sorge's Intelligence traffic was by no means all one way. He trod most delicately and shrewdly the devious path of the double agent, though he was not of course engaged by the Germans as such. He was held in high regard at the German Embassy simply because he was able to pass information on to them and to use his contacts to make inquiries on their behalf. Naturally, the Intelligence he gave the Germans was such as not to harm Soviet interests, though after the German invasion of Russia that became much more difficult. Nevertheless, despite his warm friendship with Ott, Sorge never felt too easy with the resident Gestapo officer keeping a watch on him. To dispel Gestapo suspicions, which could very easily be aroused if only because of their contempt for diplomats, he needed to acquire a reputation for being a valuable informant. Sometimes he took great pleasure in sending the Gestapo man on some false errand of inquiry. At the same time he had to ensure that the information he gave Ott was reliable and relatively valuable. In return Ott would allow Sorge to see certain highly confidential German documents.

These he surreptitiously photographed whenever possible with a specially designed flash camera made for him in Moscow. This could be fitted into a match-box. Often it was a question of split-second timing to take a quick picture in the very few moments when nobody else would be looking. One fascinating sidelight of Soviet espionage within the Sorge ring (and this also sometimes applied to other Russian networks) was that on Sorge's instructions all documents in Japanese were to be translated into English. Miyagi was responsible for these translations. Here Sorge's Teutonic thoroughness in studying the language and literature of the nation in which he was spying stood him in good stead. To translate Japanese into another language is to risk a distortion of its original meaning and Sorge realised that only a native Japanese who not only thoroughly understood the language into which he was translating, but had received an education overseas in this language, could overcome this hazard. Miyagi was such a man and English was the other language in which he was fluent. In this way Sorge believed he could best evaluate Japanese documents for transmission to Moscow, translating his own summaries into Russian.

Ott sometimes used Sorge as a courier for German dispatches to Hong Kong and elsewhere so that he was able to pass on documents to Soviet Union agents at the same time. Again, Sorge was lucky in that the task of deciphering Japanese coded messages was relatively simple because, as the Japanese alphabet consists of more than fifty letters and two thousand hieroglyphics, they sent their codes in Roman letters. The Americans could equally have deciphered much of this Japanese code traffic with ease, but their fault lay in incompetent interpretation of some messages, gross negligence and a lack of political acumen. Sorge, on the other hand, knew from personal experience and from the wisdom of Ozaki exactly what such messages implied.

Usually keeping discreetly in the background was one faithful and solitary Japanese woman who worshipped Sorge. Sometimes she was to be seen, dressed in traditional Japanese clothes, at one of Sorge's noisy parties, mingling with blonde fräuleins, diplomats, businessmen, Bohemians and Japanese artists. This was Miyake Hanako, a quiet, serious girl who was young, intelligent, beautiful and with liberal sympathies. Absolutely devoted to Sorge, she still insists today that she was registered as his common-law wife. They met when she was working as a waitress and seem very quickly to have established an easy, tolerant and happy relationship, though it was to be some time before Hanako agreed to become Sorge's mistress.

Miyake Hanako had been expelled from high school for alleged radical tendencies and activities. Perhaps this encouraged Sorge to trust her above all other women in Tokyo, for, while he never let her into the secret of his Intelligence work, he seems to have confided in her about his private dislike of Japanese militarism and Nazism. She, too, suspected that he was engaged in some kind of secret work.

It was remarkable how Sorge trusted her implicitly to such a large extent; equally remarkable was the fact that the Kempeitai never succeeded in using her to trap Sorge. Hanako did not move into Sorge's house, but she occasionally stayed there and sometimes they spent brief holidays together at a seaside resort outside Tokyo. Though she was deeply in love with him, she neither resented his mistresses, nor objected to being told to leave his house when a party was drawing to an end. 'It did not seem unnatural to me for him to have other women,' said Hanako years later. 'I always thought they had something to do with his work, and anyhow important men always have a lot of women around them.' She had some talent as a singer and Sorge encouraged her in this and arranged for her to have lessons from a German music teacher.

There was another factor in Sorge's conduct in his last two years, that perhaps increased his tendency to take risks. Miyake Hanako has since told that she recalls one moment when his mood became one of deepest depression and he felt very much alone in the world and this was when the

Germans attacked Russia. That single incident caused him to feel that he was a man of destiny, that he must risk all to save Mother.

So the radio traffic with the USSR was stepped up and the tempo of Sorge's parties became more hectic. In the small hours of the morning the laughter of the geisha girls was punctuated by the breaking of glass as well as the clinking of glasses. But when the last guest and geisha had gone, often with Sorge propelling a reeling Japanese officer down the steps, this indefatigable spy was still sober beneath his mask of revelry and so, if they happened to be present, were his agents. Only then did they get down to their briefing sessions and discussing tactics, invariably with the gramophone left playing to deceive the neighbours.

In the early autumn of 1941 it was clear that the spy ring was in danger of being discovered by the Japanese. The other members of the ring were becoming extremely anxious and it says much for Sorge's powers of leadership and his refusal to panic that he held them together. He was under pressure from Moscow to provide more detailed information on Japanese intentions towards Siberia (Stalin was still reluctant to believe that there would not be an attack on this front). But more importantly Sorge himself, taking the long view, wanted to ascertain the exact date and place from which the Japanese would launch their attack on the Americans.

About this time Mikaye Hanako was summoned to the police station and questioned. Nothing of any value was learned from her, but she was advised to keep away from Sorge. Naturally, she told him what the police had said. At that stage it was almost as though the Japanese were trying to warn Sorge through his girl friend.

While waiting to obtain confirmation of his strong suspicion that Japan would shortly attack Britain and the USA in the Far East, for which he depended on Ozaki, Sorge conducted a liaison with a Japanese girl he had only just met. He was elated because Ozaki had informed him that so far the Japanese had resisted German pressure for them also to attack the USSR.

It had been Sorge's passion for finding new girls that provided Inspector Osashi with the perfect excuse for meeting the German in the Fuji nightclub in Tokyo. Over a fairly lengthy period the inspector and the spy had become congenial drinking companions. One night – probably early in October, 1941 – while the two men were drinking together, Osashi casually mentioned that one of the loveliest girls in Tokyo was a rice-dancer at the Fuji Club.

'The lights went down,' said Sorge afterwards, '. . . and she came on with her face hidden beneath a mask of the ancient Japanese God of Rice, Ugaki. But her figure compensated for the mask. It was one of the loveliest shapes I had ever seen . . . I bombarded Osashi with questions about her. He told me her name was Kiyomi and that she was the daughter of a rich and influential Japanese.'

Thus Osashi set his trap. Yet by this time the secret police were hot on the trail of many other clues leading them to Sorge's fellow conspirators. The situation was tense for every member of the ring, for Sorge had warned them all to be on their guard against possible moves to arrest them. For his own part, wanting to celebrate the fact that his very last message to Moscow had been to pass on positive warning of Japanese plans to attack Britain and America, he met the rice-dancer at the Fuji Club.

Kiyomi was then summoned to police headquarters and ordered to report everything that Sorge did down to the smallest detail. The girl was a trained spy and she knew exactly what to look for. About the beginning of October the secret police had started making arrests of certain Japanese suspects, minor fry in the espionage game but who could, under interrogation, provide clues leading to the Sorge ring. By 15 October it was clear that the network was in imminent danger of being totally broken up, Ozaki being one of the first to be rounded up.

Yet still Sorge dallied with his rice-dancer instead of planning a getaway. As they had dinner in the club on the evening of 17 October Kiyomi did not miss the fact that the waiter dropped a tiny ball of rice paper on the restaurant table she was sharing with Sorge and that he smoothed out the paper and read a message on it. This was a warning to him that the secret police's watch was being intensified and that he must take special precautions. Little did he know that his new mistress after making an excuse to leave the table, had straightaway telephoned the Kempeitai, informing them of the incident.

Official instructions to Russian spies were that all such secret messages should be burned at the first opportunity. Indeed, as long ago as 1919 it had been laid down by the Soviet Union's first secret police chief, Felix Dzerzhinsky, that the agent who failed to observe every rule of security in all circumstances must pay the penalty with death. To ensure that agents followed out the prescribed drill (which included burning such messages), Dzerzhinsky had his agents watched. It had been the habit among Soviet spies in Paris to pass information written on cigarette papers which would be rolled into cigarettes and then smoked. One day an agent, having read his message and memorised it, rolled his cigarette and then found he had no match. He screwed up the cigarette and dropped it into a drain. His action was reported, he was ordered back to Russia and shot.

This story is of special interest in the light of how Sorge, a Soviet-trained professional agent, possibly nervous at the time, bungled the whole affair of the rice paper message. He could presumably have slipped away to a toilet and destroyed the fatal message. Yet he waited until he and Kiyomi were in his car outside the club. He flicked away at his cigarette-lighter and it would not work. Kiyomi, sitting beside him, impassive and motionless, noticed how tense he was. When the lighter failed to function, Sorge asked her for a light, but she pretended she could not give him one.

Finally, and apparently exasperated, he threw his cigarette and the rice paper out of the car window and drove off. That was his final fatal error. But at that moment he seemed intent only on spending the night with Kiyomi. As they were driving towards his house, she asked Sorge if he would stop the car at the next telephone kiosk on the road so that she could warn her parents that she was staying out all night. It was a natural request and apparently did not arouse Sorge's suspicions. So he foolishly agreed and once again she rang the secret police and told them exactly where the rice paper message had been dropped. It was recovered shortly afterwards and from that moment Sorge's doom was sealed.

It has always seemed unbelievable that so experienced an operator as Sorge could have committed two such cardinal errors for a spy within a few hours. What was going through his mind in those final hours of this drama? Did he develop a sub-conscious urge for self-destruction? He could not have been impervious to the fact that the net was closing in on him. Even at this late hour he could have thrown off his pursuers and made good his escape. Perhaps the chances of his getting safely out of the country were slim, but almost anything would have been better than to trust this girl and spend the night with her at his house. There are two possibilities: one, that he had convinced himself he was born under a lucky star, and the other, rather more nobly, that he believed that if he tried to escape he would endanger the lives of his colleagues. He could so easily have thrown himself on the mercy of his friends, the Otts, and found sanctuary in the German Embassy. But he may not have wished to compromise them with the Gestapo.

So Sorge and Kiyomi spent just this one night together. It is said that the dangers of wartime always make the pursuit of sex seem much more desirable and quicken one's sexual impulses. This is how it may have seemed to the agent as he spent his last night of freedom in the arms of the rice-dancer. At dawn on 18 October Inspector Osashi, accompanied by the Japanese Procurator, Yoshikawa Mitsusada, who was to be Sorge's chief interrogator, arrived at Sorge's home. He was promptly arrested and taken into custody. Ozaki was already in the hands of the secret police and Voukelitch, Klausen and Miyagi were swiftly rounded up. By the end of October the Soviet spy ring in Japan was virtually destroyed. Altogether thirty-five people, mainly Japanese, were arrested in connection with the Sorge case.

The real culprit in all this was not the rice girl Kiyomi, though she played a vital part at the end, but a Japanese communist, Ito Ritsu, who had been arrested by the Kempeitai in June, 1941, on the grounds that he was suspected of underground communist activities. He was not a member of the Sorge ring. To save his skin, Ito Ritsu pleaded that he had already seen the error of his ways and offered information about other members of the Japanese Communist Party. This led the police on to the trail first of Miyagi and then of Ozaki and Sorge. But even with this lead the secret police took four months before they could make arrests.

By the time Sorge was in prison, the Russians had all the vital evidence they needed concerning Japanese war plans. Thus, says Mayevsky, Sorge made a vital contribution to saving the Russian capital and helped to give the Germans their first major set-back. 'But by then,' wrote Mayevsky, 'the hero-intelligencer was already languishing in prison. The Japanese secret police had long suspected something was amiss within the German Embassy walls. But even those shrewd and skilful opponents were unable to discover anything. And there is no knowing how it all would have turned out, had it not been for a traitor [Ito Ritsu] who called himself a communist.'

The Germans were dumbfounded at Sorge's arrest and obviously knew nothing of the Kempeitai's suspicions. At first they believed the Japanese had blundered in putting their own man in prison. They made strenuous efforts to have Sorge released, but without success. Possibly Sorge was over-confident and convinced that the Germans would bring pressure on the Japanese to release him, but of course he had no knowledge of the detailed uncovering of the network by the Kempeitai. He merely thought they were shadowing him.

Among the records of those arrested by the Kempeitai on this occasion is the name of Kinkazu Saionji, described on the police records as 'former consultant to the Foreign Ministry'. He was one of a number of bright young men in what was known as Prince Konoye's Breakfast Club, and a somewhat remote member of the Sorge ring through furnishing Ozaki with information. Saionji was found guilty of 'having violated the Military Secrets Protection Law'. He escaped with a suspended sentence because he was the grandson of Prince Saionji, a member of the royal house of Japan.

A former graduate of Oxford University, Saionji was suspected of bartering some information which helped to save him on this occasion. He was rejected with contempt by the Japanese liberal-aristocratic elements whom he represented and was also expelled from membership of the Japanese Communist Party. After the war he went to Peking where he worked with the Chinese against his old Russian comrades.

Branko de Voukelitch received a life sentence for his part in the spy network and he died in 1945. Max Klausen also had a life sentence, but was released in 1945. Ozaki and Sorge were hanged on the same day, 7 November, 1944. Both men faced death with dignity and courage, according to all reports of their last hours. Sorge was forty-nine years old. Ozaki spent his last days writing exceptionally beautiful love letters to his wife. One of these letters was considered of such literary quality that it was posthumously published as a slim volume entitled *Love Was Like a Falling Star*. Sorge thanked the prison officials for 'all your kindness', but made no other statement before walking to the death cell.

The question has been raised again and again as to whether Sorge was actually executed, as officially stated, or whether he was smuggled back to Russia in some exchange deal and another man sent to the gallows in his place. It was neither in the Germans', nor the Japanese interests that Sorge should be revealed publicly as a spy. Common sense and normal diplomatic practice on such occasions suggests that the Russian Embassy should have remained ostensibly in total ignorance of Richard Sorge. On the other hand Sorge seems to have felt there might be some help forthcoming from the Russians. He requested his police interrogator to approach the Soviet Embassy in the hope that they would negotiate his exchange through diplomatic channels.

But the Soviet Embassy in Tokyo took no steps whatsoever to give any outward encouragement to such hopes. Nor did the Japanese seem anxious to make a deal. His arrest must have embarrassed both countries in their one common aim – to remain neutral towards each other. The apparent Soviet disinterest in Sorge was in marked contrast to the braver and more generous Major-General Ott who went to see Sorge in prison and who, though shocked by the disclosures, nevertheless formally saluted a former comrade in arms. Ott and his family paid for their friendship towards Sorge. Ott was dismissed from his post and his career was in ruins. He and his family made their way to Peking and remained there until they were detained by the Americans when the war ended.

It was the long delay in executing Sorge which largely led to rumours that he had been secretly exchanged for an important Japanese spy, or prisoners. Certainly the fact that he was kept in prison for just over three years strongly suggests that some kind of exchange deal might have been considered at one stage. Some people claimed they had actually seen Sorge alive in China and elsewhere and that the Japanese had secretly smuggled him out of the country to Macao in exchange for captured Japanese agents of the Kwantung Army. Hans-Otto Meissner, who had known Sorge personally, stated afterwards that there was no adequate or independent evidence of Sorge's execution and that he had met a French diplomat in Shanghai who had recognised Sorge in that city. In his book, *The Man With Three Faces*, Meissner adds: 'I think it possible that Sorge lives today directing or playing a part in Soviet espionage.'

But that was in 1955. It is an intriguing possibility, but on all the evidence gathered since from a wide range of sources, official and otherwise, it seems highly improbable. What is of interest is that it was not until twenty years after his death that the Russians suddenly awarded him the title of Hero of the Soviet Union and allowed their version of his career to be published in the form of books and innumerable articles.

There were probably two reasons for this Soviet gesture. The first was that the boosting of Sorge as 'hero-intelligencer' was part of a general campaign to publicise some of the Soviet agents of distinction and to show that espionage could be a patriotic duty. Prior to this, the official line had been that spying was a dirty word and something only indulged in by the capitalist powers and never by the USSR. But the second reason was also to counteract some of the anti-Soviet stories which arose directly out of post-war discoveries by the American authorities in Japan of the ramifications of the Sorge ring. For it was American Intelligence probes into the Sorge story which helped pave the way for Senator McCarthy's witch-hunt against communist agents in the USA. Sorge's close relationship with Agnes Smedley became a *cause célèbre*.

But the last word should remain with the ever-faithful Miyake Hanako. She was arrested after the unmasking of Sorge, but eventually released. When the war ended Miyake Hanako made a search for Sorge's remains and it is her evidence which unshakably testifies to the fact that Sorge was executed. Eventually she traced his grave in a cemetery at Zoshigaya. In the coffin was a skeleton, the size and shape of which proclaimed it to be undoubtedly that of a foreigner. Hanako also claimed to recognise the gold fillings in Sorge's teeth and from these she had a ring made. This she has worn ever since, having had the coffin removed to another graveyard to be laid to rest alongside the graves of Ozaki and Miyagi.

Münchener Ausgabe

327. Ausg. · 52. Jahrg. · Einzelpreis 15 Pf. · 20 Pf.

„Freiheit und Brot!"

Münchener Ausgabe

München, Donnerstag, 23. November 1939

VÖLKISCHER BEOBACHTER

Kampfblatt der national-sozialistischen Bewegung Großdeutschlands

Verräter Otto Strasser das Werkzeug des englischen Geheimdienstes

Wiederholte Anschläge auf den Führer

Die britische Mordverschwörung

dr. th. s. Berlin, 22. November

Die allererste Auslandsstimme, die sich in der vergangenen Nacht zur Enthüllung des Verbrechens von München meldete, war ... das britische Außenministerium. Die Verantwortlichen in Downing Street hatten kaum noch Zeit gehabt, die amtlichen deutschen Mitteilungen zu lesen, geschweige denn aufmerksam zu studieren — und schon funkten sie in höchster Aufregung das hastige Dementi in die Welt, „daß Beamte des britischen Geheimdienstes nicht für das Attentat verantwortlich seien". Genau das haben wir erwartet! Denn es ist eine alte Erfahrung, daß der Schuldige in dem Augenblick, in dem man ihm seine Verbrechen auf den Kopf zusagt, zunächst alles leugnet. Alles, auch das, was er bei ruhiger Überlegung im Interesse einer schlauen Verteidigung auf keinen Fall leugnen dürfte.

Der gedungene Mörder

Auch Georg Elser, das gekaufte Werkzeug, hat zunächst alles und jedes abgestritten. Erst dann, als die Last der Schuldbeweise ihm völlig über den Kopf wuchs, bequemte er sich zu Teilgeständnissen in der Hoffnung, sich wenigstens vom schlimmsten Verdacht reinzuwaschen. Es war zu spät, er hatte zu lange geleugnet — das ganze Lügengebäude brach zusammen und begrub ihn unter seinen Trümmern.

So mag sich ihm im Rückblick der Gang der Untersuchung heute darstellen. Tatsächlich war sein Fall von vornherein völlig aussichtslos, denn nicht der einzelne Untermensch Elser steht im Mittelpunkt des Dramas von München, sondern eine gewaltige verbrecherische Organisation, ja mehr noch, ein ganzes verbrecherisches System. Georg Elser — das ist nur ein kleines, mehr oder minder zufälliges Rad oder bestenfalls das Schlußstück jener größeren Höllenmaschine, die Deutschland in die Luft sprengen soll.

Die Mittelsmänner

In der gleichen Stunde, in der Downing Street frech und gottesfürchtig leugnen [illegible] ganzen Welt berüchtigten Geheimdienst von den Münchener Blutspuren reinzuwaschen versucht, sitzen zwei hervorragende Funktionäre dieses Instituts in deutscher Haft. Mr. Best und Captain (Hauptmann) Stevens. Der britische Rundfunk hat schon bei ihrer Verhaftung vor vierzehn Tagen zugegeben, daß diese beiden Männer, die in der holländischen Hauptstadt eine erstaunlich große Rolle spielen konnten, dem Intelligence Service angehören. Dieses Geständnis an sich hat kaum jemand überrascht, da alle Welt weiß, daß fast alle britischen Auslandsbeamten und zahllose englische Privatleute in Frieden und Krieg für den Geheimdienst arbeiten müssen.

Es gibt in der ganzen Welt keine zweite staatliche Geheimorganisation, der ein so gewaltiger personeller und finanzieller Apparat zur Verfügung steht wie dem Intelligence Service.

Der Dummkopf aber, der in der vergangenen Nacht das Londoner Dementi losließ, rechnete offenbar darauf, daß die vierzehntägige Gastfreundschaft, die Best und Stevens in Deutschland genossen, restlos durch Teetrinken und Brettspiel ausgefüllt worden sei. Er hat sich verrechnet!

Wir haben nicht nur erfahren, welche hervorragenden Aufgaben die beiden ins Garn gegangenen Burschen in der Londoner Verschwörerzentrale spielten, sondern noch viel mehr ...

In allen Ländern ist in den vergangenen Jahren und Jahrzehnten viel über die Taten des Intelligence Service geschrieben worden. Auch der „V. B." hat wiederholt auf das verbrecherische Treiben des britischen Geheimdienstes hingewiesen. Nun aber werden wir zu gegebener Stunde in der Lage sein, diesem düsteren Thema einige sehr bemerkenswerte Kapitel anzufügen.

Der schöne Haag ist von der britischen Regierung dazu ausersehen worden, Kriegszentrale des Intelligence Service und seiner mit der Durchführung von Attentaten und anderen Verbrechen beauftragten Sonderabteilung, des Secret Service, für ganz Europa zu sein. Tapferen und umsichtigen Männern des Sicherheitsdienstes der SS ist es gelungen, dieses politische Gaunernest restlos auszuheben. Wenn man sich den Umfang des Aufgabenkreises der Haager Zentrale vor Augen hält, dann kann man ungefähr ermessen, welche Bedeutung der Erfolg dieses Erkundungsunternehmens und die Dingfestmachung seiner Leiter für die deutsche Kriegsführung hat.

Dem Intelligence Service wird bekanntlich Schlauheit nachgesagt. Es ist tatsächlich richtig, daß dieses einzigartige Unternehmen seine früheren Erfolge zum Teil den raffiniertesten Gehirnen seiner Leiter und Agenten verdankte. Der Löwenanteil aber mußte der völligen Skrupellosigkeit und der hinter ihr stehenden nackten englischen Macht zugeschrieben werden. Die Unverfrorenheit, mit der die Zentrale im Haag arbeitete, bestätigt nur die alte Erfahrung, daß in vielen Ländern ein Brite, besonders wenn er sich als Gentleman aufspielt, mit anderen Maßstäben gemessen wird als ein gewöhnlicher Mensch.

Die große Pleite des Intelligence Service

Die jetzige Pleite des Intelligence Service hat einen doppelten Grund: Das nationalsozialistische Deutschland hat die „fromme Scheu" vor dem Britentum und seinen Vertretern völlig abgelegt. Wir haben die Maske durchschaut und bekämpfen die britische Arroganz mit rücksichtslosen, erfolgreichen Methoden. Dazu kommt, daß hinter dem Intelligence Service nicht mehr die alte britische Übermacht steht, ein Mangel, den London durch die Gewinnung neuer Helfershelfer wettzumachen versucht. Ein einziger Name, der in dem Untersuchungsbericht des Reichsführers SS genannt wird, beleuchtet die Art von Englands neuen Hilfskräften: Otto Strasser!

Best, Stevens und ihr Londoner Chef sind letzten Endes daran gescheitert, daß sie ihre Informationen über Deutschland aus der schmutzigen Quelle der Emigration bezogen. Sowohl im britischen Lügenministerium wie im Londoner Hauptamt des Intelligence Service wimmelt es von fanatischen Landesverrätern, schmierigen Asphaltjuden und gemeinen Geldjägern, deren Wiege einst in Deutschland stand, die aber längst keine blasse Ahnung mehr davon haben, wie es in Deutschland wirklich aussieht und was das deutsche Volk in Wahrheit denkt. Dieser Abschaum der deutschen Revolution ist es, der die englische Presse mit den albernsten Greuellügen füttert, der den Text der idiotischen Flugzettel verfaßt, der Chamberlains [illegible] Reden „An das deutsche Volk" verfaßt und dem Intelligence Service die Richtlinien für Zersetzungsarbeit und Attentatspläne gibt.

England kann nicht anders! Selbst in den Glanzzeiten, als Englands Macht in ihrem Zenit stand, hat die britische Politik die hinterhältigen Methoden einem offenen Kampf vorgezogen. Heute aber ist Britannien gar nicht mehr in der Lage, zu wählen. Frankreichs Opferblut allein genügt nicht, um Deutschlands Macht zu brechen. Englands eigene Söhne werden sorgfältig für ein schon jetzt bald menschenleeres Weltreich aufgespart. London schreit nach Bundesgenossen! Judentum und Emigration sind — neben der Schwäche und Willfährigkeit gewisser Neutraler — die einzigen, die seiner verbrecherischen Kriegspolitik restlos zur Verfügung stehen.

Der gedungene Mörder und seine Hintermänner

Das gekaufte Werkzeug Georg Elser

Die Leiter der britischen Mörderzentrale für Europa Kapitän Stevens Mr. Best

Aufn.: Presse-Hoffmann

Strassers Auftrag, den Führer zu beseitigen

Berlin, 22. November

Otto Strasser ist der tatsächliche Organisator des Münchner Verbrechens. Sein Lebensweg ergibt ein klares Bild des an Charakterlosigkeit [illegible] Emigranten.

Am 10. 9. 1897 in Deggendorf (Bayern) geboren, ist er der Bruder Gregor Strassers und Paul Strassers, der wegen homosexueller Verbrechen in das Ausland emigrierte.

Der Beginn seiner politischen Tätigkeit sieht ihn im Jahre 1919 als überzeugten Sozialdemokraten, der nach kurzem Studium der Volkswirtschaft die Leitung eines sozialdemokratischen Korrespondenzbüros übernimmt. Während des Kapp-Putsches ist er Führer einer spartakistischen Hundertschaft. Im Rahmen seiner Entwicklung zum Nationalrevolutionär stößt er im Jahre 1925 zur NSDAP. Daß die Gründe hierfür nicht weltanschaulich-idealistische und selbstlose waren, beweist sein späterer Lebensweg. Als Hauptschriftleiter einiger im Kampfverlage erscheinender Zeitungen, an der Spitze „Der Nationalsozialist", bemüht sich sein Geltungsdrang und sein zügelloser Ehrgeiz darum, politisch im Rahmen der NSDAP. eine besondere politische Rolle zu spielen.

Als der „revolutionäre Sozialist", dem das Wort vom „Gemeinnutz geht vor Eigennutz" stets ein Fremdwort geblieben war, und der sich nicht einfügen konnte, seine egoistischen Ziele nicht erfüllt sah, verließ er, um dem drohenden Ausschluß aus der Partei zu entgehen, mit der bekannten theatralischen Erklärung „Die Sozialisten verlassen die NSDAP." die Partei und gründete die sogenannte Kampfgemeinschaft revolutionärer Nationalsozialisten.

Später führte ihn der Verräterweg mit dem Meuterer Stennes zusammen. Der erhoffte Einbruch in die NSDAP. gelang nicht, so daß er lediglich ein Gerippe von persönlichen Einzelgängern im Reich zurückließ, als er im Jahre 1933 zunächst nach Wien emigrierte. Sein bisher im Reich erscheinendes Organ, die „Schwarze Front", erschien nun mit nur geringer Auflage als „Schwarzer Sender" im damaligen Österreich. Zur gleichen Zeit wurde im Reich der größte Teil seiner Organisation aufgelöst und die Prominenten seiner Mitarbeiter, soweit sie nicht emigriert waren, hinter Schloß und Riegel gesetzt.

Als ihm auch in Wien der Boden zu heiß wurde, flüchtete Otto Straßer nach Prag, wo er sich unter Abstreifung des Scheines des Idealisten eindeutig als Hoch- und Landesverräter zum Kauf anbot, ein für Geld gedungenes Subjekt fremder Nachrichtendienste und Organ der mit ihm täglich verkehrenden jüdischen Emigration.

Sein engster Mitarbeiter war der unter dem Namen Heinrich Grunow auftretende Emigrant Friedrich Beer. Seine Zeitung hieß bezeichnenderweise „Die deutsche Revolution", der Geldgeber war die damalige tschechische Regierung Benesch.

Strassers Haupttätigkeit in Prag war neben der Verbreitung von Hetzartikeln in Flug- und Zeitschriften der Versuch, eine einheitliche Ausrichtung aller Schattierungen der Emigration herzustellen. Ob er dabei die Zahl des Restes seiner Anhänger im Reich mit Wissen oder ohne Kenntnis überschätzte, ist belanglos. Es steht jedenfalls nicht fest, ob zu dieser Zeit Otto Straßer selbst auch nur im geringsten noch an die Möglichkeit einer Revolution in Deutschland glaubte.

Straßer lebte jahrelang seit Jahren schon ausschließlich von den Geldzuwendungen ausländischer Nachrichtendienste, denen er versprach, in Deutschland eine Revolution zuwege zu bringen, zumindest aber den Führer zu beseitigen. So machte er im Juni 1934 eine Reise nach Paris, um die französische Regierung zur Unterstützung eines Putsches im Saargebiet zu bewegen, durch den die Saarrückgliederung unmöglich gemacht werden sollte. Nach seinen eigenen Angaben, die in dem gleichzeitig veröffentlichten handschriftlichen Brief dokumentarisch festgehalten sind, hat damals die französische Regierung diesen Plan abgelehnt, da sie den durchzuführenden Umsturz im Reich ohne außenpolitische Belastung 1934 billiger zu erreichen hoffte.

Im übrigen kamen schon damals die gleichen Gedanken zum Ausdruck, die später den Verhandlungen mit den Leitern des englischen Secret Service in den Jahren 1938/39 zu Grunde lagen.

Im Rahmen seiner verräterischen Arbeit setzte Otto Straßer einen in Zahorí bei Prag mit Unterstützung des tschechischen Nachrichtendienstes gebauten sogenannten „Freiheitssender" ein, der neben der propagandistischen Arbeit schon damals die den Attentatsabsichten Otto Straßers und seiner Helfershelfer entsprechenden Parolen gab. So schlossen z. B. fast alle Aufrufe dieses im Jahre 1934/35 arbeitenden Senders wörtlich mit der immer wiederkehrenden Aufforderung, daß „Adolf Hitler sterben müsse".

Die deutsche Regierung hat damals offiziell von der tschechischen Regierung die Beseitigung dieses zum Mord an deutschen Regierungsmitgliedern auffordernden Senders gefordert. Nachdem die tschechische Regierung behauptete, von der Existenz dieses Senders keine Kenntnis zu haben, wurde ihr der Standort des Senders genauestens angegeben. Da Herr Benesch naturgemäß auch dann nicht bereit war, den vom tschechischen Gelde aufgezogenen Sendedienst einzustellen, mußte von deutscher Seite selbst eingegriffen werden, um diese fortgesetzte Mordpropaganda zu unterbinden. Zwei SS-Führer des Sicherheitsdienstes haben befehlsgemäß am 26. Januar 1935 diesen Sender zerstört.

In Vollzug der ihm von seinen damaligen Prager Geldgebern erteilten Aufträge versuchte nun Otto Straßer, die nach Deutschland auf dem Funkweg gesendeten Parolen auch praktisch zu verwirklichen.

1936 fanden Vorbereitungen für den ersten Sprengstoffanschlag statt. Er sollte ursprünglich im Olympiastadion in Berlin während der Olympiade, später anläßlich des Parteitages 1936 in Nürnberg und schließlich anläßlich des Besuches des Duce 1937 zur Ausführung kommen. Otto Straßer bediente sich dabei durch Vermittlung seines engsten Mitarbeiters Fritz Beer (Deckname Heinrich Grunow), eines ehemaligen Studenten der Baukunst, namens Helmut Hirsch.

Dieser Prager Jude erklärte sich bereit, den Sprengstoffanschlag auszuführen. In zahlreichen eingehenden Besprechungen war der Plan des Anschlages genauestens festgelegt worden. Als Hirsch mit zwei Höllen-

A German newspaper headlines the Venlo incident, implicating, for the purposes of propaganda, Best and Stevens in the attempted assassination of Hitler at the Munich Beer Cellar

2

The Venlo Incident

'Best and Stevens have given us a complete and detailed account of the British Secret Service in all its ramifications. . . . It still remains to be seen whether they are speaking the truth, whether they have invented anything, or whether they have left anything out of their account'

OFFICIAL GERMAN REPORT ON THE
TWO BRITONS DETAINED AT VENLO

It was shortly after five o'clock in the morning on 9 November 1939, that Captain Sigismund Payne Best, a British Secret Service operative in Holland, joined his colleague, Major Richard Stevens, to set out on a mission which, they optimistically hoped, would end World War II.

Such was the foolhardy wishful thinking of many Britons in high places in those early months of the conflict which have come to be cynically dubbed the 'Phoney War'.

Best and Stevens were planning to meet a high-ranking German officer whose name they did not know, but who had led them to believe through intermediaries that he was prepared to defect. The idea was that this mysterious Very Important Personage should be flown secretly to London where he would put forward a plan for the ousting of Hitler and the ending of the war. In the hierarchy of the Secret Service in London there was even a hope that the VIP might be Admiral Wilhelm Canaris, head of the Abwehr, Germany's Secret Service.

This was to be the greatest moment in the lives of Best and Stevens. Not surprisingly both men were feeling somewhat tense that morning. Over breakfast Best and his wife were discussing the sensational news of a bomb explosion in the Bürgerbraukeller at Munich after a speech there by Hitler. It certainly looked like an attempt on Hitler's life which had badly misfired. Best wondered whether it would affect the outcome of his meeting on that day.

If you had been in The Hague in November 1939, and asked anyone where the British espionage headquarters was, you would have been unhesitatingly directed to Number 57 Nieuwe Paarklaan. Everyone knew that the British Passport Control Office, situated in that building, was the regional headquarters of the British Secret Service. Passport control offices all over the world were used as a cover for such activities and even after

World War II the British persisted in continuing this outmoded and somewhat ridiculous attempt at camouflage which deceived nobody.

As Holland had been neutral in World War I and neutral capitals were supposed to be ideal for directional centres for espionage, The Hague had been selected as the regional headquarters for Secret Intelligence Service (usually referred to as SIS). The head of this station was Major Stevens, an ex-Indian Army officer in his mid-forties, a courteous and likeable man who lived with his English wife in a first-floor flat, controlling an impressive network of more than a hundred agents in Europe.

But there was also a second British spy network based in The Hague, quite separate from that of Stevens, but also controlled by the Secret Service in London. It was known as the 'Z' network. Its Hague office was run by Captain Payne Best, who lived in a house in the old town. Best, a Wodehousian figure who sported a monocle and wore spats, was a veteran Intelligence officer of World War I. Then fifty-five years of age, he operated under the cover of an import-export company. Because of his somewhat old-fashioned pukka manner he was regarded with mild amusement by some members of the British community in The Hague.

That morning, when he kissed his Dutch wife goodbye, Best commented ruefully, 'I shall be glad when this job is all over. I'm getting a little too old for this sort of caper.' He went on to the Passport Control Office to pick up Stevens and their driver, Klop. All three men took revolvers with them. It was noticeable that Stevens was more enthusiastic about the mission than the more experienced Best. The latter felt that there had already been undue delay on the part of the Germans in agreeing to a meeting. He was also somewhat apprehensive about the selection of Venlo as their rendezvous.

Best pointed out that Venlo was really in no-man's-land on the borders of Germany and Holland. Stevens replied that this might be so, but that officially it was Dutch territory. In any event all was ready for the reception of their 'friend' and an aircraft was standing by at Schiphol airport to whisk him away to London.

On the journey out to Venlo their car was repeatedly stopped at Dutch defence posts so that they were late in arriving at their destination. At the last moment they decided to take Jan Lemmens, another driver, with them so that he could bring the car back in case for some reason or other they decided to return by train.

Best chain-smoked furiously throughout the journey to Venlo. As they waited at one guard post Stevens scribbled on a writing-pad on his knee. To a quizzical Best he explained that he was making a list of some British agents in Holland who would have to be taken away if the Germans invaded that country. Klop had reported to them that there had been rumours of possible German moves in the border territory that very morning. Best's sardonic comment to Stevens was that if the worst occurred, Stevens had better 'eat' his list. Whether or not this list was ever destroyed before they met the

Germans nobody seems to know. It was a most unprofessional action for a spy chief to take at this particular moment.

As they drew near to Venlo, Best took over the wheel and Klop sat beside him. The sentry raised the barrier at the frontier post and the car drove through. Between the Dutch barrier and the German barrier was a stretch of roadway with a customs house on the right and the Café Backus on the left, right in the middle of no-man's-land. This is a typically Dutch stretch of countryside, very flat, sandy and with only a few gorse bushes and a clump of conifer trees. Best and Stevens had hoped that once they had passed through the Dutch barrier they could stop and await developments. But they were told that all was well and that they should 'carry on'.

Klop, a resourceful character who had considerable influence, had indicated to Best and Stevens that extra Dutch guards were on duty at the frontier this particular day and that this was some kind of a safeguard. All the same Best and Stevens would have been happier if they could have halted rather closer to the Dutch side.

'Somehow it seemed to me that things looked different from what they had on the previous days,' said Best, who knew the area well. In his memoirs, *The Venlo Incident*, he afterwards stated, 'I noticed that the German barrier across the road, which had always been closed, was now lifted . . . My feeling of impending danger was very strong . . . No one was in sight except a German customs officer in uniform lounging along the road and a little girl who was playing with a big black dog in the middle of the road before the café.'

Suddenly they recognised their German contact, the man they knew as Schaemmel, standing on the verandah of the café. He waved to them as though to indicate all was well. Best stopped his car and then reversed into the car park. He was then alongside Schaemmel's car. Then, without warning, another German car shot through the German barrier towards them, with armed SS men on the running-boards with machine-guns and revolvers pointing in their direction. Best and Stevens were brusquely ordered out of the car almost before they knew what was happening. Klop, their driver, had been much quicker to react to the danger. He had whipped out his revolver, jumped into the road and started firing at the Germans. As Best put it afterwards, Klop was 'running diagonally away from us towards the road, firing at our captors as he ran.' He was the only man to put up any show of resistance, but he only managed to escape as far as a clump of trees when he was shot and mortally wounded. Meanwhile Best and Stevens together with Lemmens were ordered to put up their hands and, having had their revolvers removed from them, were frogmarched to the German frontier post. There all papers in their pockets and wallets were taken away by the Germans.

This was how Britain's two key intelligence officers in Europe were made prisoners by the Nazi secret police. Too late did they learn that their

German contact man, whom they knew as Schaemmel, was none other than Walter Schellenberg, of the Nazi Central Security Agency, specially set up to catch spies. It was Schellenberg's first big secret service coup, paving the way to his ultimate appointment later in the war as overall head of German Intelligence.

News of the kidnapping of Best and Stevens and the shooting of Klop was swiftly passed by the Dutch frontier guards to the Netherlands military Intelligence agency. Very shortly after this, terse details of the affair at Venlo were being tapped out on the wires to London.

Colonel Stewart Menzies, the new head of MI 6, had been in his office all day, waiting for news of the expected arrival of the prominent German defector, hoping it might even be his opposite number, Admiral Canaris, which would, of course, have been a splendid start to his career as chief of Britain's Secret Service. At the very worst, he felt, it must be some leading dissident general who might have information of a new coup against Hitler inside the German Army. This might seem to be quite unjustified optimism on the part of 'C', as the head of MI 6 was known, but only the day before news of the bomb explosion in a Munich beer cellar had encouraged the belief that the Nazis had a great deal of trouble to cope with inside their own country.

Then came the devastating and totally unexpected blow. Menzies' devoted confidential secretary, Miss Pettigrew, appeared with a pink flimsy containing the terrible, indeed almost unbelievable news. For it was unbelievable in the sense that it seemed impossible that two relatively senior secret service operators should have put themselves in such a position.

Menzies knew at once the grave implications of that message and he lost no time in acquainting the then Prime Minister, Neville Chamberlain, with the facts. Fortunately, Menzies was in one respect admirably fitted to handle this highly damaging incident: he had considerable political acumen and was able to handle the prickliest of politicians at all levels as well as the intelligence chiefs of the three services. But he needed all his skill to cope with this explosive issue.

As far as the British public was concerned the disaster at Venlo, because of wartime censorship of news, rated only a small paragraph or two in most newspapers. *The Times* reported from Amsterdam that 'one man was shot dead and a number of Dutchmen were kidnapped and taken into Germany in an incident at Venlo on the Dutch-German frontier after an armed clash between German officials and Dutchmen.' There was, of course, no mention of Best and Stevens, no indication that Britons were involved. The German press naturally kept quiet about the Venlo affair, but made full use of the beer cellar explosion at Munich as an example of the 'wicked machinations of the British' against the Führer, Adolf Hitler.

The *Völkischer Beobachter* thundered, 'England threw the bomb in order to find an escape from the embarrassment caused by her reverses.' The *Deutscher Dienst* went further: 'The instigators, who paid for the work, the only people who are capable of such a revolting idea, are those who have always used murder as a political weapon, the agents of the "Secret Service" [British]. Behind them stand the British warmongers, in whose ears whispers Judah.'

Meanwhile Menzies was no doubt grateful for the small mercy of wartime censorship of news. But he waited for the further bad news which, because of his training, he knew instinctively would follow. Sure enough it did. First of all communications from the agents set up by Best and Stevens began to fail. Then the secret radio links went dead. News came that a vital intermediary agent had 'disappeared'. Worse still, there was no contact with the Abwehr, no roundabout word of solace from Admiral Canaris and no more news of a mysterious general who would defect. The last hopes of a compromise, of a patched-up peace with Germany had failed. The war which the smart alecks in the Secret Service, and indeed in some of the other Services, had said would 'end by Christmas' was not only still on, but had veered strongly in Germany's favour. As to Admiral Canaris, who had always wanted Germany to avoid going to war with Britain, he felt that if the British could blunder as badly as they had done at Venlo, then it was far too risky for him to establish even cautious links with London at this time.

To understand fully just what happened, one must look at the whole political and secret service set-up in Britain in the years immediately preceding World War II. First of all there was the question of the delicate relationship between the Prime Minister of the day and the Secret Service. Stanley Baldwin, for all his faults and alleged indolence, was not only a prime minister with an astonishing gift for achieving a kind of permanent consensus with the electorate but, while allowing the Secret Service to conduct their own affairs, also kept his own private Intelligence checks. Neville Chamberlain, on the other hand, while relying entirely on MI 6 in a much more conventional way, also had his own private advisory service on foreign affairs which had a strong pro-German bias. The latter, of course, was in no position to give him Intelligence of German intentions, but often gave him advice contrary to that of MI 6.

Menzies had inherited a secret service that was in many respects outdated, which had often concentrated on the wrong targets, had tended to recruit its members from ex-Service officers and White's Club and was an amateur rather than a professional organisation. Of course, this meant that it had the benefit of some brilliant if amateurish ideas which occasionally came off, despite professional prejudice. But it also meant that a Venlo-type operation was always a risk with the kind of amateurs employed in key posts. Admiral Hugh Sinclair (nicknamed 'Quex'), Menzies' predecessor, had been a much less forceful character who had suffered from undermanning and a lack of funds for secret service purposes between the wars.

Successive governments had been quite prepared to provide funds for MI 5, the counter-espionage organisation, but much less enthusiastic about MI 6 (responsible for Intelligence overseas). Sinclair had also failed in that he was never quite sure what the priority targets for espionage should be. Certainly Germany had not been a priority target for MI 6 and the fluctuations in policy towards Russia had also caused a great deal of confusion. As a result Menzies had started with the disadvantage of an organisation singularly ill-equipped to assess Intelligence coming out of Germany.

Sinclair, who had been in poor health for some time, had not been vigorous enough to resolve some of these problems, nor to keep a tight control over internal wrangles between his executives. He had even been so unprofessional as to share solely with his sister the secrets of where the various dead letter boxes for 'dropped' communications were sited. Had they both been killed in an accident, the whole of the Secret Service could have been in a state of chaos. As war approached Sinclair's health steadily deteriorated and so Menzies was suddenly promoted to the top seat. He was immediately confronted with one persistent and seemingly ineradicable problem – that of Colonel Claude Dansey, an assistant director of the SIS. There was a disturbing atmosphere of hostility between Dansey and the deputy head of MI 6, Colonel Vivian.

Dansey was a controversial figure and a difficult man to work with. There was a brief period when it seemed likely that he would be demoted, but he staged a comeback on a very simple and effective strategy. He had pointed out to Admiral Sinclair that, in the event of war, the whole of the British Secret Service was vulnerable because it was so obviously sited at the Passport Control Offices of every British Embassy or Consulate. If war came, argued Dansey, Britain would have no alternative secret service.

The argument was absolutely correct, but the man who was putting it over was hardly the best man to put things right. Somehow Sinclair was persuaded to acquiesce to a second string of agents, to be organised by Dansey, supplementary to the main corps, but still under SIS control. The idea was that the two organisations should be kept strictly apart. This is how 'Z' Section came into being.

Dansey was a fire-eater of an executive who could terrify all but the strongest of men. Even Kim Philby, who worked in MI 6, has admitted that the only way to deal with Dansey was 'to beard him in his office; a personal confrontation lowered the temperature and made it possible to talk common sense. . . . Happily our paths did not cross often, as he was good enough to strike me off his list of pet bugbears.'

So Colonel Dansey built up this 'Z' network, choosing his favourites together with mainly ex-military men for his agents. In The Hague Captain Payne Best was his key officer. He was not only an Intelligence officer of long standing, but had extensive social contacts in Holland, many of them due to the influence of his wife who was the daughter of a Dutch Marine general. Nevertheless he does not seem to have been a popular figure and was regarded by some of his colleagues as being already too old for work in an area in which war was almost a certainty in the near future.

When war broke out Sinclair, before he retired, sent a memorandum to Dansey saying that the problem the SIS faced was that the left hand did not know what the right hand was doing and that it was essential for the orthodox MI 6 network to combine with 'Z' network. As a result of this directive Best was told to contact Stevens.

Stevens was a different type altogether from Best. He had been an Intelligence officer in the Indian Army and had been recalled for a new assignment in 1937. He was then posted to the job of Passport Control Officer at The Hague as the cover for running a network of spies in Holland, Germany and Belgium. Stevens disliked the whole conception of his new job. He felt he was ill-fitted for the task. His judgement was sound: Stevens had only been concerned with Intelligence in the sense that he had had to deal with the evaluation of reports on the deployment of frontier tribesmen in India. This was a very different matter from dealing with the sophisticated Intelligence world of Europe. He had no specialised knowledge of Germany or adequate contacts in that country before he was posted to The Hague. He was essentially a professional soldier, highly disciplined but not so good at using his own initiative. But the powers that be twisted his arm and Stevens had to accept the assignment.

So, at the beginning of World War II, the British Secret Service had one unwilling agent, doubtful of his capacity for coping with events in Europe, and another willing agent, undoubtedly skilled in the methods of World War I, but hardly suited to those now facing him. It is not surprising that with two such ill-chosen agents the Abwehr and other German secret service organisations should have been able to step in to baffle and bewilder them.

The Germans were well aware at the outset of World War II that there were people in Britain who were prepared for peace at almost any price. For a long time before this they had been steadily preparing the ground for a fifth column which would eventually come down on their side. But the Intelligence chiefs in Berlin were sensible enough to know that this worked two ways. On the one hand there was the need to keep in touch with anyone on the British side who was prepared to make a deal for a secretly negotiated peace, especially once the Polish campaign was ended. On the other hand there was the supreme opportunity for infiltrating MI 6 and learning all its secrets simply by planting an intermediary who would suggest that a peace deal was possible. It was at this stage that Walter Schellenberg took over and planned the whole operation which led up to that disastrous day at Venlo.

'For several years a German secret agent, F 479, had been working in the Netherlands,' stated Schellenberg in his memoirs. 'He had originally been a political refugee and by continuing to pose as one after he began working for us he was able to make contact with the British Secret Service. He pretended to have connections with a strong opposition group within the *Wehrmacht*, which greatly interested the British. His influence became so great that his reports were sent direct to London and through him we were able to infiltrate a continual stream of misleading Intelligence.'

The Germans were well aware that very many of the British were sympathetic towards them and that despite the declaration of war between the two countries, there was the hope on all sides that an armistice could be arranged once Poland had been occupied. All the indications were that the British might agree to peace moves and that there was an influential minority in the British Cabinet in favour of this. On this basis Walter Schellenberg worked towards conning the British into a cessation of activities. Obviously the one factor which might swing the chances in favour of the Germans was an extensive dossier on a German intermediary who could pose as an anti-Nazi of great influence. Schellenberg was realistic enough to appreciate that the chances of a secretly negotiated peace might be slight, but that the opportunities for infiltrating and breaking the British Secret Service were considerable.

So Walter Schellenberg went to Holland, adopting the name of Hauptmann Schaemmel of the Transport Department of the *Ober kommando Wehrmacht*, with the aim of establishing top-level contacts with the British Secret Service. The Germans were in the beginning extremely doubtful about the value of this operation and it was only Schellenberg's persistence which made them consider the idea seriously. Those who were in charge of Germany's Intelligence organisations were still convinced that the British Secret Service was second to none and that it could not possibly fall for such a ploy as this. What made the Germans suspicious was that Best's service as an Intelligence officer dated back to World War I and they felt that the fact that Best wore a monocle and appeared to be such a dandified figure was all part of his camouflage.

What the Germans did not then know was the extent of British secret Intelligence which they would gather. The fact that Sinclair had told Dansey to make his men link up with those of Passport Control was a totally unexpected bonus. Best himself had this to say on the subject: 'I now decided to establish direct relations with the opposition leaders in Germany. Through a German refugee in Holland, named Dr Franz, we had for some time past received reliable and often valuable information from a major in the Luftwaffe named Solms.'

Best met Dr Franz early in September, 1939. As a result of this talk he agreed to meet the doctor's friend, Major Solms. This meeting took place at Venlo and, though Best had some misgivings, agreements were reached for coded communications in future. 'I was told that a certain German general would like to meet me, but to make absolutely sure that I was indeed a British agent, I was asked to arrange that a certain news item, the text of which was enclosed, should be broadcast in the German news bulletin of the BBC. This was easily arranged and the paragraph was broadcast twice on 11 October. About the same time, too, I received a last message from Major Solms in which he told me that he was afraid he was being watched by the Gestapo and would therefore have to lie low for a while.'

It was at this stage of the negotiations that Best brought Major Stevens into the picture. From that moment onwards they worked as partners. 'Dr Franz' was in fact Dr Franz Fischer, a southern German who had left his homeland in 1935 as a political refugee. But he seems very quickly to have regretted his decision and to have sounded out friends back in Germany about the possibility of a safe return. This, he was told, would be quite feasible if he was prepared to perform certain services for the Third Reich. It soon became clear to Dr Fischer that he was expected to make contact with certain German military men who were dissatisfied with the Nazi regime. This was the original ploy by which Franz was irrevocably trapped in the Nazi network. From then on he was used as a major source in feeding to the British bogus material about dissidents anxious to make contact with London. One of Fischer's chief contacts was Johannes Travaglio, a former film director who had been posted to the Abwehr, and who called himself 'Dr Solms'.

Major M. R. Chidson, who had been head of Passport Control in The Hague before the arrival of Major Stevens, had been warned to beware of Fischer. But it is not certain that this warning was heeded. Meanwhile Fischer and Best had established secret contacts on the basis that there was a powerful group in Germany who wanted to oust Hitler. There seems to be no doubt that the Central Security Agency of the Nazis had as their aim the penetration of the British Secret Service. What they wanted above all else was to establish links with somebody sufficiently high up in the SIS, so that eventually they could find out all about the personnel of MI 6 and its methods of operation in Europe.

The first talk between Payne Best and 'Dr Solms' took place in a hotel in Venlo between 15 and 20 September, 1939, without any Dutch authority being aware of it. From Best's viewpoint the meeting was satisfactory and it was agreed they should meet again towards the end of the month. Of this second meeting Best reported that 'Dr Solms' had 'answered one or two questions on technical air force matters which I put to him, and, in the end, told me that there was a big conspiracy to remove Hitler from power and that the highest ranking army officers were involved.'

It was here that Schellenberg took a closer hand in the whole complex game of cat-and-mouse between the rival Intelligence services. Under the identity of Hauptmann Schaemmel of the Transport Department of the OKW, he made plans to meet the British: 'I had also secured an exact and detailed report on Hauptmann Schaemmel – his background, his way of life, his behaviour and appearance – for instance, that he wore a monocle, so

I had to wear one too, which was not difficult, as I am short-sighted in my right eye. The more inside knowledge I had of the group, the more chance I had of gaining the confidence of the British.'

It was a remarkable coincidence that Payne Best should also sport a monocle. Indeed, a somewhat farcical picture is conjured up by the meeting of the two monocles. Their first rendezvous was at Zutphen where Best met Schellenberg, driving his own car. The German got in beside him and they drove off for a long talk and apparently hit it off almost immediately. Best, said Schellenberg, 'spoke excellent German, and we soon established friendly relations.' Their common interest was music and Schellenberg discovered that Best was quite a useful violinist.

But let Schellenberg tell the story of what happened in his own words: 'They accepted me apparently without reservations as the representative of a strong opposition group within the highest spheres of the German Army. I told them that the head of this group was a German general [oddly enough, it was because the Germans said he was a general that some of the SIS hierarchy in London felt sure he was an admiral and Canaris at that], but that I was not free to divulge his name at this stage of the negotiations.'

Schellenberg appeared much more tense than Best on this occasion and was obviously still nervous about the whole operation, for Best would not go into details about the proposals until he had taken Schellenberg to Arnhem where Major Stevens and a colleague joined them. The talks continued between all four while Best drove around the Dutch countryside.

Prior to this, a message came from the top-ranking German officer that he wanted to meet Best and Stevens, but that first he required proof that Best was a British agent. It was this request which led to the message being broadcast by the BBC, and also when Best reluctantly agreed to bring Stevens into the picture. This was perhaps the most disastrous move of all, as the Germans knew full well that, as the relatively new Passport Control Officer, Stevens was positively an MI 6 operator. And it was Stevens who, with London's agreement, decided that it would be essential to seek the co-operation of the Dutch, as this might well be vital if the German 'ringleaders' were to cross the border frequently for talks.

It should have been obvious by this time the whole plan was getting out of control with so many people being involved. There were grave risks that there would be leakages. The Germans were, of course, delighted and were able to concentrate on their few intermediaries against the increasing number on the other side. General van Oorschot, of the Dutch Army, agreed to co-operate with the British, but 'on one condition, one of my representatives must be there and must be able to report on what is talked about.' It was finally agreed that this man should be the unfortunate Lieutenant Dirk Klop, who acted as driver to the British at Venlo. Klop had lived in Canada for five years, his English was fluent and he was regarded as a first-class man for the job. For this role he adopted the name of Coppens.

The Germans not unnaturally were highly suspicious that their bogus peace overtures were being taken seriously. They found it hard to believe that the still much respected British Secret Service could fall for a ploy like this. So they insisted on further negotiations at the end of October. These talks seemed to carry things forward in a promising manner on both sides and Major Stevens immediately phoned MI 6 headquarters in London. Half an hour later he heard that the Secretary of State for Foreign Affairs, Lord Halifax, would shortly contact him.

There was a mood of euphoria in both camps by this time. The Germans, after having been highly suspicious of the whole operation, began to feel reassured. One night Best gave a dinner party in honour of the Germans at his elegant home in the Lange Voorhout in The Hague. Present on that occasion were Best and his wife, May, Stevens and his wife, and Schellenberg (then known to them simply as Schaemmel), Dr Franz Fischer, a man named Grosch and Lieutenant Klop. Many years later Schellenberg in his memoirs recalled the occasion and mentioned that Best gave 'a short, pleasant speech' and he remarked upon the excellent quality of the oysters and the wine.

A few days later a message from Lord Halifax was duly received. According to Best this was 'carefully worded and rather non-committal'. However, they were encouraged to maintain their links with the Germans. But, as the message stressed, neither Best nor Stevens was to give his fellow conspirators anything in writing. All undertakings must be verbal only.

By now 'Schaemmel' had outlined the situation to Best and Stevens. 'He started by giving us a clear and convincing résumé of conditions in Germany,' said Best, 'and the degree to which the Army had suffered in the Polish campaign. Losses in men and material had been high [Best should have known that this was nonsense] and the present military and economic conditions made it imperative that the war should be brought to an end quickly. Hitler, though, would not listen to the advice of his General Staff and allowed nothing to stand in the way of his ambitions. Therefore he must be got rid of. . . . The intention was to take him prisoner and force him to give orders authorising a junta of officers to reorganise the government and start negotiations for peace. But, said "Schaemmel", the plotters first want to know the peace conditions of France and Britain.'

It is true that at this time Walter Schellenberg was only twenty-nine and not yet the major figure in German Intelligence which he later became. But it is still incredible that Best and Stevens seem to have made no attempt to check on the identity of the mysterious 'Schaemmel'. It should not have been difficult to have had their contact photographed and for this to be checked back with records. Much the same applied to the other and earlier intermediaries.

Klop had reported back to General van Oorschot certain reservations regarding the negotiations. Van Oorschot expressed the view that the

Major Richard Stevens

Captain Sigismund Payne Best

Captain Payne Best at the entrance to his home in The Hague, shortly before his capture

15 Nieuwe Uitleg in The Hague where Captain Payne Best had his office

Hitler speaking in the Munich
Beer Cellar on 9 November 1939

The devastation caused by the bomb

Walter Schellenberg alias Hauptmann Schaemmel

The resourceful Lieutenant Klop

The Café Backus by the border at Venlo

The aftermath: the invasion of
Holland by air, land and water

Germans were making fools of the British and that Klop should take precautions. The General must have realised the risks to his own country by going along with the British in all this, even though the co-operation was unofficial. In World War I Holland had had no difficulty in maintaining her neutrality and keeping out of the fighting. But the Nazis had far less regard for neutrality than even the Kaiser's Germany. It should have been clear by this time that the Nazis would be eager to seize upon even the smallest breach of neutrality as an excuse for intervening in Holland. Already they had a fairly shrewd idea that The Hague was the key centre of Britain's European secret service. It is surprising therefore that the Dutch military authorities agreed to Anglo-Dutch co-operation in the matter of the negotiations with the Germans. Presumably the Dutch felt this was justified in that it seemed to offer a genuine prospect of peace. But, from their own viewpoint, they should have realised that these were not simply informal peace feelers between two governments, but in effect subversive moves by the British to ally themselves with anti-Nazi forces in Germany. The Germans knew full well that this kind of co-operation was in flagrant breach of the obligations of neutrality. From Venlo onwards the invasion of Holland was only a matter of time. The hands of those who wanted to acquire advanced bomber bases in Holland were greatly strengthened by the Best-Stevens affair.

It was at this stage of the talks between the British and 'Schaemmel' that the Germans speeded up the whole operation. Best and Stevens were informed that 'the leader of the German opposition to Hitler' wanted to give the British some very important documents personally and that he was prepared to fly to London for discussions with Lord Halifax. This was the bait on which Best and Stevens eagerly bit.

There is quite a lot of evidence to suggest that Schellenberg would have preferred to play along rather longer with the British and that he thought the Venlo kidnapping was premature. Schellenberg had had one very uneasy moment at a meeting with Captain Best. He was washing his hands in the cloakroom when Best came up behind him and said: 'Tell me, do you always wear a monocle?' Schellenberg's instant reaction was that Best was beginning to have doubts about his identity, but he recovered his presence of mind sufficiently to reply, 'You know, I've been meaning to ask you the same question.'

But that matter of the bomb explosion in the Munich beer cellar changed the whole situation overnight. Heinrich Himmler, the chief of Gestapo, telephoned Schellenberg, ranting on about the British Secret Service being behind the attempt on Hitler's life, and saying he had just spoken to the Führer. 'He now says – and this is an order,' shouted Himmler, 'when you meet the British agents for your conference tomorrow, you are to arrest them immediately and bring them to Germany.'

It was an entirely new situation for Schellenberg to cope with, but

Himmler would not listen to any objection or counter-proposals. There was no doubt that somebody else in German Intelligence had sought to stir things up against the Dutch and at the same time to try to make propaganda by suggesting that Best and Stevens had been involved in the Munich bomb explosion and had been caught by the Gestapo as they tried to escape back into Holland.

Once they were captured by the Germans the two British agents were in a hopeless position. Suddenly they realised that 'Schaemmel' was Schellenberg and that the Germans knew almost everything about them. They were, of course, separated and interrogated individually so that one agent could be played off against the other. In those days no real attempt was made to instruct Secret Service operatives in how to avoid telling the enemy too much if they happened to be caught. Such techniques as tactics against brain-washing were relatively unknown. Of course, under torture, nobody was expected to be immune. But what was totally unprofessional and unforgivable was that key Intelligence officers were allowed to know far too much about the whole set-up of their Secret Service. And in this respect Best and Stevens were so very vulnerable: each knew of the ramifications of MI 6 and the 'Z' network, but above all the entire SIS set-up was firmly implanted in their heads. They knew the top personnel in various hush-hush departments and the addresses of various sections of the Service. There was very little of vital importance that they did not know.

They were soon taken to Berlin and subjected to prolonged interrogation. There is no suggestion that they were ever tortured and after the war neither of them mentioned or even hinted at such treatment. Yet German evidence from the files of the Abwehr and the Gestapo make it abundantly clear that both Best and Stevens talked freely. Of the two men, Best was easily the more sophisticated in dealing with the Germans and, initially at least, he seems to have said very little. According to German sources, Stevens told them such a lot that the Germans more or less left Best alone for two weeks. A charitable view would be that this was due to Stevens' lack of experience, but it is possible that another factor was that Stevens actually believed that some kind of a deal with the Germans was still possible, and that he was talking in an effort to probe Nazi intentions. Best, possibly to cover up his colleague's weaknesses, stated in his own account in *The Venlo Incident* that he believed that Stevens discarded his list of agents before they were caught: his exact words were, 'I believe he tore up the paper and threw it out of the car'. But evidence both on the German and Dutch side is that the Germans secured from Stevens a list of his agents and that this was how originally they were able to break him down and make him talk.

Perhaps Stevens, fully aware of his own limitations, was ashamed of this stupid breach of elementary security precautions. This may have caused a psychological collapse on his part. He attempted suicide in Berlin and there is no doubt that his detailed confessions placed Best in a very difficult position. The Germans did not have to exercise any physical pressure on Stevens. He felt, as he wrote in June, 1940, in a short letter to Best which was sent surreptitiously, 'compelled to tell the truth. Any other line would have been useless. They already knew too much . . . I was told that if I did not talk, I'd soon be made to.'

This was the only hint of the threat of torture. The Germans seem to have appreciated his co-operation. Later in the concentration camp in which he was finally locked up with Best, he received privileged treatment. Occasionally, admittedly under supervision, he was allowed to play tennis or swim outside the camp, or even to go to theatre shows in Munich. Curiously, some of those who held SIS posts during World War II today seem intent on defending Stevens and blaming Best for giving away information to the Germans. This is possibly because Stevens belonged to the orthodox MI 6 set-up, whereas Best was a protégé of Dansey who was the *bête noire* of so many of the SIS hierarchy. Certain it is that to some extent Best and Stevens tended to blame one another for disclosures.

What is abundantly clear, however, is that the Germans obtained from both men all vital details of the British Secret Service which they had in their possession. Thus this always doubtful mission nearly caused Britain to lose the war. It proved to be a body blow for national security within the first few months of the war, and in military terms equivalent to the total devastation of several divisions. Its outcome was the destruction of the entire British Secret Service networks on the continent of Europe and the revelation to the Germans of its personnel and organisation in London as well as abroad. It was not surprising that after this the Germans seriously considered the possibility of a successful invasion of Britain. If they had not lost their nerve the following year, very little indeed could have prevented the taking over of the whole nation.

One of the aims of the kidnapping of Best and Stevens was to gain proof that the Dutch military chiefs had been acting in a non-neutral fashion. To this extent, as has been seen, the Venlo affair actually led indirectly to the invasion of Holland by the Nazis the following year. Three days after the incident Heinrich Himmler, head of the Gestapo, proposed to Hitler that the SS men who had taken part in the kidnapping should be awarded the Iron Cross second class (Schellenberg received the same award first class). What Himmler added in his recommendation was significant – 'the men had the job of using existing information connections in such a way that evidence for a continued breach of neutrality by Holland in favour of Britain could be put forward.'

Captured Gestapo records make it clear that the Germans did everything possible to exploit the Venlo incident. These reveal that Schellenberg and the chief of the Gestapo in Düsseldorf obtained a confession which they said had been made by Lieutenant Klop before he died. It is extremely unlikely that Klop was fit enough to make any kind of statement while he was mortally wounded. In the 'confession' it was stated that plans to overthrow the Nazi regime had been 'actively supported by the Dutch General Staff in continuous consultation with the British General Staff.' Subsequent examination of documents has shown that Klop's signature had almost certainly been forged and attached to a bogus confession.

From that moment onwards the British Secret Service in Europe was more or less blotted out. At the very moment that Best and Stevens were being imprisoned in Berlin Schellenberg used the wireless link to The Hague to maintain contact, this time with Stevens' deputy who, astonishingly, was not even adequately informed as to what had happened at Venlo. The deputy responded to Schellenberg's call (the latter was still operating as 'Schaemmel') by suggesting that negotiations should continue despite the kidnapping of Best and Stevens! From this it would seem that London had not even warned their MI 6 post in The Hague.

The full proof of the break-up of the British Secret Service in Europe – apart from functioning in spasmodic bursts in Switzerland – lies in a specially prepared report for the German Secret Service entitled *Der Britische Nachrichtendienst* which, by the beginning of 1940, contained an almost complete guide to the British Secret Service. Not only did it give a brief run-down of the whole set-up of intelligence services in the Foreign Office, War Office, Admiralty, Air Ministry, Colonial Office and Board of Trade, but named all the top men in all departments. On Stevens it had this to say: 'Stevens is known to have run the Passport Control Office in The Hague. Stevens and his staff were mainly concerned with the acquisition of military intelligence from and regarding Germany . . . Stevens reported either to his boss, Admiral Hugh Sinclair, or to the Admiral's headquarters housed in 54 London Broadway Buildings, near St James's Park Station. His deputy was Colonel Stewart Menzies, a Scotsman who succeeded his boss on the latter's death on 4 November, 1939. His ADCs [sic] were Captain Howard, RN, Captain Russell and Hatton Hall.'

But the details which followed this revelation prove that between them, wittingly or unwittingly, Best and Stevens must have given away their whole organisation. The German report shows that they knew that the administrative section of the SIS was on the fifth floor of the Broadway Building, that Major Hatton Hall was head of the military section and Captain Russell head of the naval section on the sixth floor. It is true that sometimes the German translations were somewhat slapdash, for example, regarding the Air Section Intelligence, there was this note: '*Leiter*: Winter-Bottom (Whing-commander?). *Er hat zwei Offiziers als Mit-arbeiter*: Adams *und*.?' This referred to Group-Captain F. W. Winterbotham who was one of the key people in the deciphering business in World War II.

The Germans obtained from Best and Stevens a massive overall picture of the whole SIS set-up, even to some extent covering the counter-espionage department of MI 5. On the political section of the SIS the Germans had these comments: 'Head of Department, Major Vivian, assisted by Police Officer Mills (Vivian calls himself Major, but he is also a police officer [he was ex-Indian Police]) . . . the handling of subversive movements, communists, fascists etc. Stevens and Best do not differentiate between counter-intelligence and espionage. Stevens says "they overlap so much there can be no division." Stevens claims that he does not know the title of this sub-section of Department Six [in fairness to Stevens it can be deduced from this that he was trying to lay a false trail for the Nazis, as MI 5 was not a department of MI 6, though there was some liaison between them].

'Cipher and Decipher Section: head of department not known. A retired colonel by the name of Geffreys works there.'

Many other names were splattered across the pages of the German Intelligence report on the SIS, and if the spelling was sometimes wrong, the identity was always clear: 'Communications section: *Leiter*: Perry, Gambier [this should have read Gambier-Parry] . . . MI 5: Colonel Sir Vernon Kell, Lieut.-Colonel Hinchley-Cook, G. Liddel [Capt. Guy Liddell] and a Mr Curry.'

Rather more fascinating is the passage in the report which names as a key man in MI 5 a 'Captain King in London, Delphin Square, Hood house, Flat 308, *bei* Coplestone.' In case this should cause some confusion because a Foreign Office cipher clerk, Capt. John Herbert King, was jailed for espionage in 1939, it should be explained that the German document does not refer to the same Captain King. 'Captain King' was in fact the cover-name used by one Maxwell Knight, of Section B 5 (b) of MI 5, a counter-espionage officer who operated from Dolphin Square.

Stevens and Best also confirmed to the Germans that plans for propaganda and sabotage were being prepared by the Secret Service. This referred to the section of the SIS known as Section D (for Destruction), which had been set up in 1938 under Colonel Lawrence Grand. It was intended, as its name implies, to be an aggressive unit aiming at inflicting damage on the enemy by sabotage. Its original purpose was not to operate outside the country, but in the event of a German invasion to organise subversive operations and sabotage in enemy-occupied territory in Britain. Grand had plenty of good ideas, but some of these went far beyond his brief. For example he put forward a scheme to stop the supply of Rumanian oil to Germany by acts of sabotage.

The Germans also learned that 'Z' Section of the SIS was controlled by Dansey from a small office in Bush House, Aldwych, and that in this entourage were fellow-workers of Best's such as Kenneth Cohen (code-named Cowan, Keith Crane and Robert Craig). From Stevens, Schellenberg had already obtained the call-sign ON 4, as well as a small wireless transmitter with a daily call schedule which enabled him to contact 'Z' Section in The Hague after the kidnapping.

The dossier which the Germans painstakingly built up from what Best and Stevens told them has never before been published in any detail. It is a classic document revealing how in a single kidnapping incident a Secret Service could be broken in an afternoon. Every important address of secret operatives in London (often with telephone numbers) was duly recorded from Queen Anne's Gate and Broadway, to plans for moving the deciphering organisation to Bletchley. One interesting sideline in the text was the naming of the new head of MI 6, Stewart Menzies, the Germans carefully noting that this was '*gesprochen Mengis*', in other words, 'pronounced Mengis'. The complete text was published in 1940 for limited circulation only in German Intelligence circles as part of a document entitled *Information – Scheft Grossbritannien*.

Did all this amount to betrayal on the part of Best and Stevens? It certainly came very close to it and, under the much more professional basis of Intelligence work today, it would have been rated as such. But the truth regarding this is not easy to arrive at in an objective way. It might even be that one or both men thought that by revealing a certain amount of the truth about the SIS they would gain access to some senior Intelligence officer who was sympathetic to the Allies and himself an anti-Nazi, perhaps even Canaris himself. If, as we now know, some leading British statesmen still clung to the idea of a negotiated peace, Best and Stevens might have had the same naïve thoughts. For some reason Stevens was treated rather more leniently than Best, probably because he was Passport Control Officer. Best undoubtedly suffered from being linked to the ill-fated 'Z' Section which, quite unfairly, was blamed more than MI 6 for the Venlo disaster.

It may also be that Best was singled out for criticism after the war on the basis of the Abwehr and Gestapo reports on him. One of these stated, 'Best is of a different opinion to Stevens. Unlike Stevens he is not a professional soldier. But he is superior to him as far as experience in the Intelligence Service is concerned, and as a result his attitude is more penetrating; these qualities he combines with considerable character defects and a complete lack of scruples. He is not a British officer like Stevens. He is a civilian who loves to live well and be a successful businessman. He may therefore see things in a clearer light in spite of a pretended lack of significance, or he may say more than Stevens. He has stated that the Foreign Office, the Admiralty and other departments have their own espionage centres and exchange information. . . .

'In this context one has to discuss once more what the British mean by counter-espionage. Stevens and Best both spoke of counter-espionage and called it either counter-espionage or counter-Intelligence, but they refused to differentiate between the two . . . Best defined it thus: "Counter-espionage includes all security and police actions which are taken to prevent events that may become the source of national or political danger." During World War I, counter-espionage was, according to Best, handled by the MI 5 in the War Office. It worked closely with Scotland Yard.'

This last claim by the Germans would seem to show that whereas Stevens had attempted to deceive them by suggesting MI 5 was a branch of MI 6, Best gave them the real facts.

Schellenberg was far from being elated about his coup at Venlo. He still felt that more could have been achieved if he had been allowed to continue the negotiations as he wished. Ordered by Hitler to assign the ablest and most experienced counter-espionage officers to the task of questioning Best and Stevens, he was anxious that the prisoners should be treated in the best way possible, but, he added, 'unfortunately, orders began to come down from above . . . Hitler demanded that every evening the reports of the day's interrogation be shown to him personally. . . . To my dismay he became increasingly convinced that the attempt on his life had been the work of British Intelligence and that Best and Stevens . . . were the real organisers of this crime.'

By the spring of 1940 Holland was invaded by the Germans and the onslaught across Belgium and France followed swiftly. The 'Phoney War' was transformed into the Battle of Britain and, with France having surrendered and Winston Churchill called to form a truly National Government, it was very much a matter of fighting for survival. Could Britain hold on long enough to restore some of the damage which had been done, not just by the German advancing armies but by the blunders of their own secret agents?

Churchill was one of the first to realise that Britain's conventional Secret Service was a dead duck and that it would be a long time before it could recover and be rebuilt. Yet not even Churchill, or any of his advisers, realised at that time just how much Best and Stevens had passed on to the Germans. More by instinct than anything else, knowing how the SIS set-up in Europe had been destroyed, the new Prime Minister decided that something needed to be built up instantly to replace that devastating loss. It had to be something new, with no links to the past, and so the Special Operations Executive (SOE for short) was created to replace Britain's intelligence network in large areas of Nazi-occupied Europe.

Without the building up of SOE Britain would have been almost totally devoid of any kind of secret service in Europe for the rest of 1940 and well into 1941. This is the situation into which Best and Stevens had landed the whole country. It meant starting almost totally from scratch, desperately improvising by using amateurs to establish links with would-be resisters in France, Holland, Belgium and more rarely in Germany. There was a desperate attempt to recruit anyone who might be able to fit into such an organisation. Sometimes the recruits proved totally inadequate for the harsh tasks which lay before them. There was Noor Inayat Khan, an Indian princess born in Russia, who joined SOE. An emotional, artistic character, she should almost certainly never have been recruited for such work. Yet she was sent into action in France, eventually arrested by the Gestapo, taken to Dachau and executed. Unlike Best or Stevens, however, this gallant young woman refused to reveal anything to the enemy, despite threats and torture. She was posthumously awarded the George Cross.

Occasionally some unexpected talent would appear to relieve the situation, like one cheerful little Cockney Jew who was parachuted into France and scored surprising successes. Churchill had decided that the task of rebuilding an effective Intelligence organisation to link up with the Resistance groups in occupied Europe was too much for the Secret Service to tackle, and he gave Dr Hugh Dalton, as Minister of Economic Warfare, the job of forming the SOE. In the early days many risks had to be taken. Among the influx of French, Belgians, Dutch, Norwegians and Poles who fled to Britain from Nazi-occupied territory were many whose aim was to infiltrate British Intelligence, and relay information back to the Germans. The influx was so great and the need for recruits so acute that not even MI 5 could spare the time to screen everybody adequately. For at this time Britain faced five years of total war, for much of it entirely without allies, not only virtually unarmed, but without any Intelligence source left behind enemy lines, to penetrate what Winston Churchill called 'the veil of the unknown'.

Best and Stevens did not fare too badly in prison, though as the war continued conditions became somewhat harsher. While they could occasionally hear the screams of less fortunate inmates who were being roughly 'interrogated', they at least were regarded and treated as 'officers and gentlemen'. Yet the Gestapo Arrest List for Great Britain, the *Sonderfahndungsliste G.B.*, reveals only too clearly the extent to which Best and Stevens provided names. Among those names, together with a good deal of factual detail, is that of Major Stevens' wife, who is listed as belonging to the '*Täterkreis* Stevens/Best', the Stevens-Best network. Yet another was David Footman, a senior officer in MI 5 and an authority on Russia.

Stevens tended to insist afterwards that he had a much worse time than Best and blamed the fact that so very many British agents were killed by the Germans after their arrest because Best had supplied all the names and numbers of SIS car registrations. This was certainly a gross exaggeration of what Best could have told the Germans, though it is true that many agents were rounded up and shot. Best, on the other hand, claims that Professor Six, a Gestapo agent, planned to take Stevens with him to Britain if and when the Germans invaded, so Stevens could act as adviser on arrests and safeguarding actions.

In his book, *The Venlo Incident*, Best was rather more charitable towards Stevens. He writes of meeting a medical officer at Dachau who had met Stevens. 'He said that Stevens himself was quite fit and that the conditions of his life were extremely comfortable; his quarters were roomy, he was allowed unlimited exercise in a garden which he shared with a number of other prisoners . . . and he was permitted to leave the camp in the company of a guard to play tennis, bathe, and even got to the theatre at Munich. I was, of course, delighted to hear that he was getting on so well, as he had really seemed to be in very bad shape at Sachsenhausen, and I had often feared that his health might have broken down.'

One ingenious ploy which the Germans used was to send one of their agents, disguised as a matchseller, to St James's Park underground station where he would be able to keep a watch on everyone at the SIS Broadway headquarters. The matchseller's job was to photograph surreptitiously all those going in and out of the building. Whether the Germans actually pulled off such a coup, or whether they pretended to do so is of little account. But they claimed that the pictures were taken and shown to Stevens who confirmed the identities of some of the people.

Schellenberg in his memoirs states that he tried several times to secure the freedom of Best and Stevens by having them exchanged for German prisoners of war, but that 'all these attempts were sharply rejected by Himmler, until finally in 1943 he forbade me ever to bring up the matter again.'

When eventually they were released both Best and Stevens were closely interrogated by the British. Stevens somewhat inauspiciously ended his career as a translator and died in Brighton in 1965. Best was reunited with his Dutch wife who had been evacuated to England, but their marriage ended in divorce. He was later married again to an English woman with whom he spent the remaining years of his life quite happily. From all accounts he was given the roughest time by the authorities in MI 6 who informed him that his services in the SIS were no longer required and they appeared to indicate that they blamed him for the Venlo affair. This was being smugly wise after the event, bearing in mind that MI 6 had gone along with the 'Schaemmel' project without giving any warnings right up to the time of the kidnapping.

Best lived on in his countryside retreat in the West Country until 1978 when he died at the age of ninety-three. Despite the ups and downs of his always precarious life, Sigismund Payne Best was the great survivor. He even managed in a dignified way to survive the indignities heaped on him by those who believed he had given away a nation's most precious secrets. His hey-day had undoubtedly belonged to the First World War when he was awarded the OBE for his intelligence work as well as the Belgian *Croix de Guerre* and the French *Légion d'Honneur*.

Earlier on, no doubt listening to those in authority who wanted to pin all the blame for Venlo and its aftermath on Best, the British Foreign Office had deliberately excluded him from a £1 million West German Fund for victims of Nazi war crimes. Perhaps there were many more deserving cases, but Best had nevertheless been kidnapped and imprisoned by the Nazis for practically six years of war. It was not until 1968 that he, along with eleven others, was paid a very modest sum of compensation by the British for 'treatment at the hands of the Nazis'. At that age the compensation meant very little anyhow.

There was one final tribute to him in a letter to the *Daily Telegraph* just after his death was announced. A Mr R. K. Sheridon, of West Wickham, Kent, recorded that Best had been instrumental in the last days of the war 'in saving the lives of some 136 other prominent hostages of the Nazi regime . . . These people had been dragged from concentration camp to concentration camp across the Third Reich, away from the advances of the Allied armies, and had finished up, at the end of April, 1945, in the charge of an SS extermination squad. Captain Best was one of these prisoners and it was, in part, due to his cool-headed adroitness in negotiation, in concert with a group of anti-Nazi *Wehrmacht* officer prisoners, as well as the efforts of the local Tyrolese Resistance, that a massacre did not take place . . . Among those saved were Dr Kurt von Schuschnigg, until Hitler's invasion, Chancellor of Austria; his wife, Vera; Léon Blum of France and his wife; and Pastor Martin Niemoller.'

3
Cynthia

'After twenty years . . . Cynthia's tiger still stalked. The electric force was undiminished. She was still beautiful . . . still restless and quick moving. How so much sheer power had been contained in the small area of a quiet, almost humdrum life was inconceivable'

H. MONTGOMERY HYDE
Cynthia: The Spy who changed the course of the War

Harking back to our last story of the Venlo incident, it was an ironic feature of the tragedy that the Passport Control Centre of the British Embassy in The Hague was actually next door to the house in which the legendary Mata Hari had lived in 1915. The name of Mata Hari lives on almost as a cliché – 'she's a bit of a Mata Hari' – but in fact Mata Hari was a novice compared with the subject of this chapter, 'Cynthia'.

Mata Hari was in contrast to 'Cynthia' a bungling, grossly over-romanticised and inefficient spy. She has survived in the history of espionage largely because she was an alluring dancer who was shot by the French for spying for the Germans in World War I. So Mata Hari became a martyr as well as a notorious spy.

'Cynthia', however, was a very different character whose activities in World War II helped to shorten the war. 'Cynthia' became her code-name and because she is best known by this pseudonym, it will be easier and certainly more evocative of her character and calling to refer to her by this name throughout the rest of this narrative. Her real name was not exactly that which a writer of spy stories would choose for his key female agent. It was the prosaic name of Amy Elizabeth Thorpe, and she was born in Minneapolis, Minnesota, on 22 November 1910, an American citizen of mixed ancestry, this being Scandinavian-Irish on her father's side and French-Canadian with an admixture of Bavarian stock on her mother's side. She was the daughter of Major George Cyrus Thorpe, of the United States Marine Corps. In her family she was known as Betty.

One is strongly tempted in writing Cynthia's story to describe her as a kind of female Sorge. In results achieved and in efficiency over a long period she certainly compared with Sorge. On the other hand she was never operating under such dangerous conditions as Sorge and her spying, generally speaking, was done in the comfort of her native or neutral countries and

OPPOSITE Cynthia as a débutante

brought to its climax in the most comfortable of beds. Nor did it ever seem possible that Cynthia was deeply dedicated to any cause as Sorge was. She seems not to have cared for politics one iota, except as a talking point. The nearest she came to giving any reason for her activities was not in referring to any political system, or a single nation, but simply in this statement to her biographer, H. Montgomery Hyde: 'I loved my own America passionately, and I loved England and Poland and most especially Spain, and later I came to love France. I look back on these countries as another woman might think back on the successes of her salad days, or a particularly rare and extraordinary love affair.'

This statement is puzzlingly ambiguous. Love and patriotism are not quite the same thing. Cynthia's achievements were incalculably valuable and she herself was brave, reckless, determined, and her spirit unconquerable. Yet in the end one comes to the conclusion that it was the game of espionage linked to sheer sexual enjoyment which counted far more than any cause. This, and her zest for excitement and adventure, was what made Cynthia tick.

She could hardly have come from a more conservative background. Her father had fought in the Spanish-American War at the turn of the century and had travelled around the world in various posts. During most of the First World War the Thorpe family was stationed in Cuba and it was here that Cynthia grew up, notably, as her friends recall, always something of a loner, despite the fact that her brother and sister were there as company. It was in Cuba that she first learned Spanish, thus paving the way to her great passion for Spain later in her life.

Later the Thorpes moved to Washington and then, in 1921, to Hawaii, where her father was in command of the Marines at Pearl Harbor. There are various stories of Cynthia's precociousness at this age. 'She was always trying to prove that she could tackle almost anything we funked doing,' said Alicia Rose, one of her schoolfriends in her Washington days, 'and that usually meant getting into some kind of dangerous mischief. We always felt it was a reaction against her mother who was terribly conventional.' It is said that she wrote a novel called *Fiorette*, when she was only ten, set in Naples which she had never visited. She herself claimed that she was seduced at the age of fourteen and that she was deeply in love. Her lover, as she put it to her biographer, was 'an old gentleman of twenty-one!' But, as her school friend commented somewhat tartly, 'if anyone was the seducer, it must have been Betty herself.'

The teenage Cynthia was certainly remarkably mature for her age and her photograph, taken when she was fourteen, shows her as strongly resembling her father, with the same rather full and firm lips, but with a curiously serious, unsmiling expression. Very few photographs of Cynthia show her smiling either at this age or later on.

It was shortly after her first affair that Cynthia was sent to Switzerland with her sister Jane to complete her education at a finishing school overlooking Lake Geneva. She was also taken on a tour of Europe before returning to Washington where she attended the Dana Hall School in Wellesley, Massachusetts.

Her mother was from all accounts somewhat of an aggressive snob, always pushing Cynthia into 'doing the right thing', attending the 'right parties' and talking the right kind of social jargon. In short, she was being rather unimaginatively pushed forward into a rigidly orthodox pattern which did not suit her and into doing all the things which the more possessive and ambitious of society mothers of the late twenties expected of their daughters. But Cynthia was emotionally and mentally ahead of all this: she was an exceptionally adult girl with a mind of her own long before she was rated a débutante.

In great demand among the young males of her coming-out period, she gave the impression of finding American boys immature and boring. It was at this time that she met Arthur Pack, the second secretary on the commercial side at the British Embassy. He was an Irish Catholic, nearly twenty years older than Cynthia, and as a result of wounds in the First World War his health had been more or less permanently impaired. It was a strange choice for Cynthia to make. Arthur Pack may have been much older and more worldly wise than the American boys she affected to despise, but he was, by most contemporary accounts, a pompous man, slow on the uptake and conventional in every respect.

It was certainly out of character for Cynthia to marry someone like Arthur Pack when she could have had the choice of so many other dashing characters of all nationalities. She was nearly twenty, strikingly attractive in a rather voluptuous way, with a slender figure, auburn hair and large green eyes which, as one admirer once described them, were 'like a dash of green chartreuse in a pool of limpid brandy'. But there was always about her that look of challenge, something in her whole demeanour that seemed to be 'permanently daring one to do something with her whether it was to play polo, go on a midnight picnic or just to leap into bed with her' (the assessment of a former British diplomat). This same close observer of Cynthia and her husband was convinced that Pack had been considering marriage not for any personal preference, but because it seemed to be the thing to do and might further his career.

There could only have been one reason why Cynthia should marry Pack and that was, quite simply, that she was expecting his child. Certainly he was not Cynthia's type and they clashed violently throughout their married life. It must have come as a devastating shock to a twenty-year-old girl that, having agreed to marry Cynthia, Pack suggested she might have an abortion and get rid of the child, a most astonishing proposal from an Irish Catholic of that era.

This might have had something to do with that objectivity towards the male sex which Cynthia developed in later years and which she never lost. Men were to her what women are to some men – almost solely sex objects, though the emphasis was on intelligent and amusing sex objects.

Once they were married, on 29 April 1930, and went to Britain Pack did everything possible to encourage her in hard riding and any physical exercises which might bring about a miscarriage. His whole attitude to the child was that it was essential to cover up this pre-marital affair on the grounds that this could ruin his career and scandalise friends and relations. He need not have worried. Pack was never in the running for any major job. Despite his attitude and because of compassionate gynaecological advice, Cynthia had a son on 2 October 1930. Even then Pack insisted on keeping the matter secret and that the child must not be allowed to remain with his mother. So Cynthia, greatly upset, relinquished the baby to foster-parents and returned to Washington for a spell.

This was a harsh introduction to England and English society and, though the latter could hardly be blamed for Arthur Pack's attitude to their child, it could very easily have been linked in Cynthia's mind with a nation which could subscribe to such views. After all, one would have expected that Pack, by reason of his religion and education alone, should have taken a more civilised view of a child of his own. To be fair to Pack, one must concede that the account of the child's birth and background is purely that of Cynthia's. There is just the thought – possibly an ignoble one – that Pack was not the father and that Cynthia had agreed to marry him because she was expecting someone else's child. What is surprising is that such a high-spirited girl as Cynthia should have agreed to this nonsense about concealing details of the child's birth.

This incident is yet another of the enigmas of the Cynthia story. According to her own account, she really loved this child. But what was the psychological effect of this on her? Did Cynthia hit back at this by treating men as sex objects, by reducing them to sexual rubble, so completely intoxicated by her own brand of charm that they would jump through any hoop she liked to hold in front of them? If so, perhaps one could hardly be surprised. As far as training for the espionage game was concerned, what she had learned by this time was how to handle problems involving secrecy and skilled deceit, which really is a job for professionals. Oscar Wilde expounded in his own inimitable manner on the art of dissembling in his essay, *The Decay of Lying*, and he might have included in his survey the art of secrecy. Cynthia possessed to an incredible degree a talent for dissembling and preserving secrets. Wilde put his finger on this most mysterious of talents when he wrote: 'People have a careless way of talking about a "born liar", just as they talk about a born poet . . . they are wrong. Lying and poetry are arts . . . and they require the most careful study.' And Cynthia was a highly skilled liar of whom Wilde would have approved, and admired. Both in her love life and in her espionage work she told lies boldly, without any attempt to explain or justify them.

From the early thirties onwards Cynthia sought consolation with a succession of lovers, though most of her affairs were conducted relatively discreetly. First, when Pack was transferred to Chile in 1931 as commercial attaché in Santiago, she had a relationship with a wealthy Chilean and, with her usual daring, started to play polo, then quite an eccentric thing for a woman to do. Later when her husband was posted to Spain she had an affair with a senior officer in the Spanish Air Force. If British diplomats' wives were all as errant as Cynthia in those days it is surprising that Britain kept any secrets at all. Was Cynthia ever vetted for security reasons? The answer was probably a dusty 'no', yet somebody undoubtedly started to keep her under observation as a possible recruit to the British Secret Service.

Here one comes back to the Venlo syndrome and the picture of a nation of amateurs mixed up in diplomacy, politics and secret service. However promiscuous Cynthia might have been on the side, she never, as far as people who remember can tell, acted other than discreetly. There were whispers about her conduct, but no more. Then in 1935 occurred the most surprising and puzzling feature of her life. According to her own version of the story, to please the husband she already despised, she agreed to become a Catholic. Much more plausible reasons are that on the last day of 1934 a daughter, Denise, had been born to her and that her life in Spain had brought her into contact with many devoted Catholics.

But was there another reason for this conversion? Had Cynthia already been lured into the world of espionage and was it thought that Catholic male might speak more freely to Catholic female when between the sheets? One man who believed that this was a major reason was the late Lieutenant-Commander Don Gomez-Beare, a Gibraltarian, who became British naval attaché in Madrid in World War II. 'Betty [as he called her] was even then a power-house of ideas and information,' he said, 'and as a Catholic she was in rather a stronger position to "confess" the men!'

Coming from Gomez-Beare, who was himself an extremely competent operative in this field, this suggests very strongly indeed that Cynthia was then already assisting British Intelligence. What one would like to know is who recruited her, for there both Cynthia herself and most of those who knew her are silent. It was certainly in Spain that she began to be positively engaged in secret operations, especially after the Civil War broke out. The priest who was instructing her in the Catholic faith was imprisoned by the Republicans and she managed not only to visit him, but to tell him how to escape through the Republican lines. After the British Embassy staff had been evacuated to Biarritz in 1936, Cynthia was involved in a border incident at Irun and was denounced as a spy, this time quite wrongly. But she did help a number of Franco supporters to escape and later displeased the British Embassy by visiting the Red Cross headquarters at Burgos and obtaining supplies for the Generalissimo's forces.

Perhaps it was just as well that in the summer of 1937 Arthur Pack was posted to Warsaw, as Cynthia was becoming somewhat of a disturbing influence with her pro-Franco activities. But before going to Poland she arranged for the release of her imprisoned Spanish lover, Antonio, and some of his fellow aviators from Valencia, then the seat of the Republican Government. All this was done by a mixture of quite astonishing bravery, in the face of all kinds of dangers, and her own inimitable quality for cajoling people into doing her favours. But it was not until she arrived in Poland that Cynthia became a secret agent in real earnest. About this time Arthur confessed to her that he had fallen in love with a married woman whose husband refused to divorce her. Shortly afterwards he suffered from a cerebral thrombosis and was critically ill for some weeks.

Very soon Cynthia was becoming as ardently involved in Polish affairs as she had in those of Spain. She quickly became a favourite with some of the young men in the Polish Foreign Office. It was a fairly casual and unexceptional item of intelligence from one such Pole that caused the MI 6 man in Warsaw to tell her to get as much more of 'such stuff as you can'. That is how she officially started as a spy, though there is little doubt that her activities in Spain had been reported back to MI 6 headquarters in London and that she had long before been used as a useful informant. But, as Gomez-Beare put it, it was not until she got to Warsaw that she 'lost her amateur status. From then on she actually got an allowance from the Intelligence boys. Long before this she had been quite a useful informant for British Naval Intelligence.'

British Intelligence was particularly weak in Poland at this period, so any help Cynthia could give was welcomed. It was, however, made absolutely clear to her that her husband must know nothing of what she was doing. This was made easier through his being away ill much of the time, so Cynthia swiftly entered into the spirit of this new adventure and became the mistress of the Polish diplomat. But her greatest triumph in Warsaw was when she determinedly set out to ensnare another young Pole who was a confidential aide of Colonel Josef Beck, the Foreign Secretary, one of the most devious statesmen in Europe.

'When I heard what his job was,' Cynthia told her biographer, Montgomery Hyde, 'I would have made a dead set at him, even if he had been as ugly as Satan. But happily this wasn't necessary.' Which remark exemplifies as well as anything Cynthia's wholehearted enthusiasm for the tasks of espionage.

What, however, has not been told before is exactly what was so very important about this Pole. Not only was he entirely in Colonel Beck's confidence, but frequently went on secret missions for his master to Czechoslovakia and Germany. He also had access to all manner of confidential documents. But far more important than all this was the tip Cynthia was given that he might also be able to give her details of the German 'Enigma' cipher machine. Thanks to British Naval Intelligence rather than the Secret Service, Britain had usually been a few jumps ahead of other nations when it came to cryptography. Thus it was realised long before war broke out that to break the potential enemy's cipher systems was worth a score of victories fought out in conventional fashion.

The tip-off was that not only were Polish engineers working on adaptations of the Enigma machine, but that Colonel Beck himself was interested in it. One of the few men who had foreseen the rise of Nazism had been a Canadian named William Stephenson, whose first-hand reports on Germany had been passed personally to Winston Churchill. Stephenson was almost a one-man Intelligence service to Churchill, then out of office but desperately anxious to warn the nation of what threatened it from without. And Stephenson had news of the new developments of the Enigma machine, partly from an anti-Nazi Pole and partly from one of his shrewdest assessors of such technical details, Charles Proteus Steinmetz, a Jewish scientist who had been forced to leave Germany because of his social-democratic views. Steinmetz was a man in advance of his time, especially in the field of electronics, and nobody was so able in analysing the reports of German scientific developments and then forecasting what they might mean in terms of weaponry. It was Steinmetz who pointed the way to the decoding of German signals of the Enigma chain.

To what extent Cynthia helped to solve the mysteries of Enigma is difficult to evaluate. The truth is that many people played a part in this. It was not until early 1939 that an up-to-date Enigma machine was captured and taken to Warsaw where it was picked up by Commander Alastair Denniston, a naval officer who had for a long time master-minded the British Government's Code and Cipher School. By this time it was realised that there was a new portable Enigma and the aim of the British was to build a replica. The Polish Secret Service had helped to capture these secrets and even to work out some of the methods by which the Germans had used Enigma.

Knowing what Cynthia achieved later, there is no reason to doubt that she did not apply herself wholeheartedly to this problem while she was in Poland. The probability is that she herself did not realise that the Intelligence she provided before World War II broke out was worth just as much, if not more, than what she supplied afterwards. She had a quick-thinking mind, an ability to absorb information in the tersest form and to pass it on accurately, even though she made no pretensions to understand what she was obtaining. It is certain that Cynthia herself had very little inkling of just how important her intelligence-gathering proved to be.

'The gossips claimed she required the most exquisite food and wine, followed by several hours of intense intellectual intercourse before she could be lured into bed, where she would make it all worthwhile,' wrote William Stevenson, Stephenson's biographer. But he added these important words: 'What the gossips did not suspect was that British intelligence was the chief beneficiary of her charms. She was in a position to help the understaffed SIS at a crucial moment in history . . . the future manipulators of ULTRA [the British deciphering establishment at Bletchley] were looking for details of the Enigma coding machine adapted for Nazi security services. Polish engineers worked on the new Enigma models, in which the Polish Foreign Minister, Josef Beck, was thought to be interested. Colonel Beck was on good terms with Nazis in Berlin. Beck's confidential aide was one of Cynthia's lovers.'

And Cynthia entered into this exciting new role in her life with great enthusiasm. Possibly at this stage she was fortunate in that Beck's aide was a highly desirable lover and she found it only too easy to persuade him to give her documents from Beck's office which were copied and returned. Cynthia herself talked very little to anyone about this episode in her life, yet from it stemmed not only one of the discoveries which helped win the war, but the realisation by British Intelligence that here was an agent of almost incredible talent.

'At first we just couldn't believe our eyes,' said one who worked on the operation to master the new Nazi version of Enigma. 'Here was the missing link in the whole chain of our intelligence on Enigma. You see, capturing the secrets of the Enigma machine was a major intelligence operation in itself, involving many people and many departments – SIS, the Admiralty Intelligence, War Office, etc. What Enigma did, to put it in terms the layman can understand, was to turn messages into an unintelligible scramble before transmitting it in Morse. Many people had played a role in obtaining these secrets, getting a detail here and another one there, both Americans and British co-operating to some extent. One of the most valuable of our contacts had been an anti-Nazi Pole who had worked in the German factory where the Enigma machine was built. And it was after this that we sent a secret service mission to Warsaw in an effort to follow up on Enigma. The trouble was, you see, that there had been several variations of Enigma over the years, with new models coming out just to cause more headaches for the I boys. And that is where Cynthia came in with the most unexpected results.'

Cynthia went with Beck's aide to Prague and Berlin and, though no cipher expert nor having any knowledge of the technicalities of this rather complex world, she discovered that the Polish Secret Service had secured the keys to German *Wehrmacht* cipher systems. Some of the Intelligence she supplied simply confirmed what the British already knew, but was none the less valuable for that. On the other hand what new Intelligence she secured was enormously important. That was certainly the opinion of Stephenson, who was an authority on both electronics and ciphers, and he unhesitatingly marked down Cynthia as a part-time agent worthy of more important work.

Indeed, so important was Cynthia even at this early stage in her career that it was considered necessary not only to withdraw her temporarily from further Intelligence work, but to put out a cover story which would help to kill any suspicions that she was working for the British. Cynthia herself had no inkling as to how she was being handled. When ordered to leave the country, she imagined that the British Ambassador's wife, whom she disliked, had engineered this on the grounds that she was passing secrets to the Poles through her liaison with Beck's aide. The truth was that the British Secret Service deliberately put around the story that she was suspected of passing information to pro-Nazi diplomats and had been ordered out of Warsaw for that reason. It was not a difficult story for people in Warsaw to swallow because Beck's aide was known to be allied to those who sought an understanding with Hitler. In any event he had made things difficult by telling Colonel Beck that he wished to divorce his wife and to marry Cynthia.

Thus it was that Arthur Pack, who had now recovered in health, was dispatched to Chile and Cynthia accompanied him. This was a country where German influence was strong and British Intelligence felt that Cynthia, with her fluent Spanish, would be an asset to them there. Stephenson, however, had other ideas. It was his long-term plan to lure Cynthia back to her native USA and to employ her talents against enemy and neutral diplomats.

Once she was established in Santiago, the Chilean capital, Cynthia launched out as a journalist, writing articles for a local newspaper. Although this brought her into contact with a timorous British Ambassador after war broke out (because she favoured the Allies in a neutral country!), she was in fact working strictly under orders from Stephenson who by this time was controlling all aspects of security and Intelligence for the British in the USA. The idea was for Cynthia to make a name for herself as a journalist and then to move to the USA where she would operate under her maiden name of Elizabeth Thorpe and make it clear that she was separated from her diplomat husband.

This may seem a very thin cover and one which would hardly work today, when to have any real chance of success she would have had to adopt a totally new identity. She was, of course, well known in some Washington circles, having lived there previously, so a disguise would not have been very reliable. Yet her highly skilled spymaster, Stephenson, worked on the principle that a brilliant amateur in espionage could get away with much more than a professional. Being full of admiration for Cynthia's achievements in Poland, he was also confident that she had not yet been marked down in the dossiers of any enemy or hostile neutral or non-belligerent country as a probable spy. So, when summoned to New York and given the code-name of Cynthia, Elizabeth Thorpe Pack cut adrift permanently from her husband, leaving behind a self-incriminating letter to enable him to obtain a divorce, if he wished.

David Kahn, author of *The Codebreakers* and a past president both of the American Cryptogram Association and of the New York Cipher Society, states that 'some of the most important British communications intelligence resulted, however, not from the scribblings and quiet cogitations of reticent crypto-analysts, but from the explosive sexual charms of a British secret agent in America. Her unlocking of several hearts gave Britain access to vast treasuries of intelligence . . . in the winter of 1940–41 BSC [British Security Coordination] assigned Cynthia the task of obtaining the Italian naval cryptosystem.'

BSC arranged for Cynthia to rent a two-storey house in the socially fashionable Georgetown area of Washington. This was the spider's web into which sooner or later Cynthia lured her potential victims. The first man to be enticed there was the Italian Admiral Alberto Lais, naval attaché at the embassy in Washington. Cynthia had met the Admiral years previously so it was not too difficult to strike up a close acquaintance. Lais was a middle-aged man with a large family, somewhat bored with the chores of a naval attaché's work and with an eye for an affair on the side. Cynthia provided him with the opportunity he needed and soon he was in her thralls, prepared to risk his career and even his life for her sake.

Cynthia had an unerring talent for knowing just how to play on a man's mental susceptibilities as well as on his emotions. It was a game of bed and brains, not necessarily in that order. With some men bed came first and the onslaught on their brains afterwards; with others it was the reverse. In the case of Lais her task seems to have been relatively easy. The Admiral had no great enthusiasm for Mussolini's partnership with the Germans and when Cynthia hinted that she had friends in American Intelligence (that proved a more profitable line than revealing the truth that she was working for the British), he showed interest. It was of course a risky tactic; had it misfired, Cynthia could have become a liability overnight. But Lais was relatively easily persuaded to let her have the Italian naval code and cipher books with the superencipherment tables.

The documents were promptly photostatted and dispatched to London. Cynthia's coup in obtaining the Italian ciphers had surprisingly quick results. On 28 March, 1941, the Royal Navy won a resounding victory in the Mediterranean when the Italian fleet was routed at Cape Matapan. Admiral Cunningham's force destroyed the Italian cruisers *Fiume, Pola* and *Zara*, an action described by Winston Churchill as disposing of 'all challenge to British naval mastery in the Eastern Mediterranean at this critical time'. The British had been able to read the Italian signals concerning their own fleet movements and Admiral Cunningham had laid his plans accordingly.

Cynthia's next problem was how to deal with Admiral Lais. He had obviously little more to offer her and in many respects could present a hazard to her personally if he remained in Washington. With total cynicism

Cynthia used information he had passed to her to get him thrown out of Washington. Lais had told her of joint Italo-German plans to sabotage ships in American ports. This intelligence was passed on by the British to the FBI who promptly informed the State Department. Admiral Lais was immediately declared *persona non grata* and sent back to Rome. Cynthia bade him a fond farewell at the quayside, taking care to get from him the address of another Italian official who could provide her with cipher information when he had left!

Admiral Lais died a few years after the war, but when news of his affair with Cynthia was first revealed the Italian Ministry of Defence loyally defended him as 'a man of the highest integrity and honour' and indignantly repudiated the allegations. Though there is no doubt whatsoever about the truth of this story, which has been verified from various independent sources, it is probably true that it was not quite so sordid as it sounds. Lais may have been infatuated with Cynthia, but it is almost certain that he longed to see Italy free from her entanglement with the Nazis. Perhaps he felt he was in some strange way redeeming his country's good name. What makes this viewpoint sound logical is that a man who was simply indulging in a foolish love affair would hardly have passed on the name of another man just to provide a substitute bed-mate for Cynthia.

British Security Coordination were delighted with their Washington spy's efforts in the Italian Embassy and they decided that it would be well worth while employing her talents in a bid to acquire the cipher secrets of the Vichy French Embassy in Washington. But this venture was a much more difficult and dangerous project than the seduction of an anti-Nazi Italian Admiral already well known to Cynthia. It was a question of starting from scratch, feeling one's way towards useful contacts and, most important of all, finding a reason for meeting the top people in the French Embassy.

Stephenson, whose code-name was 'Intrepid', decided that for the first time he had better take a look at Cynthia himself and do the briefing for this vital task. He was a small, alert man with a soft Canadian accent that blended reasonably well into the American scene. From New York, throughout World War II, Stephenson, who was later knighted, directed both espionage and counter-espionage for the British in North America. It was an assignment which in many respects was as vital as that of the head of the Secret Service in London. In fact, in the years immediately preceding the United States' entry into the war it was probably even more important. Britain's Secret Service in Europe had been more or less totally destroyed after Venlo: it was from then on that Stephenson's position in New York became a key factor in winning the war when Britain, without allies, faced the might of Nazi Germany alone.

Stephenson had to contend with obtaining Intelligence on enemy plans and, at the same time, to seek out and watch pro-Axis agents and, especially, to check the growing number of sabotage actions against British shipping. But there was also another facet of Stephenson's organisation, to which, because of his long experience of life in Europe and America, he was well fitted, and this was the use of propaganda and, equally essential, counter-propaganda. The main aim of Germany and her allies, the Italians and the Vichy French, who were operating in the USA, was to keep America out of the war. Stephenson had to use all his wiles to counter the kind of propaganda they put out.

One day in May, 1941, Stephenson called on Cynthia at her Washington house. He announced himself as 'Mr Williams from the New York office'. She had not heard of a 'Mr Williams' before and her debriefings on visits to New York had always been carried out by two other British officials. For this reason Cynthia was wary at first, half wondering whether 'Mr Williams' was an Axis agent posing as a BSC man, or an FBI agent trying to find out what role she was playing. It must have been an amusing afternoon as the two sipped their cocktails, each testing out the other. Stephenson was summing up Cynthia, watching for weaknesses, assessing her as an agent; she was obliquely trying to find out who exactly he was. Apparently each played the game to the satisfaction of the other and in the end Cynthia was satisfied from all that he told her that 'Mr Williams' was the head of BSC and he was equally convinced that she was as impressive an agent as he had been informed. There was, in fact, no need for him to reveal his identity to her, as he realised soon enough that Cynthia had worked out exactly who he was.

Stephenson lost no time in putting her next assignment to her, taking care to put the issue broadly and not to spell it out in too much detail, so that he could assess her reactions. It was the normal technique of a professional Intelligence chief testing an agent he was meeting for the first time. Stephenson knew from reports that Cynthia was good, but what he needed to know was just how good.

'It's important to understand the present position,' he told her. 'The Vichy government of France is a little short on love for Great Britain right now. Whatever the motivation, you can see their point of view. They know what it's like to have a large portion of their country occupied by Hitler's Germany. And they want the British to know what it's like, too. Their Embassy in Washington is going hell for leather to achieve this. It operates a secret police force based on the Gestapo model. Its main object is to keep America out of the war. Methods – propaganda, sabotage, assassination. Keep the latter point in mind, because it may concern you.'

It was then that Stephenson spelt out what BSC needed – nothing less than ALL – repeat all – correspondence, personal letters and plain-text cables between the Vichy French Embassy and Europe. Doubtless Stephenson made it clear that this was almost a minimum requirement and that what BSC urgently needed was the keys to the Vichy ciphers. But Stephenson did not need to spell out what might well then have sounded like the impossible. He sensed that Cynthia was the kind of woman who would gladly tilt at windmills. He also realised that if one told her half the details of the tasks which lay ahead, her intuition would enable her to guess the rest.

Perhaps Cynthia always felt the need to prove to herself that she could get any man to tell her his secrets, if she set her mind to it. In dealing with the opposite sex she had supreme self-confidence. Nevertheless in this new assignment, which was nothing less than the infiltration of the Vichy French Embassy and its secrets, the risks were considerable. For the Vichy French had their own secret police attached to the Embassy, men who would not hesitate to kill if they found a spy in their midst. And Cynthia would not even have the protection of the FBI or the American police.

She was no casual spy who just walked into embassies and relied on her charms alone. What has not been told before is how she did her homework on the French Embassy before she launched her campaign. Very wisely she undertook this not in Washington, where any inquiries could have been obvious, but in New York where at the Hotel Pierre the Vichy French were known to congregate. Here she made a point of meeting an old Chilean friend married to a French count, and an Englishwoman who was the wife of a Vichy French businessman. From them she obtained a very good picture of the personnel in the Embassy in Washington from the Ambassador downwards. She was warned that the Ambassador, Gaston Henry-Haye, was a somewhat stuffy character who was engaged in a secret liaison with a married woman, that he disliked American politicians and the Secretary of State Cordell Hull in particular. But, bearing in mind her cover as a journalist, Cynthia asked who handled public relations and the press.

'Oh, a real charmer,' she was told by her Chilean friend. 'His name is Charles Brousse. He was a fighter pilot in the French Navy with the rank of Captain. Strange he should come to Washington as this isn't his kind of work at all. I don't know about now, but he was quite fond of the British and in the early part of the war he was a member of the Anglo-French Intelligence Board. He is loyal to Vichy, as he is a serving officer, but he has no love whatsoever for the Germans.'

No doubt Cynthia secretly decided that Charles Brousse rather than the Ambassador should be her main target in the Embassy. However, on the principle that the higher you aim the more seriously you are taken, she first of all sought an interview with the Ambassador himself. There is no doubt that this assignment tested her ingenuity to the full. She knew that she was up against the most difficult assignment of her career. She checked back with the New York office on the gossip she had picked up on Charles Brousse, and it was fully confirmed that he had been on friendly terms with some RAF officers in the months prior to the fall of France.

So, while seeking an interview with the French Ambassador as a freelance journalist, Cynthia took care that she made the approach directly

RIGHT Colonel Josef Beck, the Polish Foreign Minister in 1939

LEFT Arthur Pack, Cynthia's first husband

BELOW Charles Proteus Steinmetz

The Vichy French Embassy in Washington

The Italian cruisers *Pola*, *Zara* and *Fiume* at Naples in 1941, before their destruction by the Royal Navy

Sir William Stephenson, Cynthia's Controller

December 1941: the attack on Pearl Harbor

Cynthia at the Château de Castellnou with Charles Brousse

One of the last photographs of Cynthia before her death in 1963

through Captain Brousse, the press attaché. But on her first attempt to arrange an interview she failed to speak to Brousse on the telephone and, though the answering voice offered to deal with the request himself, she insisted on calling back when Brousse would be in. Eventually she spoke to Brousse and the interview was fixed.

Cynthia took great care with her dress and general appearance for this first vital meeting. She was immaculately groomed and her dress was sober and discreet, though with unmistakable *chic*, for she knew that Frenchmen paid great attention to a woman's dress sense. On her arrival at the Embassy, having presented her passport for identity purposes, Cynthia was received first of all by Brousse himself. She said afterwards that she had matched her green dress to the colour of her eyes, and that she was convinced this was a wise move when Brousse looked her up and down with approving eyes 'as though he was inspecting a new mare'.

Before she saw the Ambassador, Cynthia and Charles Brousse had quite a lengthy chat. She learned about his service as a naval air pilot and the awards made to him for his relatively brief wartime service and also that he had been married three times. This last item of information was given as an indication that he was well versed in the ways of women and deeply devoted to the fair sex. They took to each other from the moment they met and Brousse went out of his way to brief Cynthia on how to approach the Ambassador.

It was pointed out to her that the Ambassador was a prickly character who did not understand Americans and regarded them as having no understanding of or feeling for Europe or European culture. But, inquired Brousse quizzically, how was it that an American woman came to have a British passport, especially at a time when Britain was at war? Cynthia explained that her husband was British, but that they had separated and she had reverted to her maiden name. Brousse learned that she had travelled widely and he suggested that 'the way to play it with the Ambassador' was to appear to be the detached cosmopolitan observer.

At last, thought Cynthia, the fish is about to bite on the hook. He was actually trying to make things easier for her.

There was some further subtle badinage and exchange of information. Brousse asked if she had any children and Cynthia, to win sympathy, played on the story of the long-lost son she was not allowed to see. This was enough to draw from Charles Brousse the observation that she must have personal reasons for being out of sympathy with Britain.

Cynthia retorted that one personal tragedy was nothing compared to the fate of a whole nation. Reminding Brousse that he had worked with the British, she tried to bring the conversation round to his own opinion of that nation. Brousse admitted that he had enjoyed working with the British while he served on the Anglo-French Intelligence Board, but added that as a result of the 'unforgiveable attack' on the French fleet at Mers-el-Kebir and Oran he now felt profound hostility to Britain.

Cynthia's perception of things political was as acute as her sensitivity to sensual atmospheres. She had already decided that once the ill-advised British attack on the Vichy fleet became a subject for discussion she must play the conversation as coolly and sympathetically as she could. This was easier than it might sound. If she agreed too readily with the Vichy viewpoint, then she automatically ruled out any possibility of discovering the secret and personal sympathies and antipathies of the Vichy French. On the other hand, if she appeared to side wholeheartedly with the British, they might well become suspicious and talk less freely. Cynthia had to steer a middle course and this meant she had to be fully acquainted with the facts of what must still be regarded as one of the most foolish actions of the British in World War II, one which possibly delayed the end of the war and in no measure helped to win it.

When Cynthia interviewed the Ambassador he was in an angry mood. He had just seen Cordell Hull who had accused France of pursuing a pro-German rather than a neutral policy. Cynthia played along with him tactfully, and she noted that Brousse who sat in on the interview had nodded approvingly. By this time she felt sure that Brousse was the man on whom she had to concentrate.

From this moment onwards the story of Charles and Cynthia ranges from that of improbable fiction to farcical fact. If any self-respecting spy fiction writer today presented the truth about this pair in the guise of a novel, any equally self-respecting publisher would tell him to re-write large sections of the book. 'In real life,' he would be told, 'spies don't behave like that, nor do Embassy officials. Your readers won't feel the story is credible.'

Well, it started with a nice fictional touch: Cynthia was sent a bouquet of red roses by Captain Brousse, together with an invitation to lunch the very next day. She had no doubts whatsoever by this time that she had made a favourable impression on the press attaché. Within a matter of hours Brousse had been invited back to her house and that was the beginning of a long affair.

It was from all accounts a rumbustious liaison which Brousse seemed to savour all the more because this was something that had to be kept secret from his third wife. It is said that war and the imminence of danger of any kind – marital or otherwise – create the kind of atmosphere in which love flourishes. This certainly was the case with both Cynthia and Charles. For Cynthia their love-making proved rather more genuinely enjoyable than some other encounters in the cause of espionage. Charles was a man of the world, shared her love of good food and wine, was passionate and yet witty and humorous and altogether a likeable companion. Her chief problem was how to hold this philanderer long enough to be able to win secrets from him.

And Stephenson in New York was making sure that, through his intermediaries, Cynthia got the message that he was impatient for results. From naval Intelligence sources both in London and Washington BSC was convinced that information about the movement of convoys was being passed from the Vichy Embassy to the German naval authorities. It was essential to know just what was being passed on and when.

But so far Charles Brousse had been very correct and cautious in discussing the war and political matters generally. He had shown that he felt anger against the British for their action against the French fleet (that was understandable), but he had also expressed a dislike for Pierre Laval, the most ardent collaborator in the French Vichy government. Once, recognising one of Vichy's secret police agents at a table in a restaurant, he had confided in Cynthia that there were risks in their relationship as 'men like that one are always watching us and trying to create trouble. They do not like us associating with Americans.'

Then, about two months after their first meeting, in the blazing Washington summer of 1941, Cynthia was presented with an extremely tricky situation. It occurred when the Ambassador, Gaston Henry-Haye, sent for Brousse and informed him that Vichy had insisted on staff economies being made in Washington. Brousse would have to go back to France.

Brousse, who had no desire to do this, protested that this meant either some desk job in Vichy, which he hated, or, worse still, to join some ship lying alongside a quay, with nothing to do. Henry-Haye replied that he was extremely sorry, but the only suggestion he could make to help Brousse was that he might be able to retain his services on half-pay.

The prospect of living in an expensive capital like Washington on half-pay with a wife to keep and bearing in mind his own gourmet tastes and fondness for social life did not appeal to Brousse. The only compromise he could think of was that he should ask Cynthia to return to France with him. At least she would be some compensation for the drastic rationing under the Vichy regime.

So naturally he went round to see her as quickly as possible after his talk with the Ambassador. He explained the situation in detail, said he could not possibly afford to stay on in Washington on half-pay, but, to put him out of his misery, would Cynthia agree to go to France and join him there.

Cynthia knew that before she could take any decision she must get in touch with BSC New York. So she promised Charles she would think over carefully what he had suggested and, though she held out little hope of going to France, would give him an answer within a few days.

Her New York contact at first thought that when Cynthia meant that she could not let Brousse go back to France, she had become too personally involved with him. Indignantly, Cynthia replied that of course she had become extremely fond of Brousse, but that what she meant was that he was the best possible informant inside the Embassy for the kind of intelligence BSC needed.

The British contact man then suggested that if Brousse had been given the chance of staying on in Washington on half-pay, this might be the chance they had been looking for – to land him on their side. In that event it might be worth while providing Cynthia with the money for her to make up his pay. To this suggestion she reacted strongly that Brousse was not some kind of cheap gigolo and that this was not at all the way to set about things.

Finally, it was agreed that Cynthia should reveal to Brousse that she was a spy, but for the neutral Americans, not the British. At the same time the offer of making up his pay would have to be put in such a way that it was clear this was remuneration for his promise to let Cynthia have copies of all Embassy correspondence concerning the war and of plain-text cables. It was a gamble, of course, but well worth trying, and Cynthia felt certain that Charles was sufficiently lukewarm in his feelings for the Vichy government to agree.

Yet Cynthia knew that in putting this project to Charles timing was everything. First there must be a gradual leading up to the intimation that she was a spy. Then, even if he acquiesced to her plan, there was one question he was certain to raise: what was he to tell his Ambassador? She played her role skilfully, but Charles guessed that she was involved in 'some espionage game' before she had revealed the full facts. She pretended that the US Treasury was the secret paymaster.

There were, naturally enough, some arguments, a few heated words and then all was silenced by Cynthia leading Charles to the bedroom and convincing him that this was the only way they could stay together. But for a few days it was touch and go as to whether or not he would change his mind and decide that such conduct would make him a traitor. At the back of his mind that business of the attack by the British on the French fleet still rankled, an action which Admiral Sir James Somerville later declared to be 'the biggest political blunder of modern times'. Had he guessed that Cynthia was working for the British, his answer would undoubtedly have been 'no'.

Suddenly there arrived on Brousse's desk a copy of a naval signal from Admiral Darlan, French Minister of Marine, requesting information on British warships and merchantmen awaiting repairs in American dockyards. It was quite clear that Darlan wanted this Intelligence to pass on to German Naval Intelligence. That single message angered Brousse and he took it straight round to Cynthia that very night.

The die was cast. He looked grim and subdued, but said nothing. Then he handed on copies of the replies to Darlan from the naval attaché. They showed that the battleship *Repulse* was in Philadelphia, the cruiser *Malaya* at New York and the aircraft carrier *Illustrious* in dock at Norfolk, Virginia, for repairs. Either by sabotage, or by keeping these ships under observation until they sailed and then flashing instructions to waiting U-boats, three Royal Navy vessels could have been destroyed within a matter of weeks.

When Cynthia inquired why he was giving her this information, he somewhat grimly and evasively commented that he did not see it as a

Frenchman's job to spy for Germany. From then on he was Cynthia's most diligent supplier of Intelligence. Everything that might be of interest to her he passed on: letters, cables, dossiers from Embassy files, as well as many personal details such as who the Ambassador was seeing, what the naval and military attachés were doing. Brousse played his part superbly well and was invaluable in that he was able to answer queries raised by some of the cables and to fill in the missing details. While some of this was done verbally, he also gave Cynthia a daily written report.

A female spy who uses lovemaking as part of her craft should take precautions that she is not temporarily put out of service. This Cynthia seems to have failed to do. She became pregnant and, not wishing to complicate the situation further, neither informed BSC nor Charles, but went off to New York, ostensibly to visit friends, and had an abortion. Only when it was over did she inform Stephenson of what had happened.

Cynthia was by no means the only woman spy being employed by BSC at this time. There were at least two in New York and another who commuted regularly between New York, Washington and Boston. Two of these were British, one was French; all three used their sexual charms to obtain information. But it was Cynthia who impressed Stephenson most by her knack of spotting the likeliest source of information speedily and then setting out to snare him with a subtlety and professionalism that set her apart from all others. When Stephenson heard of her cool resourcefulness in solving her pregnancy problem with the minimum of fuss, his admiration for her was increased. At the same time he was somewhat worried that the American FBI, known for extraordinary clumsiness in handling some of their counter-espionage activities, might compromise his agent.

Cynthia was therefore warned that, as she was seeing Captain Brousse so regularly, and if the FBI were keeping a watch on her, they were almost bound to suspect that she was not only having an affair with him, but probably engaged in espionage as well.

So it was agreed that Cynthia should give up her Georgetown house and move into the Wardman Park Hotel (today the Sheraton Park) where Brousse and his wife were living. Though this might on the surface seem to be a dangerous move, bringing Cynthia so close to Brousse's own wife, it made it much easier for them to see one another frequently without being observed by outside watchers. Of course, they never met in the hotel bars, only in Cynthia's room. The FBI were on the lookout for Nazi agents and if they saw Cynthia in too close contact with a Vichy diplomat, they might well suspect her of being a Nazi agent, not knowing of her work for BSC.

There was great pressure from Britain's Naval Intelligence Division at this time for information that would lead to the capture of Vichy French naval ciphers. This was reinforced by Churchill himself, not only on account of the plan to seize French-occupied Madagascar to prevent it from becoming a base for Japanese submarines, but also to help the slowly developing scheme for a landing in French North Africa. At the end of 1941 the United States had been reluctantly forced into the war by the Japanese attack on Pearl Harbor. Their immediate preoccupation was with the Far East; the British were wisely determined to see they gave equal attention to the war against Germany. One of the best ways of doing this was to provide sufficiently accurate Intelligence of the highest quality to demonstrate that an invasion of Algeria and Morocco was feasible. The Vichy naval ciphers, it was felt, were an essential ingredient in this intelligence.

So New York's BSC office contacted Cynthia with the blunt demand that she should try to get these ciphers. She was ordered to New York where her contact man put to her Stephenson's request. Anyone but Cynthia might well have reacted that what BSC wanted was the impossible. But Cynthia revelled in attempting the impossible.

Returning to Washington, she lost no time in putting the request to Charles. He was more exasperated than angry, declaring that Cynthia's employers must be madmen and that she herself was not much better than a raving lunatic. Did she not realise that code-books consisted of several heavy volumes, that they were secured in a safe in the code-room which was always kept locked? Did she not also realise that only the Ambassador and the Chief Cipher Clerk knew the combination?

Cynthia knew she must press her case with vigour and not let Charles get away with the excuse that he was already giving her as much information as he dared. She reminded him that she knew all about embassy code-rooms from the time she was in Chile with her diplomat husband, adding that she sometimes helped with enciphering and deciphering. If Charles would not help, then what about the Chief Cipher Clerk.

He was an old man, replied Charles, and nothing could be done with him. Besides, he was about to retire. And who, asked Cynthia, was to take his place? Charles made a grimace and indicated that his successor was to be a career diplomat who had the reputation of being a shrewd and wily operator.

This was one of those remarkable stories which occasionally enliven the pages of British espionage in which amateurism triumphs over professionalism. True, this works both ways: as one has seen in the Venlo affair amateurism can produce appalling disasters. It should have been obvious to any professional that the ageing Benoit, the Chief Cipher Clerk, was absolutely incorruptible, a confused old man, saddened by the German occupation, but determined to end his career as he had lived it with a reputation for unswerving loyalty to the French government of the day, whatever its colour. Cynthia tried to persuade him, but failed. In this instance there was no question of trying to seduce the man: he was equally incorruptible in this sphere, too.

But she was very, very lucky. In nine cases out of ten any loyal official would have felt it his duty to report Cynthia immediately to his superiors.

Benoit, however, while loyal, was not altogether unimaginative. Maybe he felt a certain disinterested gallantry towards the female sex, or possibly, while taking his own firm stand, he disliked the idea of making an attack on neutral USA. He kept quiet.

So, with Charles still protesting that it would be madness to think of trying to steal the cipher books, Cynthia, quite undeterred and not even unnerved by Benoit's refusal, turned her attention to Benoit's successor, who had a wife and child staying in the country outside Washington while he maintained a modest apartment in the capital itself. Cynthia discovered that his wife was expecting another baby and her past experience told her that not only was a husband at his most vulnerable at such times, but even more so when he had an apartment on his own. But only an amateur – perhaps even only a woman – would have dared after one failure with Benoit to have made approaches to the new attaché without contacting her controllers in New York.

But this is just what Cynthia did. She did not even wait for a fortuitous meeting with the attaché. She rang him up, merely saying that she wanted to see him urgently. Now in wartime, with officialdom always warning diplomats to beware of spies and to take adequate precautions against them, this should have alerted him sufficiently to be on his guard. Certainly today any such proposal would be followed up by the switching on of a concealed tape-recorder, or hidden microphones. But the attaché, while undoubtedly suspicious (it is just possible that Benoit, without having named names, had hinted at attempts to capture cipher secrets), encouragingly replied that he was alone and would she come around right away.

Here was the classic male–female confrontation in which two experts in the field of seduction were thrown together. The scales were evenly balanced for a battle of wits. On the one hand, Cynthia, quite prepared to go to bed with the attaché if he would provide the Intelligence she wanted; in the other corner of the ring the attaché was anxious for an affair on the side, discreetly conducted, but with no intention whatsoever of letting this jeopardise his diplomatic career. So the immovable object met the irresistible force and the attaché as the irresistible force triumphed.

Cynthia's highly desperate ploy was to tell him at once that she was working for the Americans, that she loved France and wanted to see that country restored to total independence, and that, above all, she wanted the naval ciphers. She also indicated that she was prepared to see that he was financially rewarded for all this, with a regular retainer if he kept her informed of all changes in the cipher keys. She was counting on the fact that the attaché was relatively lowly paid.

But it seemed that she had failed. The new man in charge of ciphers indicated that so delightful a woman should not be bothering her head about such things as espionage. That was her second blunder. And this time the extent of her blunder was going to be rubbed into her mind in a most sadistic fashion. For the French diplomat was a man for whom *l'amour* was a game; one played it like chess, with just such concentration and the added enjoyment provided by being able to remove a piece from the board. Cynthia was in this context a queen.

So one night, without warning, he greeted Cynthia as she approached the escalator in the Wardman Park Hotel. She was taken unawares, instinctively alarmed that somebody might have noticed their meeting in the hotel, but realising that she must ask him to her room. Perhaps Cynthia, always an optimist, though taken unawares had convinced herself that the attaché had changed his mind and was prepared to go along with her. Then she committed her third blunder: she let him make love to her without having a firm assurance with positive proof in the shape of a glimpse of the cipher keys that he was prepared to help her. In this one instance Cynthia for once slipped below her normally efficient standards.

Up to this point the story is clear enough. Cynthia's problem was that she was tackling a job that was essentially that of a professional and which, despite her sexual attractions, might have been more competently performed by a male agent. The point here, of course, is that nobody believed a female spy really had control of the purse-strings of a secret service. Where money was concerned, man spoke more effectively to man. Obviously, from what Cynthia herself admitted to her biographer, she made a monumental blunder in going to bed with the attaché before he had given some firm assurance about the naval ciphers.

But what exactly happened after that? Cynthia's story is that just as she and the attaché were arranging a further meeting, the telephone rang and Charles announced that he was on his way to see her. She said that she hustled the attaché out of the room, but that Charles saw him leave and there was one hell of a row when he arrived. On the other hand there is another version – from another SIS source – that declares that for the first time in her life Cynthia was totally outwitted, that the attaché not only made love to her, but while dressing casually told her that he had changed his mind and was not prepared to betray Vichy secrets. What was more, he added menacingly that he was afraid that duty made him feel compelled to inform the Ambassador as to the approach she had made to him.

The confrontation between Cynthia and Charles was, however, not quite like that of a Ben Travers farce. Charles was enraged at the idea that his mistress had been deceiving him with one of his colleagues. He gave her what must have been one of the very few thrashings of her life and it had the effect of silencing any fight she might otherwise have put up.

The only consolation which Charles extracted from this situation was that Cynthia managed to indicate to him that the sexual gambol had not been particularly agreeable and that if he had agreed to help her in the first place, all this need never have happened.

It was a catastrophic situation. Each had put the other in a highly hazardous position. Charles Brousse had no doubt that the attaché would tell the Ambassador about Cynthia and do his best to enhance his career prospects through doing so. And, as he warned Cynthia, she was in danger of being assassinated by the Vichy secret police and ending up in the Potomac River, a fate which he thought might even be possible for him as well. Cynthia equally risked having jeopardised the whole British Secret Service operation as well as rendering herself useless for further approaches to the Vichy French Embassy.

By normal standards most, if not all, of these dire prospects should eventually have befallen them. But luck always seems to shine on lovers who do not lose heart and, in their respective ways, neither Charles nor Cynthia accepted defeat. Cynthia retired for a while to rethink the whole project in the light of her humiliating defeat and Charles came round and apologised for his behaviour and sought to make up their quarrel. One must draw the conclusion that at this stage Charles was probably more deeply in love with her than ever she could be with him.

Their immediate task was to counter any vindictive moves which the attaché might make against them. Here Charles was more than a match for his colleague whom he held in great contempt: the naval air pilot felt effortlessly superior to the career diplomat. He did not have long to wait. Soon afterwards the Ambassador sent for Brousse and mentioned that the attaché had told him about his rejecting a large bribe by Elizabeth Thorpe for betraying Vichy's secrets. What did Brousse have to say about this?

Charles played it cool. He pointed out that Cynthia was an American of some distinction, from a good family, father in the US Marines and all that. It would be rash to stir up a hornet's nest now that America was no longer neutral. The attaché was a notorious gossip and his chatter could rebound against French interests.

The Ambassador agreed that they did not want to go out of their way to have trouble with the American authorities. Cynthia might have protectors in high places in Washington. Brousse agreed with alacrity, but added that what worried him most was the attaché's chatter and malicious talk. Possibly, he suggested to Henry-Haye, Cynthia had rebuffed his advances and this was his idea of seeking revenge. Then Brousse played his trump card with devastating effect. When the Ambassador inquired what other instances there had been of such malicious gossip by the attaché, Charles replied that he had spread stories around Washington about Henry-Haye and the Baroness de Zuylen.

He could tell instantly that this item of tittle-tattle had done the trick. The Ambassador looked most embarrassed, thanked Brousse for his confidences and declared the interview closed. Within twenty-four hours the attaché was told that he would no longer have charge of the code-room.

So Charles and Cynthia were able to head off their more obvious anxieties, but there remained the problem of how to get hold of the ciphers.

It was Cynthia who, after a further talk with Charles, decided that the only way to secure them would be by burgling the code-room and this meant they must have co-operation from inside the Embassy. She reported this view back to New York, giving them a plan of the Embassy and the exact position of the code-room. Fortunately this was on the ground floor with a window facing a lawn fringed by trees.

No doubt the BSC's first reaction was that any attempt to burgle the Embassy would be the quintessence of Secret Service madness. But two factors weighed with Stephenson: first, Whitehall was renewing its demands for the ciphers and, secondly, it did seem as though there was a slight chance of success in that Brousse was now a willing accomplice on the inside. But it was realised that he could only act as adviser and possibly as a decoy for the operation. In other words what BSC needed was a professional safe-cracker.

If London wanted those ciphers so urgently, it is somewhat surprising that the SIS in London did not send over one of their own highly competent safe-crackers. During World War II they shared with the Army some of the best of this type in the whole of Europe, released from jail for that very purpose. Presumably this would have meant inevitable delays. Anyhow, not for the first time BSC collaborated with the US wartime Intelligence organisation, the Office of Strategic Services, and obtained the loan of a cracksman from this body.

By doing this Stephenson was in fact insuring his organisation and Cynthia in particular against the FBI. For though the USA were now allies of Britain, the FBI, under the direction of the xenophobically suspicious and jealous Edgar J. Hoover, was still behaving at times as though Britain was one of the enemies. Fortunately the OSS had no love for Hoover's organisation and they not only kept the burglary project a secret from the FBI, but promised that Cynthia would somehow be given legal cover if by any mischance she was caught. Charles Brousse, on the other hand, was very much on his own and by agreeing to join in talks with Cynthia and the OSS cracksman was risking his life as well as his career. However, the OSS promise to protect Cynthia seems to have been rather a thin one. Protect her from the FBI they almost certainly could, but it is doubtful if they could have stopped her going to jail – at least for a short while.

The safe-cracker was a Canadian, who, like some of his British counterparts, had been let out of jail after he had volunteered for the dangerous task of cracking enemy safes. They were among the unsung heroes of the war and some of them deserved high honours for their services. This man, for some unknown reason nicknamed the Georgia Cracker, inspired confidence in Cynthia from the very first moment. He was coolness personified and so obviously proud of his particular craft that he appeared to be a professional to his fingertips in the most literal sense of that phrase.

After a conference it was decided that more information was needed about both the safe and the code-room. So Cynthia prevailed upon Charles to find some excuse to enter it and make mental notes of all he saw. Benoit was just about to retire so Brousse made a point of dropping in on him to say farewell. Even then Benoit, acutely conscious of the strict rules about unauthorised persons going into the code-room, begged him not to stay. 'You know the rules, Monsieur Charles, you are not supposed to be here.'

'But it's a special occasion, Benoit, and we can't talk in the corridor.'

Brousse only had a few minutes to take in the safe, its position, telex machines, coding machines, telephones and filing cabinets. He was not an expert on such things and when questioned later by the Canadian cracksman, realised he had been unable to acquire as much information as was vitally needed. To listen to the cracksman was almost as enthralling as to hear of Cynthia's amorous escapades in the cause of His Majesty's Service. This alert, slightly built man with hands as sensitive as those of a professional pianist, could develop a composite picture of a safe from the barest of details simply by careful and patient cross-examination and sheer technical instinct.

'Draw me a sketch of this safe,' he asked Charles.

Brousse took out a pen and readily complied. Where were the hinges? He indicated on his sketch pad all points asked for by the cracksman, pausing occasionally to think back on his all too quick reconnoitre of the code-room. Where was the bolt-throwing handle? Where was the dial? In the end the cracksman summed it up as being 'a Mosler with a click-click com lock, probably four wheels'. He reckoned he could probably crack the safe in about fifty-five minutes.

The plan for the burglary and safe-cracking which Charles and Cynthia evolved was that Charles should pretend he had to stay behind at the Embassy for some nights as he had a heavy backlog of work. Fortunately there was only one security man at the Embassy and Charles had advised him of the fact that he would be staying late and, for company, bringing Cynthia with him. The security man was reputedly vigilant, carried a revolver on his hip and made regular rounds of the premises during the night. But he was not above accepting a bribe to agree to letting Cynthia into the Embassy: presumably *l'amour* was a safer excuse than anything else. It was at least something most Frenchmen understood.

So Cynthia's visits went on for a few nights until the security man had accustomed himself to seeing her around and she and Charles had noted in detail how often he made his rounds and at what times. The next step was to drug the security man. So one night they made a point of being seen drinking champagne together when he made his rounds and offered him a glass, into which Cynthia had slipped some Nembutal. This was certainly not the most efficacious drug for this purpose, but it was the one BSC provided. Cynthia was also worried because the security man had a very fierce dog which followed him around.

Yet luck was with them. All went according to plan and, as soon as they knew the security man was asleep, they let the safe-cracker in through the Embassy front door. But the safe took a long time to crack and Charles and Cynthia had to sweat out the minutes, worrying whether the security man would awake before the job was finished. By the time the safe was opened there was no time to deal with the cipher books. So the cracksman wrote down the safe combination on a slip of paper and handed it to Cynthia. It was now a question of Cynthia trying to open the safe on her own, the cracksman promising to make for her duplicate keys for the code-room.

The cipher-books now looked to be within their grasp during the next twenty-four hours. BSC was expecting to have photographs of them very soon. But Cynthia failed to open the safe. She was summoned to New York by plane where at a secret rendezvous she was again coached by the cracksman, this time on a model safe identical to that at the French Embassy. She returned to Washington and once again failed.

It was hardly very professional of BSC to have expected Cynthia to achieve all this on her own. It would have been more sensible, as well as saving valuable time, if they had ordered the cracksman to return the following night. The only problem with the cracksman was getting him into the Embassy without the security man knowing. But this is what they had to do in the end. To discourage the security man from disturbing them too frequently on the next vital night Cynthia and Charles discarded all their clothes and lay on the carpet together completely naked in a tight embrace. Needless to say, it was Cynthia's idea and it served its purpose for the security man was duly embarrassed and hastily withdrew.

This time the safe was opened and the books removed and passed through the window of Brousse's room to a BSC agent. He arranged for them to be taken by car to be photographed page by page and the books to be returned to the safe before dawn. It is said the books were taken to a studio to be photographed. My own guess, judging from other operations of this type, is that the books were photographed in a car nearby, probably employing three cameras to do the job, so that they could be smuggled back into the Embassy within an hour. Then the photographs were developed, taken by hand to New York and from there sent to the Ultra establishment at Bletchley where the British handled all enemy deciphering work.

The Vichy signals were of incalculable value to the British and, indirectly, to the Americans, despite the fact that Hoover's FBI men had been shadowing Cynthia's nocturnal visits to the French Embassy. David Kahn has stated: 'It was by then too late to help with the capture of Madagascar, which had gone off without a hitch the previous month. But plans were now afoot for the Allied landing in North Africa and the photostatted code helped keep the Anglo-American forces informed of the movement – or, rather non-movement – of the units of the Vichy French fleet at Toulon, Casablanca and Alexandria during the invasion. Thus was England once again helped by a Lady Godiva.'

There was, however, another important role which Cynthia had played. This was to help disguise the major source of intercepting enemy messages which was through Ultra itself. In due course news of the burgling of the Vichy Embassy in Washington was leaked to the Germans in a deliberate attempt to mislead them about the vital work of the Bletchley team.

Enough was enough. Even BSC did not commit the folly of pushing Cynthia into other highly risky assignments after the affair at the French Embassy. Brilliant amateurism had won one battle and though Cynthia herself was soon eagerly seeking new thrills in the espionage game, Stephenson held her on a tight rein. But it had to be a very tight rein indeed, for Cynthia herself had ideas of training to be an assassin and then trying her luck inside Nazi-occupied Europe. She even suggested one or two names of notorious collaborators as possible targets. Whether the idea was to seduce them first and kill them afterwards one does not know. But though she was sent to London and attached to one of the SOE offices in Dorset Square, she was never sent to France.

After the North African landings the United States broke relations with Vichy France and the Washington Embassy staff were interned in a hotel at Hershey, Pennsylvania. Cynthia kept in touch with Charles and together they went to Lisbon in the summer of 1944, not returning to France until after the liberation of Paris. Brousse obtained a divorce and on 3 November, 1945, news came from Buenos Aires that Arthur Pack had been found dead in his apartment with a gunshot wound. It was clearly a case of suicide. Charles and Cynthia were married during the following year and went to live in a romantic medieval castle, the Château de Castellnou in the south of France, perched high up in the Pyrenees.

It should have been a fairy-tale ending to a thrilling story. But, alas, after some years of happiness disaster hit both of them. First Cynthia contracted cancer of the mouth (she blamed it on her chain-smoking habits) and her last months must have been agonisingly painful. She died in October, 1963. Charles Brousse was heart-broken. He lived on for another ten years and then was found dead in the charred remains of his bed, electrocuted by his electric blanket, and half his château was burned down with him. Whether this was an accident or suicide nobody could tell.

4

Double-Cross: Camp 020

'TATE . . . became one of our most trusted wireless agents, and held the long-distance record as such . . . His work was of great value, first for counter-espionage purposes and later in deception, and he was instrumental in securing large sums of money from the Germans.'

SIR JOHN MASTERMAN, CHAIRMAN OF THE TWENTY COMMITTEE, WHICH CONTROLLED DOUBLE-CROSS AGENTS

It was on the night of 6 September, 1940 when, under cover of one of the Luftwaffe's dusk raids on Britain, a 27-year-old Swedish mechanic jumped from his plane and parachuted down towards the Oxfordshire countryside.

Conditions were ideal for an undetected landing and Agent 3719, as he was known in the Abwehr's register, had no qualms about making the attempt. He had jumped, pulled the rip-cord and experienced a sense of exhilaration at the prospect of arriving in enemy territory. He had been put aboard one of ace Luftwaffe pilot Major Karl Gartenfeld's all-black Heinkel IIIs, and dispatched to fulfil the role of an infiltrated agent.

Gartenfeld was specially selected for the task of ferrying German spies into Britain and his reconnaissance operations squadron, the second Test Formation, was used for this purpose.

Agent 3719's real name was Gösta Caroli. He had lived in Birmingham for a short while before the war and was well acquainted with the English language. Caroli's mother had been German and he threw in his lot with the Nazis when they came to power. He was dropped in a field not far from Aylesbury in Buckinghamshire, well within the target area indicated in preliminary messages. He might well have evaded the vigilant net of observers which MI 5 had set for him, but for the fact that as he hit the ground the special telefunken suitcase with which he was provided gave him a nasty blow on the head, knocking him out for a short while. When he recovered he hid his parachute and made his way to a lane beside the field. There he was immediately spotted by a farmer's daughter who, only the day before, had been warned by the local police constable about keeping an eye open for strangers in the area. She was suspicious of the man, partly because he was wearing an overcoat on a warm autumn day, and she called the police. Within an hour Caroli found himself inside Aylesbury police station where he was immediately collected by MI 5 officers.

OPPOSITE the former double-cross agent no 3725 TATE with the Mayor of Mainz in 1959

Caroli had been one of a number of eager young men who had been brought to the attention of Dr Karl Praetorius, one of the recruiting scouts for the German Secret Service, the Abwehr. He had been selected for special training as a member of the advance team of German spies who were to precede the invasion forces to Britain. Training for these future espionage tasks had been carried out in Hamburg, where recruits were first of all interviewed by Abwehr officers in a small office run under the cover of an importer's business near the Rathausmarkt. He was stationed at the Phoenix Hotel while undergoing his training. This was thorough, if somewhat unimaginative: it took into account all the obvious details a prospective spy should know about England, but was sadly lacking in preparations for the unexpected. The trainees were all given to understand that when they landed, all Britain would be in a state of confusion and it would be simple for them to operate undetected; that they would have plenty of help from agents who would be told to expect them; and, finally, that within days of their arrival – well, perhaps at the worst a few weeks – the German invasion forces would arrive and take over. They were given detailed instructions on how to operate a portable wireless transmitting and receiving set and such equipment of the parachuted spy as secret inks, communication techniques, codes and ciphers.

Caroli had been assigned to what had become known as the Lena Team, a group of spies who were to be dropped by air in a triangular area of England extending from Birmingham to Bristol and London. The man in charge of the airborne spies was Major Nikolaus Ritter (alias Dr Rantzau) of Section 1 Luft Hamburg of Department Abt. I of the Abwehr. The major had lived in the USA for some years and spoke English perfectly. His organisation came under Abwehr II, responsible for sabotage plans and insurrections, led by Colonel Erwin von Lahousen. There were several military experts involved in this ambitious project which was, in fact, only a small part of Operation Sea Lion, the code-name for the invasion of Britain. Admiral Canaris, chief of the Abwehr, had indicated that the invasion would probably take place sometime in September, 1940. A great deal of work had been done in the two years immediately preceding the war to build up the nucleus of a spy network in the United Kingdom, primarily to prepare the ground for the landing of airborne spies.

What, however, the Germans had not realised was that both MI 5 and the Special Branch of Scotland Yard had already penetrated the network and in the case of one of their spies were manipulating him as a double agent. It was a risky game and they were never too sure as to how it would work out, or on which side this Abwehr agent would eventually come down. But ultimately it produced some worthwhile intelligence as to what plans the Germans were making to put spies into Britain. In the months leading up to World War II MI 5, Britain's counter-espionage organisation, under Major-General Sir Vernon Kell, had prepared a special list of 'Category A' suspects who were to be picked up under Emergency Regulations the moment war was declared. Collaborating effectively with the Special Branch, the Germans were effectively robbed of their main, long-term spy network in Britain. On 4 September 1939, all enemy aliens in the United Kingdom were ordered to report to the police and, out of some 62,000 Germans and 12,000 Austrians, 6,800 were considered 'uncertain' and 600 positively unreliable.

All this, however, did not touch the Abwehr's invasion plan. What drew MI 5's attention to the possibility of airborne spies being sent in was the arrest of a Welsh electrical engineer named George Owens at the outbreak of war. He had spent much of his time travelling around the Continent in the pre-war years, selling his company's equipment. While doing so he picked up a certain amount of low-grade technical intelligence which he offered to the Admiralty in London. Eventually the Admiralty passed him on to MI 6. However, Owens was swiftly disillusioned with his new Intelligence masters and not only felt that what he was likely to get out of it would be 'peanuts', but became uneasy about what he regarded as their slackness in security measures. He feared that some kind of carelessness on the part of MI 6 would betray him to the Germans. Somehow the Abwehr got to hear of this (possibly through the very carelessness which Owens feared); at any rate, hoping to turn him to their advantage, they made him an offer.

But it was carelessness on the German side in not guarding their cover addresses sufficiently well which proved Owens' undoing. His links with the Abwehr were discovered when a routine mail search revealed a highly compromising letter sent to a known Abwehr cover address – Box 629, Central Post Office, Hamburg. The contents clearly showed that Owens was in contact with the German Secret Service. After that MI 5 kept a watch on Owens' post and referred the matter to MI 6. When questioned by the latter Owens confessed to his dealings with the Abwehr and suggested that through these he could learn a great deal of value to Britain. After consultations in which both MI 5 and the Special Branch were concerned, Owens was astonishingly allowed to continue his work for the Germans. Between 1936 and the outbreak of war Owens (he was given the code-name of SNOW as partial anagram of his own name) built up a network of disgruntled Welsh nationalist sympathisers, covering thirty-five strategically placed towns.

The Germans, having failed to make much headway with Irish nationalists, had begun to pin their hopes on a Welsh underground movement which, in the event of war, could be used against the United Kingdom. This project was largely based on the activities of its own agents and the misguided political zeal of certain Welsh nationalist extremists. It should, however, be made clear that this in no way concerned the Welsh Nationalist Party. One Hans Kuenemann, who represented a German firm in Cardiff, was nominated head of the Nazis in Wales in September, 1938.

Kuenemann built up a network of informants in Wales. The long-term plan was for Ireland to be invaded by German paratroops and for a base to be established here for making landings in Wales. This was part of what the Nazis called 'Operation Green'. To intensify preparations for this operation, as was revealed in the Abwehr official War Diary, 'an attempt is made to set down the agent Lehrer [code-name] with a wireless operator on the coast of South Wales in order to establish better communications with the Welsh nationalists.'

In the case of Owens – fortunately for MI 5 who had connived at his carrying on working for the Germans – his instructions from Hamburg were to lie low until his favourite song, *Du liegst mir im Herzen*, had been played twice in succession on the midnight programme broadcast from Berlin to Britain. He was then to begin his transmission schedule, but he only had the chance to radio three times before his arrest at Waterloo Station. Owens was taken to a cell at Wandsworth Prison and it was then suggested that he might play a double game. There was some opposition to this proposal by MI 6 and the Army, but members of MI 5 eventually persuaded the authorities to accept this ploy. This resulted in the Germans being fed a mass of deceptive information through Owens' radio and it eventually paid off by the British receiving information on the plan for sending in airborne spies.

The leading light in this deception exercise was a young Scot, Major (later Colonel) T. A. Robertson, of the Seaforth Highlanders. He was the link-man with MI 5, having become enthusiastic about various schemes for double-crossing the enemy in discussions with an Intelligence team from the French *Deuxième Bureau* early in 1939. The idea was simple: instead of locking up spies, one harnessed them to supply their masters with false information.

Through this early and very haphazard experiment Gösta Caroli had been caught in the Buckinghamshire countryside. Owens had been ordered to deceive the Germans by reporting an elaborate and completely fictional network of agents all over the country. The Germans radioed back to Owens (with MI 5 listening in, of course) that they proposed to parachute an Abwehr agent into England in the first few days of September. There had been some conflict of opinion between the experts as to whether spies should be dropped singly or in pairs. The overall Abwehr view was that single 'drops' were preferable.

So the British had news that Abwehr Agent 3719 should arrive in Britain early in that fateful month in which the Battle of Britain was won. Luckily they also had details as to where he would land and Major Michael Ryde, MI 5's Regional Liaison Officer, was able to alert the Chief Constables of Oxfordshire and Buckinghamshire, Eric St Johnston and Colonel Tom Warren. They in turn warned their men to be on the look-out for the expected German. At the same time it was made clear that 'this pigeon is

MI 5's, so take care there is no spectacular arrest which all can see.' This was a very rough guide to what was happening and nobody could have complained if Caroli had slipped through without anyone spotting him. There were several false alarms, but eventually Owens' new 'helper' arrived.

Meanwhile Major Ritter sat back contented in the knowledge that his superiors had had sufficient confidence to name him as the chief-designate of the Abwehr branch in England once the invasion was made.

The British idea of employing double-agents came from a variety of sources – the universities, psychiatrists and enthusiastic amateur Intelligence officers brought into MI 5 with the advent of war. Probably the scheme would never have got off the ground if it had not had the wholehearted backing of the Prime Minister, Winston Churchill, but it is equally possible that the project might not have succeeded but for the arrest of Owens and the subsequent capture of the agent Caroli. Then it became clear that there was a strong case for a highly specialised section of Intelligence to deal with this venture alone. MI 5 insisted that they must have control of any system concerning the re-employment of enemy agents. MI 6 were equally clamorous that they must be consulted. The War Office, Home and Foreign Offices all had their own viewpoints to express.

But the one stark fact which clinched the issue in favour of those who advocated using double-agents was that the British Secret Service had been totally destroyed in Europe after the Venlo incident. The situation in the middle of 1940 was that the only source of Intelligence that was swiftly available came either from people who had just escaped from Nazi-occupied Europe, or from enemy agents smuggled into Britain in the guise of refugees or by parachute. Britain's one main hope of success in staving off an invasion attempt was by being able to deceive the enemy – in short, to convince the Germans that her defences were much stronger than they actually were.

Thus what was in effect a special section of MI 5 was set up to cope with these matters. This was Bl (a), the nucleus or embryo of what eventually developed into the Double-Cross System. It was a modest experimental beginning to a new chapter in counter-espionage and the arts of disinformation. In essence what it amounted to was a combination of spy-catching and provision of a regular stream of false Intelligence to the enemy. But because this impinged on the preserves of so many departments – the Foreign Office, MI 6 and MI 5, the War Office, Admiralty, Air Ministry and the Ministry of Home Security and the police – it proved that much more difficult to implement. It was a revolutionary tactic in the history of secret service in that never before had this been applied as an organised system of espionage involving a completely new body to administer it.

In 1940 MI 5 was in a turmoil. Sir Vernon Kell, the chief who had survived since World War I, had been retired, but he had left a legacy of industry without talent. It was a tradition of the Kell days that promotion in the Service, certainly as regards the girls (of whom there were quite a number) depended on 'good legs, the right kind of figure and a sound military or naval background'. When at the outbreak of World War II, MI 5 moved one section to HM Prison, Wormwood Scrubs, in the days when even fashionable society still travelled on buses, conductors on the route delighted in calling out 'All change for MI 5!' when they came to the prison stop.

It was from the new amateur talent brought into MI 5 that what came to be known as the Double-Cross System drew its strength. It started cautiously with the Bl (a) section of MI 5 and then developed into an organisation controlled by the Twenty Committee (XX = Double-Cross). The chairman of this committee was the late Sir John Cecil Masterman, an Oxford University don who had become a lecturer at Christ Church, shortly before World War I, during which he was interned in Germany for four years. In between the wars he had even indulged in writing some spy fiction, including *The Case of the Four Friends*, which in its sub-title Masterman described as 'a diversion in predetection'. He also portrayed a centre where 'secrets and information – true and false, but mainly false – were being bought and sold'. This may well have played a part in his being drafted to the chairmanship of the Twenty Committee, whose task was the manipulation of double-agents.

The Bl (a) officers who interrogated Caroli took him back to the point at which he had landed, insisting on his pointing out to them where he had hidden his parachute. This may have appeared to be merely a point of academic interest, but for MI 5 it helped to show what future parachutists might do. It was noticeable at this stage that Caroli, always regarded in Germany as the daredevil type of operator who would win against all odds, had visibly wilted and shown a willingness to co-operate.

He was swiftly whisked away by car to Camp 020, the top secret MI 5 detention centre at Ham Common, near Richmond. Here at Latchmere House, an ugly Victorian building which had formerly been a home for shell-shocked officers of World War I, a thirty-cell top-security block had been added to the western wing of the house, incorporating all the most modern recording and listening devices. It was controlled by Colonel 'Tin-Eye' Stevens, a fearsome, monocled commandant who struck terror into his own men, let alone the prisoners. This gloomy institution was ideally suited for its purpose, surrounded by four fences and armed Intelligence Corps guards. Thick woods shielded the compound from prying eyes and the inmates had no idea where they were. Interrogations took place on the ground floor, conducted by a team led by Stevens and his deputy, Major 'Stimmy' Stimson, aided by the resident medical adviser, Dr Harold Dearden, the well-known criminologist and psychiatrist.

Caroli's extrovert character was pricked very swiftly. Not suspecting that Owens had betrayed him, he was quickly reduced to a state of pliable shock by his interrogators. They did not need to put much pressure on him. It was enough that they totally demoralised him by revealing how much they knew. He had been told that he could expect to arrive in a rapidly disintegrating Britain; instead he found himself rounded up shortly after landing and confronted with detailed knowledge of the people behind him. He had the shock of his life when he learned the extent of MI 5's knowledge. Very soon his one thought was how he could manage to survive and avoid execution. After a fairly brief talk a bargain was struck: he agreed with Major Robertson, the resourceful ideas man who was now at the centre of Bl (a), that he would co-operate with the British on the understanding that he was saved from the hangman. To clinch the issue he made another offer. If MI 5 would agree to make the same bargain for a comrade of his, he would give full details about his projected arrival in Britain in a few days time.

How many of these promises could be relied upon? That was the problem for the men of B1 (a). Owens, despite all the evidence against him, had at last proved his value. Could Caroli be trusted to do the same? But, as one member of MI 5 said at the time, 'Look, we are right up the creek, entirely at the mercy of Germany. All we can beat them on is by our wits. What have we to lose? SNOW has given us one present – Caroli. Why shouldn't we see if Caroli can give us others?'

So in the B1 (a) book Caroli was registered as Agent SUMMER and he was ordered to signal back to Hamburg his safe arrival in England, with MI 5 keeping a close watch for any trickery on his part. It was then that Hamburg indicated that Agent 3725 was the next to arrive and where he was supposed to land. This time there were more details and MI 5 not only had a more accurate idea where the agent would land, but some indication of his background and training.

There was a lot to learn, but the experiment which so many of the hierarchy of the Secret Service had decried was beginning to pay off. The Afu wireless sets with which the spies were equipped needed to be examined and tested. Moreover the great worry was to what extent a captured agent who appeared to agree to sending bogus messages to his masters might not introduce some code note of warning into his transmissions. At this time such tests had to be made by trial and error, but it was fully realised that the individual transmitter had his own special touch by which he could be recognised by his own side. All these things posed problems – not least the question of some possibly deliberately prearranged interruption of transmission which could give a warning.

Caroli had actually trained with Agent 3725 and the two had become close friends. So he was able to provide some useful information on the awaited spy. Caroli had considerable knowledge of Operation Lena and he had also lived in the same hotel as Agent 3725 while undergoing training. It was soon evident that the new agent was going to be much more of an enigma, more difficult to handle than Caroli. The latter was athletic and seemingly outwardly tough, extrovert and full of fun, but he had proved surprisingly easy to 'turn'. From all accounts the new man was much better educated and very dedicated to the task set for him.

The new agent in question was Wulf Schmidt, the son of a German father who had served in the Luftwaffe and a Danish mother. His parents were married at Nykobing in Denmark in 1911 and though they went to Germany shortly afterwards, Wulf's mother took him back to Denmark at the beginning of the First World War in 1914. He came from the Schleswig-Holstein area on the Danish-German borders and was himself not only a German citizen, but had joined the Nazi Party. Slim, but sturdily built, blond and good-looking, he was a highly intelligent cosmopolitan who had allowed a youthful enthusiasm for the philosophy of *Mein Kampf* to obscure his powers of reason. This was a pity because he was a likeable chap, thoroughly responsible and well-balanced. Yet, even though he had studied for the law at Lübeck University, the aura of phoney Wagnerian romanticism which the Nazi Party conjured up, turned his mind to indulging in stirring activities on behalf of his country. He was at heart an incorrigible adventurer and so he became a natural target for those who were recruiting secret agents.

Schmidt first came to the attention of Dr Karl Praetorius who believed that his knowledge of Denmark would be invaluable to the Nazis when they invaded that country and so, indeed, it had proved. Wulf had joined the Nazi Party in Denmark and, while happy to be a minor agent for the Abwehr, had actually volunteered for the work of a spy overseas. For this purpose he had acquired a number of aliases and it is these which have frequently confused and bewildered earlier writers who have tried to trace the strange story of Wulf Schmidt. He had the name of Hans Hansen, the idea being that he might be able to bluff the British authorities that he was a Dane if he was caught at any time. He was also known as Schmidt-Hansen. The variety of aliases, combined with the fact that Schmidt and Caroli were both in the Lena Team, may have been responsible for the totally inaccurate statement in some versions of German espionage activities in this period, that they were parachuted into England together.

Speaking a certain amount of English as well as being able to read and write the language, Schmidt set out to improve his accent and fluency. Though a natural linguist, he had never had much opportunity to perfect his English. His accent was still markedly foreign, so that it says much for his reputation that Major Ritter was confident he was an ideal man for the job. He had travelled widely in Europe, Africa and elsewhere. When asked by Ritter what name he would like to choose to have on his forged British identity card, he said that the only British-sounding name he could think of was Harry Johnson, the name of a District Commissioner in the Cameroons, where he had been posted for a while before the war.

Ultimately Schmidt passed his parachute-jumping tests with ease and was ready for action. The Abwehr report on him was exceptionally flattering: '. . . well-equipped mentally, energetic and with a good bearing and all signs of a first-rate upbringing.'

It was on the night of 19 September, 1940, that Wulf Schmidt stepped into a Luftwaffe plane and headed towards England. 'It should be a cake-walk, as they say in England,' he told himself. 'After all in a few weeks' time the Third Reich will have installed their own government in London.'

But as Agent 3725 jumped from his plane and parachuted towards the borders of Cambridgeshire and Hertfordshire his elation turned to apprehension. For he found himself drifting dangerously close to an anti-aircraft battery at the end of an airfield. Fortunately the battery crew seemed completely unaware of his arrival and the thought crossed his mind that possibly the airfield had been taken over by other advance Nazi agents. In landing he hit a tree where his parachute got stuck and, in climbing to the ground, twisted his ankle which soon became swollen and painful. But he was able to bury his parachute and limp across the fields in the direction of a nearby village which he located simply by listening to the chiming of the church clock. Those sweet, peaceful and unhurried chimes striking the hour of ten were distinctly reassuring.

For the previous two months Britain had taken an almost nightly bashing from the Luftwaffe. Under cover of these raids a few Nazi agents had been dropped at various sites in the countryside, mainly in the south of England. The Germans, intent on softening up the inhabitants of the United Kingdom and destroying their airfields one by one, had maintained a series of bombing raids throughout the months of June, July and August. British fighter planes had bravely contested the Luftwaffe, but suffered heavy casualties in doing so. On 15 September, 1940, Fighter Command was claiming with some justification that it had finally won the Battle of Britain in the air by having destroyed 1,753 German planes against RAF losses of 915. Nonetheless British fighter strength was reduced to a dangerous level and at the time when Agent 3725 landed there was optimism among some of the German High Command that an invasion of Britain was feasible and could possibly be launched within a few weeks.

The young German secured his Afu wireless-transmission set before seeking shelter for the night in a hedge on the outskirts of the village. At dawn he tried in vain to find his pistol which had fallen out of his pocket during the drop. Eventually he decided to hide his wireless set and explore the village, which he discovered was a small hamlet not far from Cambridge. This much he learned as a result of visiting various shops in which he bought a new watch and a copy of *The Times*. Then he had breakfast.

Before heading for the nearest railway station, however, he made a fatal mistake. He went to the village pump to bathe his foot. This attracted the attention of a passing Home Guard patrol who asked to see his papers. His foreign accent, combined with the fact that he bore the name of Harry Johnson on his forged British identity card, aroused suspicions. The patrol detained him and took him to the police in Cambridge.

Unknown to Agent 3725 his arrival in Britain by parachute had not only been expected, but interrogation officers had actually waited for him to arrive. From a nearby barn an Army officer and a corporal had heard the aircraft approach in the darkness. Their information was that a 'drop' would be made in this area and, as the officer remarked to the corporal, 'luckily we know that Jerry can put these agents down in a precise position. It's very rarely they are off target.'

It was the corporal who suddenly spotted a parachute and saw it disappear into a clump of trees. They were anxious not to act precipitately: it was important to be sure whether this was the man they were expecting before they confronted him. Also they wanted to watch what his first moves would be, where he would try to go and whether he would attempt to contact anyone, so he needed to be kept under observation.

It was not long before the watching officer and corporal were aware that the Home Guard had stepped in first. Then they had to move in speedily to ensure that the German was handed over to MI 5. When the latter had a tip-off about such an important arrival as Agent 3725, it was very often a case of racing both the police and the Home Guard to capture him. Once a spy was caught in public circumstances the publicity could ruin everything. It meant that there was more than an outside chance that the Germans would hear he had been arrested.

Eventually they confronted the young German, addressing him in his own language. At first he thought he was being greeted by other German agents in disguise. When he realised that he had been captured he was deeply shocked. He was bundled into a plain black van and driven away, first to a house in the neighbourhood, where there was a brief examination, and then to MI 5's interrogation centre at Camp 020.

But Wulf Schmidt's war was not over. It had, in fact, only just begun. He was astonished at being arrested so quickly and even more surprised at being handled in a relatively polite manner, polite at least compared with Gestapo tactics. But it was borne in on him from what he had seen – and he hadn't seen very much – that Britain was far from being a defeated nation ready to capitulate to the Third Reich. He had expected to see signs of a population on the run, as had happened in France, Holland and Denmark. Instead what little he had glimpsed *en route* to Camp 020 was of a calm, orderly community. He understood English well enough to grasp some of this from the casual conversation of the guards.

Had he been deceived by his controllers? Had they painted for him a false picture of a Britain where a cowed population was only too ready to accept Nazi rule? These thoughts must have passed through his mind on his journey to Camp 020 and they left him somewhat bewildered. Nobody had ever suggested he might be caught at once, or that he would find any kind of serious resistance. Very cleverly, too, he had been brought to Camp 020 by a circuitous route, taking in Whitehall, the Houses of Parliament and Westminster, with the deliberate intention of showing him places he would recognise and see that they were undisturbed and still standing.

MI 5 regarded Schmidt as their supreme test case. They were prepared to take infinite pains with this Nazi interloper. For the first time, thanks to Caroli's detailed information, they had a complete dossier on an incoming spy. When this was revealed to Schmidt in cross-examination, it should undermine his moral defences.

Years afterwards Schmidt said: 'Gradually I realised that the picture that had been given me of a totally defeated Britain, with the people on the run and resistance to Germany nil, was entirely misleading. As a trained spy I was able to observe how calm the country was, how orderly and – at that time, at any rate – what comparatively little bomb damage London had suffered. There was a small window in the van in which they took me to Ham Common and, as we came near to London I could see all the balloon barrages in place, the people going about their business normally. It depressed me to think I had been so misled.'

No time was lost in interrogating Schmidt. He was confronted by two Army officers and Dr Harold Dearden. The last-named had taken a lifelong interest in criminological mysteries from Jack the Ripper to the Sidney Street siege and the mysterious 'Peter the Painter'. He was dressed in civilian clothes, and his general appearance must have bewildered Schmidt. For here was no frightening figure in uniform, but a man casually, almost shabbily dressed, with cigarette ash all down his suit, generally untidy and with a mop of unruly white hair.

'When I was brought in for interrogation,' says Schmidt, 'I was fascinated by the strange old man in civilian clothes. He was reading a magazine. He looked at me briefly as I came in and then went on reading. I couldn't take my eyes off him.'

The first stages of the interrogation took the form not of direct questions to Schmidt, but a few polite exchanges and the casual dropping of various hints as to how much the MI 5 people knew about him. Wulf Schmidt mentioned that he was somewhat confused when he arrived and was not sure whether he had been dropped in the right place. 'Oh, but I'm sure Major Gartenfeld wouldn't make a mistake like that,' commented one of his interrogators.

'Gartenfeld?' exclaimed Schmidt incredulously (then they knew the name of his pilot). But he was determined to try and bluff this out. After all, they might be guessing. He went on to say, 'I am Danish. I have managed to escape from Germany and I'm seeking asylum.'

After this German agent (Karl Richter) had been intercepted by the police, the Double-Cross committee took him back to the field where he landed, to find his parachute. Top left: from l. to r. Colonel Stevens, Major Samson, Major Short, Karl Richter, Major Stimson, Captain Goodacre

LEFT Camp 020, the top-secret MI 5 detention centre at Ham Common, Richmond

UNDER-SHERIFF OF THE COUNTY OF LONDON

P. K. METCALFE

TELEPHONE No. MANSION HOUSE 8564

SECRET

Dear Sir,

13961. K. R. RICHTER

I have today heard from the Home Office that there will be no respite in this case, and that the law must take its course. I shall therefore expect you to attend at Wandsworth Prison on Tuesday next the 9th inst., for the execution on Wednesday the 10th inst.

Yours faithfully

Deputy Under-Sheriff

A letter to the chief executioner, Albert Pierrepoint, detailing him to hang the unfortunate Karl Richter

OPPOSITE The beginning of the German air attack on Britain in September 1940

His interrogators pointed out that they knew full well that this was his cover story. Schmidt remained silent. It was obvious that he would not be a push-over. Unlike Caroli, it was not easy to turn him into a double-agent. No doubt in time he could have been worn down by constant questioning and a mixture of threats and bribes, but time was not on the side of MI 5. The one thing his interrogators did not know was how long Schmidt's German controllers had given him to settle down in Britain. Their calculations were that they probably expected to hear from him by wireless within three days. As one of them said, 'unless he taps out a message to them very soon now, the Abwehr are going to assume that he is either dead or captured. And they will write him off. Any belated communication with them will make them instantly suspicious.'

So there was an interval while the interrogating officers consulted with Dr Dearden as to how he visualised their problem in terms of Schmidt's psychological reactions. Was it possible to turn him round into co-operating with the British? Could he be trusted to do so?

Dearden pondered for a few moments. Then he pointed out that Schmidt was not as easily frightened as Caroli and was quite a different character from Owens. He thought that in some respects Schmidt was unique which might just make him worth more than Owens and Caroli put together. In the first place he was very well-educated. Then again he was tough and had a strong character. It was always possible to turn an agent within two days, if one knew how to do it, and if the person was normal. Schmidt was normal, but the question was – how to do it.

Dearden thought the one great advantage which MI 5 had over Schmidt was that he was completely shattered in that he expected to see Britain in chaos and that he had admitted he had been told the invasion would start within three weeks. On the other hand he was still truculent. But once he realised MI 5 had a complete dossier on him, he had crumpled – not visibly, but inwardly. His pride had been badly dented. He was in a very bad mood, argued Dearden, in that he was angry with his interrogators and also, though he wouldn't admit it, angry with his Nazi bosses.

There was, however, one thing about Schmidt on which they must play. He probably did not show it, or feel like revealing it at the moment, but to a trained psychologist it was clear that he had a sense of humour. On this factor he might be turned.

That was Dearden's advice. Colonel T. A. Robertson, one of the most brilliant of B1 (a)'s directors, reacted instantly to Dr Dearden's comments by exclaiming, 'My God, how right you are! D'you know, I kept asking myself who Schmidt reminded me of. Now you mention a sense of humour, I know who it is. He is very, very like Harry Tate, the music hall comedian. So, if we do turn him, I suggest his code-name be TATE. What better?'

'Good idea,' replied another officer. 'And we could even flatter him by saying it is the name of one of England's best bowlers!'

Thus it was that in due course Abwehr Agent 3725 became double-agent TATE of the British-controlled enemy agents. But it was a hard battle to win him over. He proved singularly stubborn for some hours longer, but ultimately agreed to co-operate well inside the week. Slowly his outward braggadocio evaporated and the inner uncertainties became more obvious. Only once more did he try any truculence and that was more a humorously sardonic effort than an arrogant one: 'If we all wait a short while longer, you will all be *my* prisoners.'

Schmidt possibly guessed that he had been betrayed by his friend Caroli, but may also have wondered whether the British had obtained German ciphers and codes. Already the British Secret Service had broken the German coding system known as Enigma, and the Ultra organisation which intercepted and deciphered their communications was being run from Bletchley Park. For Schmidt the crunch came when his cover story was completely broken in every detail. If arrested after being parachuted down, he had been told by the Germans to claim that he had been an aerial photography interpreter in Denmark. Slowly it dawned on him that no purpose could be served by further denials and that, if he did not co-operate, the likely outcome was that he would be sentenced to death as a spy and saboteur. And he was intelligent enough to know that in wartime Britain spies were hanged. Indeed, once they had established in Wulf's own mind that his name was not Hans Hansen, but Wulf Dietrich Schmidt, the issue was clear: he could play ball with the British or end up in a condemned cell.

But Schmidt was impressed by the relatively mild treatment he had received and the patience of his interrogators, their politeness and the fact that there had been no hints or threats of torture, if he did not comply. It was, he reflected long afterwards, 'all very civilised and friendly – at least sometimes there were friendly jokes, often at my expense.' But it required a judicious mixture of alternate kindness and toughness to break down Schmidt's resistance to being turned. 'He was,' said one interrogator ruefully, 'a very tough nut to crack. It was hard going questioning him and very wearying. But in the end it turned out marvellously – much better than other spies who gave in at once and then tried to double-cross us afterwards.'

Eventually Schmidt admitted what his tasks in this country were to have been and how he was to pay special attention to dockyard intelligence in various centres. His chief interrogator then delivered the *coup de grâce* by informing him that Caroli had been picked up and had talked freely. But he kept his interrogators on edge right up to the very last moment with his insistence that he would never betray his country. In the process at least one of his interrogators was beginning to lose his cool and to risk losing a potential convert in the process.

Once Wulf agreed to co-operate he was transferred from Ham Common interrogation centre to Roundbach House near Radlett in Hertfordshire. As he had landed in that county it was important that he should transmit a message back to Germany from that area. He was assigned a case officer, Bill Luke, and a wireless operator, Russell Leigh, and told that he would be required to make a wireless transmission to Hamburg-Wohldorf and was asked who his control was. He gave the names of Major Ritter and another officer.

'You will be given a message to transmit. Send it accurately and without any fuss or hesitations and you will have no problem. But if you try to alter it, to make unnecessary pauses which might be construed as a warning, or by making a small mistake in the message try to indicate that you are not a free agent, you will be shot. Or hanged. Do you understand?'

Schmidt assented with alacrity that he had indeed got the message. It was lucky for him that those in charge of this embryonic Double-Cross system of turning enemy agents felt they might be on to a winner with Schmidt. They realised that Schmidt's clinging on to a patriotic motive was a sign of integrity and that all they had to do was to show that his patriotism was being exploited by unscrupulous men. But the verdict as to whether or not he should be used as a double-agent rested with what was called the 'Hanging Committee', who had the task of deciding if an enemy agent should be spared or should die.

Before the first message could be sent to Hamburg by TATE, as from now on he will be called, his case-officer needed to know just how he would be likely to phrase his communications. Here again was something of a problem because TATE was rather an eccentric in his communication language according to those who have studied his wartime messages. It was in this field that he showed most of all a remarkably versatile sense of humour ranging from the ironic and sardonic to the occasional bawdy or irreverent comment. It was one way in which he felt he was expressing his individualism. Some doubt was expressed by one of his interrogators as to whether an Abwehr agent would dare to address his controllers in such a manner, but Dr Dearden insisted that this made sense and was indicative of what he had proclaimed already as TATE's vital asset – a rather special brand of humour. 'Remember,' said Dearden, 'he is radioing the relatively civilised Abwehr, not the sadistic bully boys of the Gestapo. And I rather think you will find that the Abwehr have a less pompous and rather more imaginative approach to their agents than MI 6.'

Thus the first message that TATE sent under the control of MI 5 was to the effect that he had settled in satisfactorily in a farm in Hertfordshire, but that he needed money urgently. This was put tersely and in the kind of vernacular which TATE claimed the Abwehr would recognise as essentially his own mode of communication. To that extent TATE was on trust. But if his captors were on tenterhooks, TATE himself felt a certain amount of tension as he tapped out the Hamburg call-sign and put on his headphones. To transmit at any time required intense concentration, but to do this while being monitored by a sergeant radio-specialist and two officers in attendance was a considerable ordeal. But there was another problem: it was soon discovered that the Afu radio sets given to spies to bring over in the Telefunken suitcases were inefficient and not adequate for the purposes for which they were intended. So TATE had to contact his German masters on a specially provided British radio transmission set. The British had learned from Owens and others that the wireless sets given to German spies posed more problems for the spies than for MI 5. Later the sets were considerably improved, but by that time more often than not MI 5 were ready and waiting for the spies as they landed.

TATE tapped away as competently as he would have done in normal circumstances, despite his feeling of apprehension. Eventually he got a reply and he was so relieved that he held up a thumb to indicate that all was well. Then he spelt out his message and when he had finished the monitoring sergeant informed the officers that all had gone according to plan. TATE had passed his first test, but it was essential to see whether, despite all precautions, he had managed to signal to the Abwehr that he was held captive.

It took time for MI 5 to convince themselves that TATE had been turned in their direction. Robertson, now promoted to colonel, had taken a liking to TATE from the start and early in 1941 brought him to live with his family in a small house near Radlett. Previously he had been allowed to join his former friend, Caroli, for Christmas in a 'controlled' country house near Hinxton, Cambridgeshire. Then, the very next month, occurred an incident which threatened to upset all the carefully laid plans of B1 (a). Caroli, having already made a suicide attempt, tried to escape. He attacked his two guards one afternoon, nearly strangling one, and stole a motor cycle, heading towards the Fens. It was presumed afterwards that he hoped to steal a boat and make his way back to Germany. It was a ridiculous attempt and one doomed to failure. The motor cycle broke down and Caroli was recaptured at Ely. He was sent back to Camp 020 and, after further interrogations, confined to a specially constructed MI 5 'cage' at Hunterscombe Place near Henley. Yet another blow was when Owens came under suspicion after a trip to Lisbon to meet an Abwehr contact. He was confined in Wandsworth Prison and not allowed to continue as a Double-Cross agent after March, 1941.

Thus, although TATE had behaved perfectly, it was not always easy to convince the other members of the Twenty Committee at this stage of his absolute reliability. The chance to establish this did not come until May, 1941. TATE had only been given limited funds when he landed, mainly because the Germans expected to invade shortly afterwards. Therefore, to convince the Abwehr that he was still operational he needed to ask for more funds. But after the fright over Caroli's attempted escape (had he got away the entire Double-Cross operation would have been ruined), B 1 (a) had to be very cautious.

Sir John Masterman said afterwards that there were lessons to be learned from the slip-up over Caroli, or SUMMER: 'his escape, had it succeeded, would indeed have wrecked all our schemes . . . A double-agent is a tricky customer, and needs the most careful supervision, not only on the material, but also on the psychological side. His every mood has to be watched and his every reaction to succeeding events studied. For this reason we always afterwards insisted that a case officer should be responsible for each agent.'

So TATE's officer included in one of the signals for Hamburg a request for urgently required funds and an extra valve for his transmission set, hoping that this would be brought over by another agent and not dispatched by some shadowy intermediary over here. Luckily, the Abwehr had decided at the same time to try to increase the number of their agents in Britain by sending in new men. One man so chosen was an old colleague of TATE's, a twenty-nine-year-old *SS Obersturmführer* named Carl Richter. A Sudeten German, Richter had volunteered for the work of an agent in Britain, despite the fact that he spoke the language badly.

Back to Britain came a signal that Carl Richter would be parachuted into the country with both the funds and a valve for TATE. Various rendezvous sites and times were indicated for TATE to keep at places as diverse as the Regent Palace Hotel, the British Museum and the Tate Gallery (an ironic touch, this!).

Richter was dropped by parachute near a wood in Tyttenhanger Park not far from London Colney in Hertfordshire on the night of 13 May, 1941. He brought with him the radio valve, £500 in cash and 1,000 American dollars as well as a map of East Anglia, a compass, a wireless set and an automatic weapon. The Double-Cross Committee were expecting Richter and an elaborate trap had been set to catch him when he arrived at the first of the three rendezvous sites arranged with TATE. Unfortunately, when Richter landed he was picked up within a very short time by an alert police constable and taken into custody. His arrest was too well known for MI 5 to try to keep it a secret from the Germans who would have become suspicious if their man suddenly obtained his release. So Richter was not 'turned', but tried as a spy at the Old Bailey and hanged at Wandsworth Prison at the end of the year.

By this time the Double-Cross Committee was convinced that TATE was unlikely to trick his new masters and that the Germans really believed he was acting as a free agent on their behalf. They decided to build him up so that he would appear to the Germans as an ace of spies. To help create this illusion in Hamburg B1 (a) invented a number of fictitious sub-agents for TATE. Once he could claim that he had a spy ring of his own inside Britain, TATE was also in a position to ask the Abwehr for more funds and this he did on frequent occasions with terse and sometimes saucy radio communications. 'How much longer will you delay sending a courier with the money?' he asked once, and, on another occasion, he sent the astonishing demand to Major Ritter that – to translate it into the English vernacular – 'unless you send me £4,000 immediately, you can get stuffed.' And Sir John Masterman made it abundantly clear more than twenty-five years later that TATE received more than £80,000 from the Abwehr, money which, of course, was used to finance the Double-Cross system.

In that 'darkest hour' of the war when Britain alone, and without allies outside of the Commonwealth, faced the might of Germany, it was often a question of whether brains could successfully overcome an inferiority in arms and manpower. One possible answer to this was to use British Intelligence to deceive the enemy and, taking things a step further, to lure enemy agents to change over to the British cause. And TATE was to be the one shining light, the one supreme example of such a policy.

'But for TATE,' said one of the operatives, 'we might well have had the whole operation called off after SUMMER tried to defect. Whenever anyone came up with criticisms of Double-Cross we just said "take a look at Harry".'

There is no question that Masterman regarded TATE as his prize double-agent. He admired what he called TATE's 'terse and virile telegraphese' and added that 'he became one of our most trusted wireless agents, and held the long-distance record as such, for he transmitted and received messages to us from Hamburg from October 1940, until within twenty-four hours of the fall of that city in May 1945. His work was of great value, first for counter-espionage purposes and later in deception, and he was instrumental in securing large sums of money from the Germans. He was . . . to the end regarded by the Germans as a "pearl" among agents.'

That this was no exaggeration is borne out by the Abwehr files for that period which show Major Ritter, his controller, writing of him that 'shortly after his arrival, Agent 3275 was active on our behalf and henceforth worked exceptionally diligently. Apart from sending us regular weather bulletins, he radioed observations of airfields and other strategic targets, all of which was rated extremely valuable by the competent authorities in Berlin.'

In the early days TATE was closely watched while he lived in relative comfort at a 'safe house' in Hertfordshire. Some lurid stories have been told about his behaviour while staying there, still under the tight control of the Twenty Committee. But, as far as can be ascertained, these yarns are at best highly embellished and at worst grossly inaccurate. TATE had a sense of humour which could in private be Rabelaisian, bawdy and indelicate, but which was held well in rein in public and especially when women were present. The truth is that to survive as he did TATE had to behave well. He has suffered in the past from snippets of malicious gossip about him largely concocted by enemies in Germany rather than over here.

If TATE had radioed some of the outrageous signals to the Germans which he is supposed to have sent, he would not have lasted as an Abwehr agent for the whole of the war. Equally, he would have been discarded hastily by the British. Quite a few Double-Cross agents were suspended from such operations through faulty judgements, or erratic behaviour. TATE, on the other hand, demonstrated that he would not abuse freedom and hospitality, that he was not only trustworthy, but competent as well. So, despite the treachery of Caroli and a few other Double-Cross agents, TATE was given an increasing amount of freedom as the war progressed. Eventually he was free to come and go more or less as he wished from his 'safe house'.

The view was that, while TATE had started brilliantly in deceiving the Abwehr, much greater care would need to be taken if this deception was to be maintained over the years. Unless he was free to move around and observe life in Britain at first hand, as an agent at large would do, sooner or later someone in Hamburg was going to suspect that all was not well. True, B 1 (a) could furnish him with bogus intelligence for the Germans, but this needed to be personalised – 'to be TATED up', as one case-officer put it – if it was always to appear the genuine thing. So it was essential that TATE should see for himself something of the life of the country, including arms factories and aircraft production and the everyday living conditions in large cities. There were many excellent reasons for this. Perhaps most important of all was the need to show TATE that Britain was a free and happy country even in wartime, despite bombing and rationing, that people still laughed and sang and, above all, that they seemed to be on the way to winning the war. Being a highly intelligent and observant man, TATE could also make suggestions as to what kind of intelligence would impress the Germans as being genuine, while still ensuring that it was deceptive. In other words a great deal depended on TATE's advice, his own ingenious and inventive mind and his knack of phrasing his messages in such a way that they were not only recognisably his, but that they made the Germans feel he was their top agent in the United Kingdom.

More than forty agents passed through the hands of the Twenty Committee with varying degrees of success. Among the items which TATE radioed to Hamburg were those of exaggerated reports of bomb damage at airfields, thus luring the Luftwaffe away from civilian targets, which were difficult to protect, to the more easily defended fighter bases; a bogus shipbuilding programme reported to have added three new carriers to the British Fleet in the Indian Ocean; performance of new aircraft and equipment was consistently underestimated. The result was that by the end of 1941 the Twenty Committee was able to indulge in self-congratulation at the success of their policy which by then was effectively giving them control over most if not all German agents in Britain. Of these TATE was far and away the outstanding performer.

He had always been an excellent photographer with standards equal to those of a professional, a talent he very quickly developed in Britain. So he was allowed to apply for a job as a photographer on a local newspaper. Later he travelled widely in the United Kingdom. With the concurrence of MI 5 he was actually allowed to go on holiday in Scotland on another occasion, mainly to glean some local colour and to be able in his own inimitable way to suggest some new material for Hamburg. Later he received more important assignments as a photographer. He was even asked by an unsuspecting firm if he would go to Normandy for the 'D' Day landings! Naturally he had to refuse, but today he recalls how once he was within a few yards of King George VI when the sovereign was visiting troops before the invasion of Normandy.

Early on TATE had minor battles with his case-officer over making inquiries about his family to the Abwehr. Not unnaturally, in the early stages when TATE was very much on probation, there was always the risk that this was a ploy to send some hidden message to Hamburg. However, eventually he was allowed to send such queries along with his other messages and Hamburg not only passed these on to his family, but occasionally replied with news from home.

None of the many friends and acquaintances he made in Britain knew that he was a German, let alone an agent of any kind. One such was a girl worker on a farm in Hertfordshire. Eventually he married her and later reported to the Abwehr 'I have just become the father of a seven-pound son.' One might think that the Abwehr would be highly disturbed by such intimate fraternisation with the enemy as this and worried about the safety of his communications, but what served the Double-Cross Committee so well was that Hamburg was apparently fully aware of TATE's highly individualistic methods of operating, his anxiety about money and his zany and forthright sense of humour. This again is some indication of the fact that TATE was already an agent of repute when he was parachuted into Britain. One cannot help wondering whether, if Caroli had not betrayed him, he would have remained free for the duration of the war.

As it was, his reputation in Germany not only remained high, but was enhanced as the war continued. In some of the earlier histories of espionage in World War II he was described as the Germans' outstanding spy in England. On MI 5's instructions, he had, of course, warned Hamburg that Caroli was no longer operative after the latter's attempt to escape. Among the many thousands of words which TATE tapped out to Germany on his wireless set was the news that Caroli had been 'compelled to suspend security operations for pressing reasons'. He added that his radio was in the safe hands of another agent: that 'agent' was MI 5.

Long before the end of the war Major Ritter had recommended TATE for the Iron Cross, First Class, and, though technically a Dane, he was specially naturalised by wireless so that he could be given this award. The Iron Cross, First Class, is quite a cherished medal, despite the fact that it has been distributed liberally. To make the award in wartime and, what is more, to use up valuable wireless time in announcing it was something unique in the annals of espionage.

TATE always did his own radio work, even though he had an operator attached to him. He claimed that 'nobody can fit my finger', as they say in the jargon of the spy world. Once when he hurt his finger and could not operate effectively for a brief spell, he had to make excuses to the Germans.

It is often said that honours in wartime go to the 'yes-men', to the conformists rather than the heroes. This might be true of the British, but it was certainly not true of the Abwehr. One can only think that the British must have handled TATE in a psychologically brilliant manner, as his German masters gave him a remarkable display of loyalty and understanding. The award of the Iron Cross might have made some agents feel guilty about betraying their fatherland. Yet TATE, the patriot who was so difficult to 'turn', was oblivious to such blandishments. Is there perhaps a lesson in the fact that TATE could be rude to his employers, even tell them he was 'going to get drunk tonight' when he received some money from them, and again 'think it's time I took a holiday', and yet still be rewarded? Abwehr signals show that TATE was notorious for his frequent demands for money, often brusquely phrased. The money he received from Hamburg, or rather the funds which Double-Cross handled, came from a variety of channels, sometimes through agents parachuted in, sometimes via contacts in London. Once, before Japan entered the war, TATE received instructions from Hamburg to go to London to obtain funds from an intermediary. The money was passed to him in notes hidden inside a copy of a newspaper while TATE was a passenger on a bus sitting alongside a Japanese attaché from the London embassy.

By the end of the war wireless deception had become quite a sophisticated development. Not only did special units broadcast dummy signals to mislead the enemy, but telephone lines were established to different parts of the country, terminating in wireless sets, to simulate the location of agents. Thus TATE was confirmed by German direction-finding as being at Wye in Kent when in fact he was operating from Hertfordshire.

All manner of queries were fired at TATE by the Abwehr once they positively accepted that he was their best agent in Britain. As early as December, 1940, they were asking him whether there were 'any constructions or mechanisms to prevent air landings' in the area of Folkestone, Lyminge and Aldington and this was followed by a list of questions about the material used and whether it was electrically charged. Hence the need for a 'visit' to Wye. On another occasion TATE was asked whether an underground factory of Vickers had been built at Hawarden, west of Chester. Other queries put to him were requests for lists of food prices and any information on stocks of various commodities. From the various questions put to TATE by the Germans it was possible for Intelligence to gain some insight into their plans and whether or not an invasion was still envisaged. Occasionally these questions were so frequent and persistent, especially following those dates when TATE was due to receive money from the enemy, that to provide him with an excuse for not giving all the answers, a cover story had to be invented. For example he had been asked why he had not registered for military service in the United Kingdom; TATE said that to avoid this he had secured a job on a farm which, as it was vital work, exempted him from being called up. But, said TATE in explaining this to his masters, 'I can only leave the farm at weekends and so cannot undertake long journeys for you.' When, of course, B1 (a) wanted him to undertake a long journey to provide some bogus intelligence of their own, then TATE signalled that he was going on holiday.

None of these deception ploys was as easy as it sounded. Having provided such vast sums of money for TATE, the Germans began to suggest that, as he had ample funds, he should be moving in more influential circles, even if he had to work on a farm. This poser was resolved by giving TATE a fictitious girl friend named Mary in General Eisenhower's invasion headquarters who was supposed to be indiscreet enough to leak intelligence to him. 'Mary' was, in fact, only partly fictitious: it was necessary to have a real person playing this role just in case the Germans wanted to check TATE's highly misleading information prior to 'D' Day. She was a girl who worked in a cipher department of one of the ministries who at weekends used to visit the farm where TATE resided. She was transferred to Eisenhower's HQ to lend some substance to TATE's cover story. In his radioed messages to the Abwehr he raved excitedly about 'Mary', on one occasion giving an accurate description of what she looked like and adding, 'Don't you think she is quite a tasty dish?'

TATE would appear to have been used to give the Germans certain accurate intelligence, on the principle that he needed from time to time to provide intelligence that was valuable to the Germans, if only to convince them of his reliability. According to the German writer, Gunter Peis, TATE was allowed to leak accurate information on the Dieppe raid in the hope that they would believe his later disinformation on the landings in North Africa and Normandy. This TATE himself flatly denies, as do those associated with him on the British side. It is true that there was appallingly bad security prior to the Dieppe Raid. Some attempt was made to devise a cover story that a raid was being planned for the Channel Islands and this was certainly passed to the Germans. But what positive pointers they got to Dieppe would have been from leakages from naval and military personnel discovered by MI 5 as early as the end of June, 1942.

As late as the spring of 1945 TATE was sending messages regarding minefields at sea which were instrumental in closing an area of 3,600 square miles to U-boats. In the last months of the war a vast amount of deception work was carried out by double agents for the Admiralty. By then it was realised that German submarines no longer came to the surface to recharge batteries as the snorkel apparatus enabled them to do this underwater. This made the hunting of U-boats difficult and the only solution to the problem was the laying of deep minefields which would trap the U-boats, but over the surface of which other ships could pass in safety. The Naval Intelligence Division needed to convince the Germans that there were far more of these deep minefields than in fact existed. TATE was the instrument for carrying out this deception, which consisted in his reporting to the Germans the details of totally fictitious mine-laying in certain areas. It would seem that the Germans were still sufficiently impressed by TATE's reports to act upon them for, as late as 2 May, 1945, he received a message from Hamburg in which German Naval Intelligence urged him to maintain contact and keep them informed on mine-laying.

Gunter Peis has suggested that the Germans knew TATE was double-crossing them from sometime in 1943 onwards. This, however, is not borne out either by Abwehr reports or, as has been seen above, their continued reactions to his messages. His source of information on mine-laying was, he told the Germans, an indiscreet captain of a mine-layer. The story that TATE may have been suspected has arisen from the fact that after a German War Graves Commission employee had been repatriated from his internment camp on the Isle of Man (the Red Cross had been heavily infiltrated by the Germans), it was thought that he might have been an Abwehr agent who had been in contact with one or two other captured German agents interrogated at Ham Common. But if the Germans had received reports which cast suspicion on TATE, they do not seem to have believed them. Indeed, to be absolutely fair, one must admit that the Abwehr control-officers of TATE behaved towards him throughout the whole of this period with a courtesy, loyalty, compassion, consideration and understanding far greater than that shown by most spy-masters in wartime. They, too, deserved his thanks.

In the fatally insular minds of most British there was never a sensible appreciation of the fact that there were 'two Germanies' and that the Nazis only represented one side of the coin. Similarly the Abwehr was totally different from the Gestapo. The Abwehr, as Ladislas Farago has stated, 'had none of the cynicism and hypocrisy' of the British Secret Service, but was 'a plodding, utilitarian and rather mild-mannered organisation whose plots seemed – and often were – naïve and diffident.' The Abwehr of Admiral Canaris was always an ambiguous service and it sometimes seemed as though its devious master was less inclined to defeat the Allies than to ensure that his own secret service remained free from Gestapo interference. But there can be no doubt that those in Abwehr control in Hamburg treated TATE almost more as their master than their servant. To them he was the sublime individualist and hero, their chief ally in the heart of enemy country.

With the end of the war, Caroli was sent back to his native Sweden, but TATE showed no desire to return to Germany. No doubt, as a double agent, he felt it would be adding insult to injury to return home and gloat over his deception, more especially as his German masters had been so good to him. The decision must have been hard to reach, as TATE was devoted to his family. He sought and was given permission to stay in England, though he has on a few occasions visited Germany to see his family. Today he lives within three miles of the Tower of London where several of his co-agents were executed as spies during the war. He was given British citizenship and a new identity, and he has since avoided any of the publicity which so many ex-spies indulge in. TATE is now divorced from his wartime bride and leads a discreet and highly respectable life in what might fairly broadly be described as the legal profession.

5

Stashinsky: The Murder Machine

'At that moment Stashinsky suddenly realised with horror that the purpose of his task in watching Rebet was to prepare the latter's murder . . . The weapon was a metal tube, about as thick as a finger . . . the firing pin caused a metal lever to move; it crushes a glass ampoule . . . this vapour leaves no traces, it is impossible to ascertain death by violence.'

THE US SENATE INQUIRY INTO 'MURDER AND KIDNAPPING AS AN INSTRUMENT OF SOVIET POLICY'

For some months a strange young man might have been seen hovering around the streets of Munich, sometimes as though he did not know quite where he was going. He was slim rather than athletic, with sloping shoulders and a flat chest, but the thing about him which struck one most was a queer agitated flickering of his eyes, almost like those of a frightened bird.

But he was not really such a frightened character. A closer look, or perhaps after a few drinks with him, and one would deduce that he was a remarkably controlled person and an easy conversationalist. Above all else he was an adaptable character.

He needed to be, for Bogdan Stashinsky – that was his name – a Ukrainian employed by Soviet Intelligence, had been asked to keep watch on Ukrainian exiles in West Germany who were believed to be hostile to the Soviet Union. There was nothing particularly unusual in this: the Ukrainians had always had a hankering for independence and some of them still regarded the Ukraine as quite distinct from Russia. In World War II many Ukrainians had sided with the Germans.

Stashinsky had made diligent reports to his Soviet masters on some of these Ukrainians when, on their instructions, he went to Munich on a Soviet Zone travel permit made out in the name of 'Lehmann'. The main target of Stashinsky's attention was an exiled Ukrainian politician named Lev Rebet, editor of the paper *Ukrainski Samostinik*, who lived in Munich.

Then in September 1957, Stashinsky was ordered to report to his Soviet controller. He was greeted dramatically with the words: 'The time has come. A man from Moscow is here.' There was something in the controller's tone of voice which sent a shiver down the Ukrainian's spine. As he later testified, Stashinsky suddenly realised with horror that the purpose of his task in watching Rebet had been to prepare the latter's murder. It was with growing uneasiness and alarm, which he tried hard to disguise, that he

OPPOSITE Bogdan Stashinsky and Inge Pohl at their wedding

met the KGB man from Moscow who was to demonstrate the death weapon to him.

The meeting with the KGB man took place in Karlshorst, the section of East Berlin in which the Soviet administration headquarters was sited. There the KGB man showed him 'the weapon which is to do the job for you – the perfect weapon for the perfect murder. This is what you will use on Rebet.'

The weapon looked harmless enough at a superficial glance. It was a metal tube, about as thick as a human finger and about seven inches long, consisting of three sections screwed together. In the bottom section there was a firing pin which ignited a powder charge. This caused a metal lever in the middle section to move; it crushed a glass ampoule in the mouth of the tube. This glass ampoule contained a poison that in appearance resembled water and escaped out of the front of the tube in the form of vapour. If this vapour was fired at someone's face from a distance of about one and a half feet, the person would drop dead immediately upon inhaling the vapour.

The KGB man grinned at Stashinsky as though taking a huge delight in shocking him. 'Quite simple, you see, and much better than this. [He drew a finger across his throat.] The vapour leaves no traces, and it is quite impossible to detect that murder has been done. But you yourself will need to be careful. You must guard against the possible effects of the vapour on you. We do not want two killings – that would give the game away.'

Again there was that wicked grin. 'Look,' said the KGB man, 'here is the safeguard,' and he handed Stashinsky a tablet. 'You swallow this as an antidote beforehand, and immediately you have fired the weapon, you crush an ampoule which is sewn up in gauze and inhale its vapour. Then you just get the hell out of it – fast.'

The poison used in the gun was said to be prussic acid, the colourless liquid form of cyanide. The antidotes prepared by Soviet chemists and given to Stashinsky were sodium thiosulphate, a white powder which is known to amateur photographers as hypo, and, with this, amyl nitrate, a yellowish liquid used medically to dilate the blood vessels, this being inhaled as a precaution.

The KGB man gave him a demonstration with the gun and then said that next day Stashinsky must practise with it himself. 'The next few hours were a living nightmare,' said the Ukrainian afterwards. 'I was so filled with loathing at the thought that I was to kill somebody with this weapon and at point blank range at that. I just wanted to get the practice over as speedily as possible. I hoped that somehow I should be able to dodge this assignment, yet I knew that the KGB man would be watching all my reactions and especially having me shadowed to make sure I did not escape.'

Next day he went with the KGB man, whose name was Sergey, to a small wood nearby. Sergey had brought a small dog which he tied to a tree. He then gave Stashinsky an anti-poison tablet and handed him the weapon, which was ready for firing.

'I was so upset I could harldy bear to look at the dog. Sergey must have noticed how I felt: he was the sort of man who would miss nothing. The dog sniffed around my feet trustingly. I turned my head away and fired the weapon about a foot in front of the dog's muzzle. There was hardly any detonation and the animal fell over immediately in a brief convulsion and died.'

The dog's carcass was left on the ground, but Sergey took away the leash, collar and muzzle. It was then made absolutely clear to Stashinsky that he was to carry out the killing of Rebet without further delay. On 9 October 1957, he flew by Air France from Berlin to Munich under the name of 'Siegfried Drager', taking a room at the Stachus Hotel. According to the detailed instructions given him by Sergey, he swallowed his antidote pill each morning for the next three days, periodically stationing himself in the Karlsplatz waiting for Rebet to appear. All kinds of wild thoughts passed through his mind during those three days. He supposed the antidote pills were safe enough, but this did not prevent Stashinsky from an uneasy feeling that the last pill he took might not be an antidote at all, but a killer tablet to silence him after he had murdered Rebet. Such things had happened before. 'I kept hoping that Rebet would not appear and that then there would be no need for me to carry out the deed.'

Shortly after ten a.m. on 12 October he caught sight of Rebet as the latter dismounted from a tram and headed for the building, No. 8 Karlsplatz. On hearing Rebet enter the building, Stashinsky took the weapon, which was wrapped up in a sheet of newspaper, out of his coat pocket and went towards his quarry who suspected nothing. As he drew level with Rebet he pointed the weapon at his face and fired. There was no noise as he pressed the trigger, no screaming and, of course, no blood. Rebet tumbled to the ground and Stashinsky rushed down the stairs. In the entrance hall he crushed the antidote ampoule and inhaled the vapour. He ran out of the building and threw the weapon into a stream at the rear of the Hofgarten.

'I was distressed at what I had done. I suddenly noticed that the sun was shining and that people looked happy,' said Stashinsky. 'I felt as though I had been dreaming . . . I went to the station and caught a train to Frankfurt. I stayed there overnight and then flew back to Berlin. In the jargon of the KGB such a killing was "to greet an acquaintance". In my report to the KGB I wrote that I met my acquaintance and that I was sure the greeting was a success.'

The branch of the KGB for which Bogdan Stashinsky worked was almost certainly the greatly feared OKR (*Otdely Kontrrazvedki*), the counter-espionage killer brigade which in 1946 took over *Smersh* (*Smyert Shpionam*), which means 'death to spies'.

* * *

Bogdan Stashinsky was born in 1931 at a village in the West Ukraine near Limburg (Lvov). He was the third child of Ukrainian parents who belonged to the Greek Orthodox faith. When the Germans invaded Russia in 1941 they occupied Stashinsky's native village.

It was at this time that some of the Ukrainians saw a glimmer of hope for escaping Soviet rule for all time. They had suffered greatly from Russian persecution and, though they did not like being occupied by the Germans, many of them felt that this was preferable to being dominated by Stalinism. In fact, since the Treaty of Pereyaslavl in 1654, Moscow had done everything possible to deny the proud Ukrainians any kind of autonomy and to stifle their own distinctive culture. After the Russian Civil War of 1917–20 life became much worse for the Ukraine. Following his armistice with the Central Powers Lenin officially recognised the Ukraine as a completely sovereign state. But this was mere window-dressing hypocrisy. At the very same time the Bolsheviks presented an ultimatum on the grounds that the Ukrainian Central Rada was acting in 'a bourgeois manner' and could not be accepted as an 'authorised representative of the labouring and exploited masses of Ukraine'. After the collapse of the Central Powers a directorate of five assumed power in Kiev.

Civil war followed, but while the Ukrainian Army, such as it was, fell to the Soviet armies after a valiant struggle, an independent Ukrainian government was set up in the Western Ukraine. For some time the situation in the Ukraine as a whole was extremely confused. On 7 May 1920 the Poles under Marshal Pilsudski occupied Kiev. Eventually, however, Poland was forced to sign a peace treaty with the USSR under which Russia retained control of the bulk of the Ukraine, but Eastern Galicia and Volhynia were recognised as part of Poland. Afterwards, a series of Ukrainian underground movements were formed to try to undermine Soviet influence and, where possible, to win aid and sympathy from the Western world. There were, at various times, the UVO (Ukrainian Military Organisation), the OUN (Organisation of Ukrainian Nationalists), the UPA (Ukrainian Insurgent Army) and the UHVR (Ukrainian Supreme Liberation Council). Many of the early Ukrainian patriots were wiped out in Stalin's purges of the late thirties, but the persecution was being relentlessly continued long after Stalin's death. What so angered the Soviets was that a document entitled *The Shame of the Twentieth Century* was smuggled to the West, giving an account of the various Soviet methods of oppression in the Ukraine.

Bogdan Stashinsky was quite a bright boy and he obtained his school leaving certificate from Lvov Gymnasium in April 1948, and then began a study of mathematics at the Lvov Teachers Training College. When he had started his schooling the chief foreign language that was taught in the Ukraine was Polish, but when Poland was divided up between Hitler and Stalin at the end of 1939, his native village came under direct Russian rule.

As far as he was concerned, this meant he had to learn Russian. Then, when the Nazis invaded Russia in 1941, the village changed into German hands. So the young Stashinsky had seen a bewildering change in the fortunes of his homeland and his family. Some of his family strongly supported resistance to the Soviet Union and were devoted members of the Greek Orthodox faith.

Young Stashinsky had first wanted to be a doctor, but had failed the examinations for the medical school. It was after this that he decided to try his luck at teaching and went to the Teachers Training College in Lvov for this purpose. Once or twice a week he used to travel home to obtain food and money from his parents who were still supporting him. Then, in the late summer of 1950, he was caught travelling on a train without a ticket and was ordered to report to the transport police in Lvov. This summons was enough to alarm even the bravest Ukrainian, as the transport police formed a department of the Soviet State Security Service actually operating under the MGB (the then Ministry of State Security).

Stashinsky was interviewed by an MGB captain Sitnikovsky, who was clever enough to question him without mentioning the fact that he had been caught travelling without a ticket. Sitnikovsky wanted to know all about Stashinsky's family and conditions in his native village. He warned the young man that he was fully aware that his family was involved in the OUN and he emphasised the 'senselessness' of this Ukrainian resistance: 'they will most certainly be caught, arrested, punished and deported.'

Soon the implications of this talk were obvious to this young man. If he really wanted to protect his family, then he could do so by giving the USSR information on who was who in the Ukrainian underground. In return his family would be given immunity from arrest. Maybe later they would realise that their son was their saviour. Stashinsky was only nineteen at the time, and he promptly agreed; to a large extent he had already been brainwashed at school and college where OUN supporters were designated as traitors and their leaders said to be in the pay of the Americans.

Shortly afterwards Stashinsky signed a written declaration binding him to work for the MGB and pledging him to complete secrecy. He was given the alias of 'Oleg'. During the next few months, in keeping with the instructions that he had received, he informed Sitnikovsky about all the incidents of note in his local village. By January 1951, the Russians had formed the opinion that Stashinsky had the makings of a good secret agent. He had been frank with them about Resistance activities in his village, he had shown intelligence and discrimination, so Sitnikovsky told him he must join a Resistance group of the OUN in order to learn details about the murder in 1949 of the Ukrainian pro-Soviet, anti-Catholic poet, Garoslav Galan, at the instigation of the OUN.

By this time Stashinsky was afraid that if he did not fall in with the MGB proposals, he might find that his course of studies had been discontinued.

But the Russians made their demand and the consequences of its refusal a little more brutal this time: only by helping them, he was informed, could he save his parents and sisters from being deported to concentration camps.

On the pretext that he was about to be arrested by the MGB, he managed to get into an underground group of the OUN. He reported back to the MGB who promptly informed him that, as the Ukrainians now knew all about his involvement with them, it would be impossible for him to return home. If he wished to remain safe and free, he must give up his studies and enter the service of the MGB. The fact was that the Russians had decided that Stashinsky was worthy of more important employment. Until then he had simply been rewarded by the occasional payment of a small sum of money and a pat on the back. But after he had persuaded his sister to introduce him to some partisans hiding out in the forest near Lvov, he had impressed Sitnikovsky enormously with the extent of his information. He had given the Russians the name of Galan's murderer, as a result of which he was put on the Soviet pay-roll at a salary of nine hundred roubles a month. And the truth was that Stashinsky rather revelled in having some kind of authority, even a delegated authority, and in playing the role of the 'big-shot'.

So Stashinsky was sent to Kiev for two years training as an agent. His alias was then 'Moros' and in addition to political instruction he was also taught German. The MGB (about to be merged with the KGB) made one concession in 1954; they allowed him to make things up with his parents and simply to tell them that he was living in Kiev and had a job there.

This was a classic example in modern times of how an insignificant person can inexorably be drawn into an espionage net before he realises what is happening. About the middle of 1954 he was given a completely new identity, that of Josef Lehmann, a German national born in Lukowek, Poland, on 4 November 1930 – exactly a year before Stashinsky's own birth date. The training Stashinsky was given for this new role in his life was extremely thorough. Accompanied and supervised by Soviet and Polish secret service officers, and using the name of 'Katshor', his mother's maiden name, he had to visit and memorise the places in Poland which played a part in the whole Lehmann story. Subsequently taken into the Soviet-occupied zone of Germany, near Frankfurt-an-der-Oder, he was handed over to his future Soviet superior officer, Sergey Alexandrovich. Needless to say, Josef Lehmann, whose role he was to fulfil, had long since 'disappeared'.

The KGB must have formed a high opinion of Stashinsky, because they ensured that his training continued even after this date. After he was sent out under his new identity, Stashinsky was watched, given additional training in trips to Bautzen and Dresden with a whole variety of jobs and assignments to test him out. He worked for a time as a press operator in a factory in Zwickau close to the Czech and East German borders to obtain his labour papers. After that he moved to East Berlin where he took a furnished room and worked as a freelance interpreter in German and Polish at the East German Ministry for Home and Foreign Trade. It was not until the beginning of 1956 that he started his real work for the KGB. Then he was sent to Munich to keep watch on Ukrainian exiles hostile to the Soviet Union. As 'Lehmann' he had to establish contact with a Ukrainian emigrant named Bissaga who was working in Munich as an agent for the KGB while serving on the staff of the anti-Soviet newspaper *Ukrainski Samostinik*, published by a Ukrainian exile organisation in the German city. This was the beginning of the watch being kept on Lev Rebet, the Ukrainian exiled politician and Resistance leader who was also editor-in-chief of *Ukrainski Samostinik*.

Little did Stashinsky know, however, that he had already become known to the West German Secret Service as a Soviet agent. They had photographed him talking to Bissaga, who was then known to be an agent of Moscow, and from this they deduced that Stashinsky (or Lehmann, as they knew him) was working for the same masters. But by this time the West German Secret Service had been infiltrated by the KGB and the man in charge of the Russian section of this service was himself a Soviet agent, Heinz Felfe. He may well have suppressed the intelligence on Stashinsky.

By now Stashinsky had almost convinced himself that he was a dedicated Soviet agent and believer in communism. Indeed, unless he had given this impression the Russians would never have considered giving him assignments to kill. Nevertheless, their handling of the Ukrainian was both subtle and skilful and they played carefully on the prospects of promotion. Originally it had seemed to Stashinsky that all that was required of him was to shadow Lev Rebet, who, in due course, would be abducted back to the Ukraine. At this time it must have seemed to the KGB that Stashinsky was a much better prospect than Bissaga who appeared distinctly nervous about any deeper involvement. But perhaps Bissaga had sensed rather more quickly than Stashinsky that in the end murder had to be committed.

Yet Stashinsky as the probationary KGB agent still had much to learn. He was expected to find out everything possible about Rebet's movements and his daily routine. In his preliminary reconnaissance of Rebet he followed the Ukrainian editor when he left his office in the Karlsplatz. Rebet got on a tram and Stashinsky followed him as far as the stop at the Münchener Freiheit. 'If one is pursuing a person,' said Stashinsky afterwards, 'one has the feeling that everyone else knows all about it. It is almost like being pursued by the whole world oneself. I had a fleeting impression that Rebet might have recognised me. Then I suddenly realised what was wrong and why I had this feeling. According to the "classical" training I received in Kiev, I had put on my dark glasses. I then realised that I was particularly conspicuous and that other people in the tram noticed this because I was the only person wearing them.'

Feeling uncomfortable, Stashinsky took off his glasses, for he was, he said, 'much more disguised without them than with them. But I was unhappy at that time because I felt that I had a lot to learn in this espionage game. Not only did I not know which tram stop to ask for, but I didn't even know how much the ticket should be.'

But eventually Stashinsky overcame his fears, got to understand the environment in which he had suddenly been placed and managed to track down Rebet and observe all his movements and daily habits without being detected. It was at this stage that he was ordered by the KGB to carry out Rebet's murder.

Meanwhile another and keener interest had entered into Bogdan's life. During a visit to an East Berlin dance hall he had met a German girl named Inge Pohl, who was twenty-one years old and had the same birthday as himself. She lived with her parents in Dallgow, a small village in East Germany, situated not far from West Berlin. It was about as far west from the centre of Berlin as Karlshorst is in the eastern sector and in those days there was a direct rail connection between Dallgow and Central East Berlin of a dozen or so stops. Inge Pohl worked as an apprentice hairdresser in West Berlin. She was quite an ordinary German girl, hearty and convivial, with limited intellectual interests. But she was emotionally an intense type and in some ways a stronger character than Bogdan. Soon the two young people became strongly attracted to one another.

This posed a moral problem for the already very confused Stashinsky. He had introduced himself to the girl as Josef Lehmann, a German national from Poland, and he realised that both she and her family were opposed to the communist system. He became even more worried about their relationship after he had killed Rebet. Then in May 1958, Stashinsky was sent to Rotterdam for three days with instructions to keep a watch at the graveside memorial service for Colonel Konovalec, founder of the OUN, who had been murdered in 1938. Stashinsky photographed all those attending the service, taking particular notice of a blue Opel Kapitan with a Munich number plate parked outside the cemetery. This he found belonged to the principal speaker at the memorial service, Stefan Bandera, a Ukrainian writer who used the pseudonym of Stefan Popel. Bandera was not only the leader of the Munich branch of the OUN, he was the most energetic and oustanding of the Ukrainian Resistance leaders and the one who had the closest links with the West. Of all the Ukrainians desperately wanted by the KGB, Bandera was top of the list. But above all they wanted him liquidated with the minimum of attention; it was essential, as in the case of Rebet, that his death should appear to be an accident.

Both the American and the British secret services had close contacts at one time with Bandera. Indeed, the British had kept contact with him since before World War II. 'A Ukrainian nationalist of marked fascist views,' was how Kim Philby described him in his book, *Silent War*, in which he gives a most misleading picture of the Bandera tragedy. However, as this false picture paradoxically throws much light on subsequent events, it is worth quoting:

'. . . although Bandera was quite a noise in the emigration,' writes Philby, 'his claims to a substantial following inside the Soviet Union were never seriously tested, except in the negative sense that nothing much ever came of them. A first party, equipped by the British with wireless-telegraphy and other clandestine means of communication was sent into the Ukraine in 1949, and disappeared. Two more parties were sent the following year and remained equally silent. Meanwhile the Americans were beginning to nurse serious doubts about Bandera's usefulness to the West which the failure of the British-sponsored parties to surface did nothing to allay.'

As Kim Philby was at this time in a key position inside MI 6, actually keeping a close watch on Soviet affairs, one wonders how much he had to do with this alleged failure. But he goes on to say that 'the American attack on the alliance between Bandera and SIS [British Secret Service] gathered strength in 1950 and much of my time in the United States was spent in transmitting acrimonious exchanges between Washington and London on the rival merits of obscure emigré factions. . . . The British plea that Bandera was being used solely for the purpose of gathering intelligence, and that such a use could have no real political significance, was brushed aside by the Americans who argued that, whatever the nature of the connection, its very existence must inflate Bandera's prestige in the Ukraine.'

There were certainly differences of opinion on policies towards the Ukraine between the USA and Britain, but it should perhaps be made clear that the British then regarded Bandera sufficiently highly to refuse to jettison him. Indeed, they continued parachuting agents into the area. To all this Philby adds this totally misleading statement which no one better than he should know is far from the truth: 'Some eight years later I read of the mysterious murder of Bandera in Munich, in the American Zone of Germany [as it was then]. It may be that, despite the brave stand of the British in his defence, the CIA had the last word.'

What *did* happen to Bandera?

Well, far from there being any American CIA involvement or otherwise, in his end, the vital instructions came late in 1958 when Bogdan Stashinsky was informed by Sergey that he was to liquidate Bandera.

By this time Stashinsky had tracked down Bandera and in the course of doing so had been given a new cover identity, that of Hans Joachim Budeit, of 69 Knappenweg, Duisburg, who had been born in Kassel on 12 April, 1927. This was an unusual and even dangerous step for the normally cautious KGB to adopt, as Budeit himself was still alive. But this may well have been their own devious method of keeping a blackmail hold on Stashinsky, for by now they must certainly have known about his friendship with Inge Pohl. Slowly, but surely, the remorseless process of espionage was forcing Bogdan into an impossible position. Either he had to continue as a killer and become a slave of the KGB, without any possibility of escape, or, so it seemed to him, he could continue seeing Inge Pohl and ultimately face total discardment, if not death.

Bandera, using the identity of Popel, had been an elusive character. Not even the KGB was certain just where he lived until they had sent Bogdan on repeated missions to make inquiries. Eventually he tracked down Bandera to No. 7, Kreittmayerstrasse in Munich, for which he obtained a skeleton key. Bogdan had been trying to deceive himself. Foolishly, he had been hoping that he would not be asked to undertake another murder job. His ears were always alert to that dread expression in the world of Soviet espionage – *mokrie dela*, meaning literally 'wet or bloody affairs' and referring to espionage missions involving bloodshed.

Bogdan was torn between conflicting loyalties, a desire not to destroy his family through refusing KGB orders, along with a strange wish to conform to Soviet teachings that men like Bandera and Rebet were simply a menace to a settled society and enemies of national security, and his childhood Christian teaching that 'thou shalt not kill'. If Bogdan analysed his feelings at all, he probably felt the greatest repugnance at killing someone in what he felt was an extremely cowardly and unforgivable manner.

No doubt Moscow had been fully informed on Bogdan's surreptitious love life and possibly all that had saved him from liquidation was the fact that he had at least scrupulously preserved his false identity with Inge. She called him 'Joshi' as an abbreviation of his original espionage cover of Josef Lehmann. By April 1959, they were secretly engaged. Before he was finally told that he must kill Bandera, Stashinsky was ordered to Moscow and told by Georgy Aksentivich of the KGB that 'sentence of death' had been passed on Bandera. More in self-defence than anything else Stashinsky pointed out that Bandera usually had a bodyguard with him, which made the killing much more difficult. The Soviet reply was to give him a double-barrelled pistol with which to defend himself.

There seemed no way out for Bogdan. He was also told that since Rebet had been killed there had been a considerable improvement in the technique of these death-dealing weapons. 'The gun you used before produced a small shower of glass splinters. The new gun has a specially fitted filter to hold back the glass.' Aksentivich suddenly produced a bottle of champagne with which to celebrate 'the fact that this time you are moving into a flawless murder situation. You realise, I am sure, that you were not found out last time. The West Germans still think that Rebet died a natural death – a heart attack.'

But behind all this bonhomie Stashinsky had the feeling that he was himself just as much under threat of death. It was a case of kill, or be killed;

indeed, worse still, it was kill cleanly and undetected and you will survive, but botch it up and the KGB will gladly drink to the end of Bogdan Stashinsky.

So Stashinsky kept constant watch on Bandera in Munich, waiting for the right opportunity. He had been warned that he must finish his mission within ten days. In the middle of May 1959, a favourable chance presented itself. Bogdan noticed that Bandera was actually driving to his garage alone. He held his weapon in readiness as the Ukrainian drew up, but suddenly he was seized both by doubts and fear. He just could not carry out his orders. For a few moments he felt like fleeing.

But common sense and logic prevailed. If he fled, how was he ever going to be reunited with Inge? How indeed could he escape beyond the reach of the KGB? He had no contacts with the Western world. Instinctively, Bogdan Stashinsky realised belatedly that this was not the moment to try to escape. Yet he felt he had to make a gesture. So, as he ran away, he threw his weapon into the Kogelmuhlbach, just as he might have done had he committed the crime.

These are the kind of moments which are testing for the most devoted of spies. Sorge might have survived such a moment quite easily because he believed in the cause of communism. Cynthia, who devoured her victims in a sexual way, was never put to such extreme tests. Nor was TATE. But Stashinsky looked immediately for excuses as to why he had not carried out his mission. He examined the lock on the door of the house in which Bandera lived in order to produce some evidence of his activity as an agent and thus to try to pacify Moscow. In doing so he broke two key-bits, which were found two and a half years later in the dirt and dust that had accumulated in the large box of the lock.

There is conflicting evidence as to how Stashinsky made his excuses to the KGB, but it would seem that the latter were lenient with him because they wanted his aid in tracking down other Ukrainian exiles. Then in August 1959, the KGB made a generous gesture to their protégé: he was sent to see his parents and told that, ostensibly, he could be reconciled with them. The probability is that this was a psychological exercise to keep Stashinsky under their control. In October 1959, he once again received orders that he must kill Bandera. This time Stashinsky was left in no doubt as to what was expected of him, or what would happen if he failed. It was, he said, 'once again the old conflict between discipline, the pressure of orders and my better feelings. The Soviet authority then triumphed.'

So on the morning of 15 October, Bogdan Stashinsky kept watch for Bandera from an entrance door opposite Zeppelinstrasse 67, which was the office of the Organisation of Ukrainian Nationalist Revolutionaries which Bandera headed. This time there was no looking back, though Stashinsky's tongue went dry as he swallowed the antidote tablet. Once again he had wrapped the weapon in a sheet of newspaper and removed the safety-catch to be in absolute readiness. He was well aware that Bandera would be permanently alert for a possible Soviet killer: his life had been threatened before.

Then he saw Bandera arrive alone in his car and drive into the adjacent yard. Bogdan heaved an involuntary sigh of relief; at least there was no bodyguard to worry about. He turned round and entered the building and, as he went up the stairs, heard the footsteps of a woman coming down from a floor above. So that she should not see his face, he turned towards the lift and pressed the button. At this point acute agitation seized Stashinsky just as it had on the previous occasion when he evaded killing Bandera. But this time there was a difference. Though agitated, he acted like an automaton: 'It was,' he said, 'almost as though I were two persons, my real self holding back from the job and not wanting to remember anything about it, another self like a robot or a human machine . . . I did not remember afterwards whether I went up in the lift, or climbed the stairs.'

When he heard the entrance door open, he knew that Bandera had come in and he turned down the stairs so that he would face him. He then noticed that Bandera had a little basket with 'something red in it – like tomatoes' on his right arm and that he was struggling to pull the door key out of the keyhole in which it had apparently stuck.

As Stashinsky drew level with Bandera he does recall saying to his prospective victim, 'Won't it work?' He stepped forward and swiftly discharged the contents of the gun in Bandera's face. Then he took the gauze-covered phial containing the second antidote, crushed it swiftly against the entrance door and inhaled the fumes. He lost no time in getting away from the building, disposing of the cloth and glass splinters down a drain and flinging his gun over a bridge into the waters of the Kogelmuhlbach in the nearby Hofgarten. Next day he took the first flight to Berlin, crossed over to the Soviet headquarters in Karlshorst and reported that his mission was completed.

He was introduced by Sergey to a Soviet general whom he suspected was the KGB chief of East Berlin. They had quite a cordial talk and the general then turned to his desk, took out a bottle of cognac and poured two glasses, handing one to Stashinsky. 'I now have a very pleasant task to perform,' he said. 'In fact, some very good news indeed, and it calls for a toast. Because of the very important government business you have so successfully concluded, you have been awarded the Order of the Red Banner. But you must go to Moscow to receive this award.'

Bogdan should have been delighted, but his heart sank when he heard that he had to go to Moscow. It meant being separated from Inge Pohl once more and in recent months there had been too many of these separations. He tried to console himself that he had come a long way since that day when he was caught travelling without a ticket. But deep down he knew that such promotion was illusory as regards living a better and freer life.

Stashinsky was also nervous because this time he had been questioned much more closely about the killing than about the previous murder of Rebet. The Russians, who had made their own checks on Bandera's death, informed him that this time it had 'not been quite the perfect murder it should have been'.

'Why not?' asked Stashinsky, momentarily put out.

'Because you may have been just a little careless. Oh, nothing too serious, but still. . . . You see the German police made an inquiry into Bandera's sudden death when he was found outside his door. With Rebet they assumed it was simply a case of "natural causes", but they knew that Bandera was a possible target for assassination. And when an autopsy was carried out, the glass splinters had caused cuts on his face. That wasn't very clever. What happened to the special filter? Or were you in too much of a hurry to get away? Anyhow, the German police now suspect prussic acid poisoning.'

So, as the Bandera death had created somewhat of a sensation in West Germany, the KGB thought it advisable that Stashinsky stay in Moscow until things had quietened down. In December Bogdan was sent for by Alexander Shelepin, who was not only head of the KGB at that time, but also a leading member of the Central Committee of the Communist Party of the USSR. Shelepin personally conferred on him the Order of the Red Banner and then interrogated him in great detail on the killing. From the questions he was asked, Bogdan felt sure that the KGB had watched all his movements both before and after the killing of Bandera. He was even made to draw a sketch-map of the scene of the crime.

If Kim Philby implied that the CIA had killed Bandera, he was only fulfilling the wishes of Moscow. The Russians were all along seemingly desperate not to be suspected of planning the murder, for they feared repercussions in the Ukraine if such a rumour got around. To try to ensure that they were not blamed for the Bandera killing, the KGB cleverly planted their own cover story for the crime. This was to use other agents to put around the story that the Ukrainian exile, Myskiw, had killed Bandera on 15 October at the instructions of the German Federal Intelligence Service of General Reinhard Gehlen, and that afterwards Myskiw himself had been murdered by West German agents, working with the American CIA. So, to some extent, Philby's own story tallies with that put out by the KGB. This story in one form or other was repeated over the next few years, every time that the Bandera tragedy came into the news again.

Bogdan was also worried at this time by a lie he had told to Inge Pohl. He did not want to admit that he was going to Moscow, so he pretended that he was travelling to Poland on a business trip. He had already begun to think about escaping from his now hated job and had promised himself that never again would he agree to carry out a killing. But he did not dare to confide in Inge as yet, however much he loved and trusted her. If she knew he was a killer, almost certainly she would have nothing more to do with him.

It was his KGB controller Sergey who reported to Moscow that Bogdan had been seeing rather a lot of a German girl. He was warned that such a friendship was not altogether 'suitable' for a KGB man and that he should not attempt to marry a foreigner. Stashinsky, however, was quick-witted enough to argue that he had known the girl for a very long time now and that it might be more awkward if he was to jilt her. She would talk and then his cover might be broken. He also argued that, as the KGB wanted him to carry out other assignments for them in Western Europe, a marriage to this German girl could be helpful as a cover and also pave the way to the legalisation of his cover in the West.

The KGB controller then began to change his attitude. Perhaps he saw the force of Stashinsky's arguments, or possibly he felt that it would be a mistake to upset an agent by demanding he got rid of his girl. Or it could also have been that it was suddenly realised that if Bogdan married Inge, she could later be used as a hostage to ensure he fulfilled his assignments. The KGB man did not acquiesce to Bogdan's suggestion that he should go on seeing the girl, but told him to 'think the matter over carefully'. This was almost as bad as ordering him to give up Inge.

However, such was Bogdan's love for the girl, as well as his determination to escape to the West when an opportunity presented itself, that he courageously persisted in putting a special request direct to Shelepin that he should be allowed to marry her. Shelepin tried to dissuade him, but Stashinsky lied so convincingly about how good a communist she was, that eventually the KGB chief agreed to a marriage, but on condition that his fiancée should visit Moscow so that they could assess her reliability.

Stashinsky was taking an enormous risk in pressing his case both for himself and Inge for the Soviets could very easily have insisted, once she arrived in Moscow, that she must agree to stay there permanently. But for once luck was on his side, though he was somewhat apprehensive as to whether the KGB would find out that she was anti-communist. A few days later Bogdan was told that he must inform Inge that he was not working as an interpreter for the East German Trade Ministry, but was a member of the Soviet State Security Service.

'You must ask her if she is prepared to help you in your work after you are married. If she agrees, then you can both come to Moscow in January,' Bogdan was informed. 'You must on no account tell her about the two murders you have committed.'

It was Christmas 1959 when Stashinsky returned to East Berlin. He was still under orders not to go back into West Germany, or even to try to enter West Berlin. But he took a great risk. He headed east, quickly looked round to make sure nobody was following him, and then doubled back swiftly on his tracks. By now he was fully experienced in knowing when he was being watched or followed, and how to throw his pursuers off the track. This time, however, he felt sure he had not been observed, and he made for Inge's place of work, a hairdressers in West Berlin.

Having been reunited with Inge, he decided to risk all by telling her his full story. Once again he disobeyed KGB orders, and the only thing he omitted telling her then was about the two murders. One shock at a time, he felt, was quite enough. Inge took the news surprisingly well, but her first reaction was that if Bogdan seriously wanted to escape to the west, why not do so at once. This, after all, was a natural response.

With some difficulty Bogdan explained to her that such a move would need to be planned very carefully indeed, or it could go hopelessly wrong and he might be traced by the KGB and murdered. The free world of the West was still a very strange place to him. Somehow its very freedom seemed a frightening thing after the restrictions of the Soviet Union and her satellite states. He said he wanted to improve his knowledge of the German language first so that it would be easier for him to start a new life in the West. In fact, at the back of his mind, he was thinking of a new life in the United States rather than in West Germany. That was further away from the USSR and much safer. He recalled that the KGB had insisted that he must also learn English when he returned to Moscow and this he was anxious to do.

Fortunately for Bogdan, Inge proved a sensible, level-headed girl with remarkable courage and determination to see this extremely risky project go through. Indeed, in this whole story of Bogdan Stashinsky it is Inge Pohl who stands out as a most capable young woman with an astonishing and enchanting trust in her boyfriend. Without her capacity for deception, which matched his own, Bogdan Stashinsky would probably never have got away from the clutches of the KGB. They both agreed that as far as Inge's parents were concerned, the truth must be kept from them. To them, for the present at least, he must still be Lehmann, the interpreter. Inge also agreed to conceal from the KGB all she knew about Bogdan's real identity. Both of them had to pretend to Inge's parents that they were going on a business trip to Warsaw, when in fact they were bound for Moscow. For this reason the KGB sent all their mail via Warsaw and on their eventual return to East Berlin gave them postcards with views of Warsaw as well as small present which were clearly marked 'from Poland'.

They spent two months in Moscow, much of the time wondering whether the KGB would learn of their deceit, but maintaining, outwardly at least, all signs of calm and contentment. Stashinsky was able to convince his superiors that Inge was genuinely pro-Soviet and obtained permission to marry her. But it was probably only because Inge actually lived in East Berlin, even if she had worked in the West sector, that they finally, if reluctantly, agreed to the marriage. Even then there was nearly a last minute hitch. Bogdan said that it was his fiancée's wish, because of her parents, that they should be married at a Protestant Church. The Russians were highly suspicious of a religious ceremony, but Bogdan pointed out that with such a

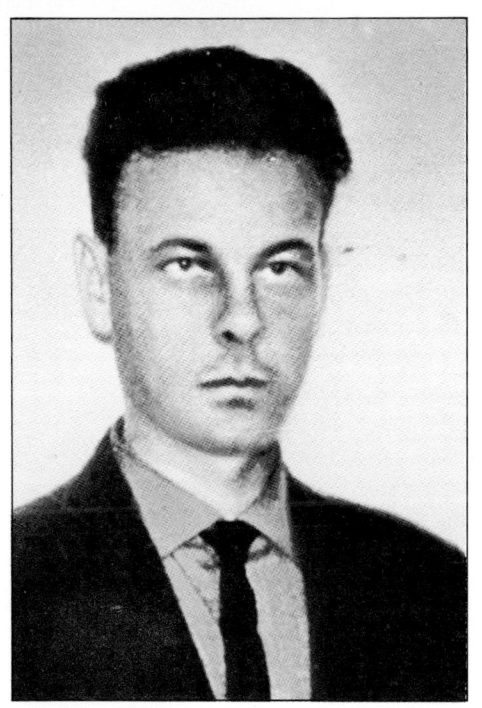

Bogdan Stashinsky

Stefan Bandera

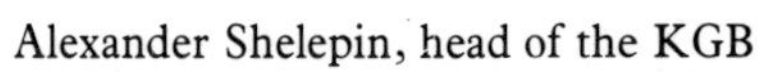

Alexander Shelepin, head of the KGB

Lev Rebet

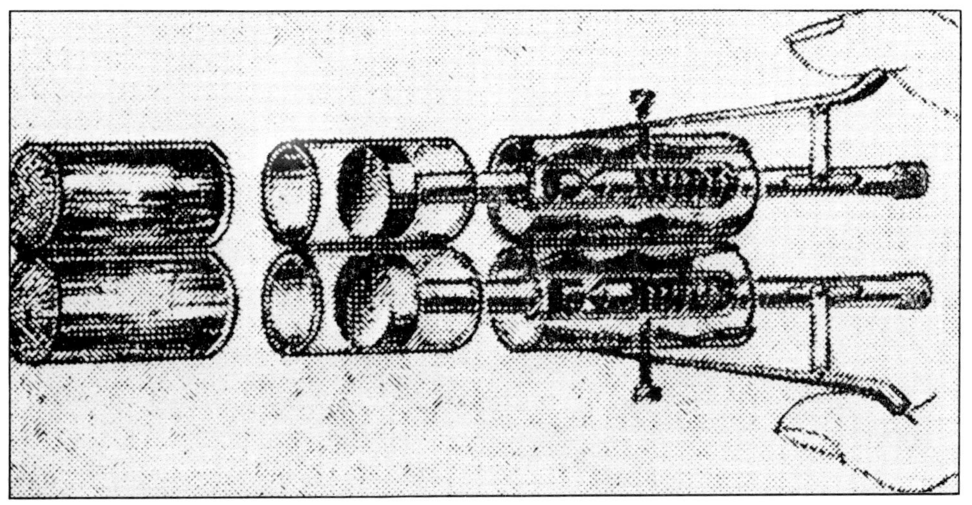

The revolutionary murder weapon – the cyanide gun

Stashinsky re-ènacts the moments leading up to
the murder of Rebet: the gun is hidden in his newspaper
as he walks down the stairs at no 8 Karlsplatz

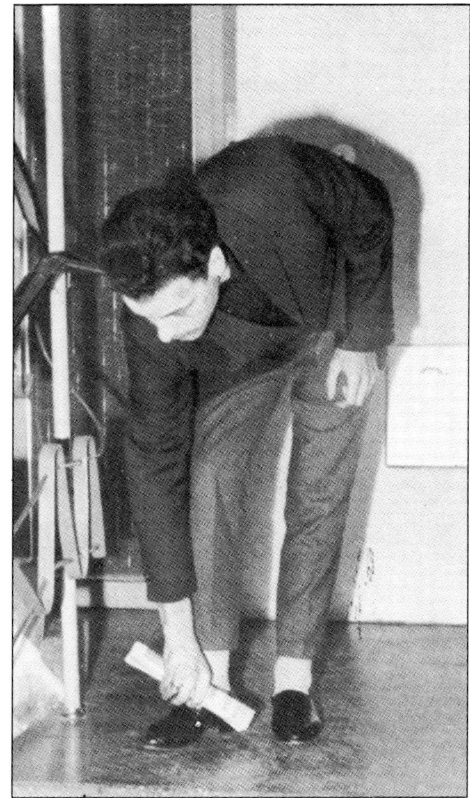

The bridge in Hofgartenstrasse where
Stashinsky disposed of the murder weapon

The funeral of Stefan Bandera, 20 October 1959

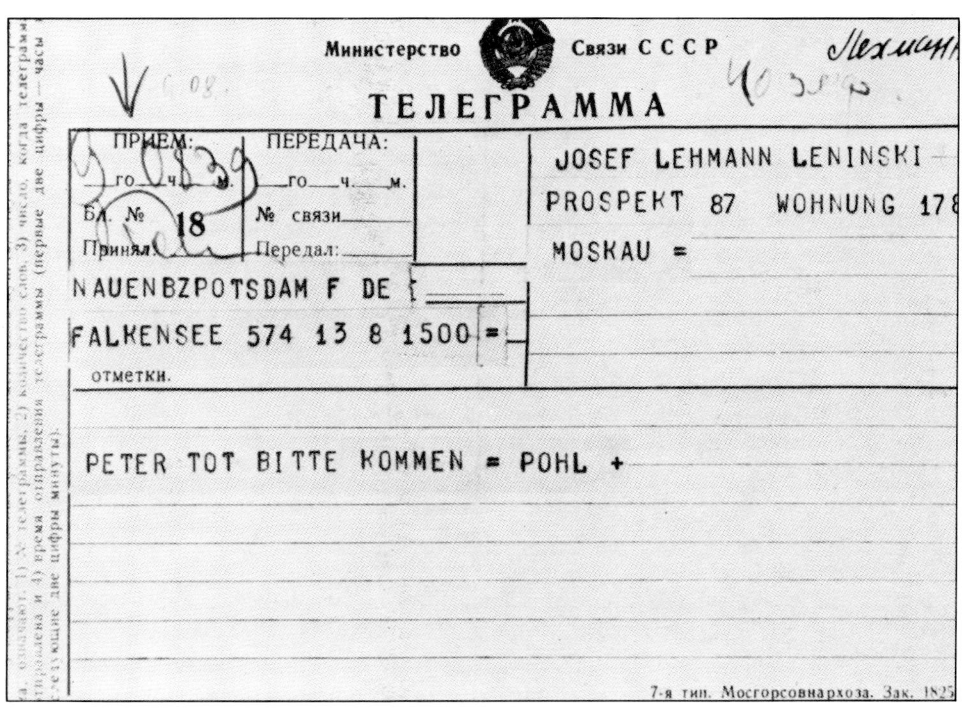

Министерство Связи СССР

ТЕЛЕГРАММА

ПРИЕМ: го ч. м.

ПЕРЕДАЧА: го ч. м.

Бл. № 18

№ связи

Принял:

Передал:

JOSEF LEHMANN LENINSKI

PROSPEKT 87 WOHNUNG 178

MOSKAU =

NAUENBZPOTSDAM F DE

FALKENSEE 574 13 8 1500 =

отметки.

PETER TOT BITTE KOMMEN = POHL +

7-я тип. Мосгорсовнархоза. Зак. 1825

The fateful telegram informing Stashinsky alias Lehmann of his baby son's death

The Berlin Wall

ceremony he was much less likely to be suspected of being a KGB agent.

Then in May 1960, husband and wife were both ordered back to Moscow where a woman from the KGB gave Stashinsky lessons to improve his German and especially his accent. He also took pains to acquaint himself with English. All the time both had the uneasy feeling that they were being watched and their behaviour was being assessed. This had the effect of making Inge increasingly hostile to the Soviet regime in secret and impatient with Bogdan for constantly delaying his escape to the West. The truth was that Bogdan was almost as frightened of escape as of staying with the Soviets. He had been conditioned by his intensive training to believe that the long arm of the KGB could reach out anywhere and grab him, if he tried any tricks. In addition, lengthy brain-washing had drained him of independent powers of decision. He was a creature moulded entirely in the ways of the Soviet Secret Service.

Also, to be fair to Stashinsky, what were his prospects if he did try to escape? If he gave himself up to the West Germans, he would certainly be interrogated and, if they found out about the murders, put on trial. Either that, or the KGB would find him out. And what chance had he got of persuading the Americans that he was a worthwhile person to grant asylum to? The only big secrets he could bring over with him were those of the crimes he had committed and they were enough to damn him.

He pointed all this out to his wife, but she insisted that anything was better than life in the Soviet Union. Their living conditions in Moscow were not particularly good. One day Inge, who had long suspected that their apartment was being 'bugged', urged Bogdan to search the place thoroughly. Sure enough he discovered a tape-recorder concealed there. It was now obvious that not only was their correspondence with their relatives being censored and every expedition watched, but that there must be secret microphones as well in the apartment. From that moment on whenever either of them had anything confidential to say, they either waited until they were out on a walk in the park or they scribbled down questions and answers on pieces of paper, taking care to burn them afterwards.

'This is not life,' Inge wrote down one day, 'it is a living hell. You must get us away.'

But there was a further shock in store for them. In September of that year Inge discovered she was pregnant. Both of them were delighted and Bogdan casually mentioned this to his KGB controller. He was horrified when this official scowled and said that Inge should immediately have an abortion as it was 'highly undesirable that they should have a child'. Otherwise, he added menacingly, 'you will have to put the child in a home and let it be brought up there'.

'I did not know that even in the Soviet Union, officialdom could be quite so brutal to their own employees,' was Inge's response. This incident does seem to have had the effect of making Bogdan now fully determined to make a break for it as soon as possible. However, as long as they were both in the Soviet Union, there was no chance of that. Only if he could get another assignment outside Soviet territory and take Inge with him, did they have any real chance of getting away. What made things seem worse was that by now Stashinsky was sure that the KGB were beginning to have doubts about him, especially after he had expressed his outrage at the abortion proposal. It began to look as though the KGB plan would be that one of them was always to be kept behind in Moscow as a hostage for the other. Why he had not realised this before they went back to Moscow does seem very surprising but one must remember that Stashinsky had lived as one of the oppressed and hunted all his life. It was not easy for him to take bold decisions for himself.

Having at last decided to make escape their number one priority, Stashinsky steeled himself to the necessary effort. He set out to be as cunning as the KGB, by being extra diligent and co-operative to show them that he could still be a valued agent. Pointing out to the Russians that Inge's parents might begin to ask awkward questions if they did not see their daughter soon, he managed to persuade them to let her go on a brief holiday to East Berlin. With some subtlety such as he had not shown previously, he even managed to hint that, with his wife away, he would be able to work harder and more efficiently. To his surprise this ruse worked and suddenly Inge was given an exit permit. This was, at least, a step, albeit a small one, in the right direction. The next problem would be how to prolong Inge's stay in East Berlin until he had found some pretext of joining her. Privately they had a plan which they hoped would work. This was that she should somehow manage to prolong her stay in East Berlin until her confinement was due and then send a begging letter to Shelepin, asking for her husband to join her.

For a while it looked as though the KGB had had second thoughts about their treatment of Stashinsky. At any rate there seemed to be an attempt to make amends for their harsh reaction to the news of the expected baby. He was given a certificate in the form of a testimonial from the 'Director of the Scientific Research Institute, PO Box 946', which was in reality a KGB department. This document stated that, 'for successful activity in working out an important problem, in accordance with the decree of the Praesidium of the Supreme Soviet of the USSR of 6 November, 1959', he had been decorated with the Order of the Red Banner.

Close contact with Inge was maintained by the KGB in East Berlin, but she managed to prolong her stay. On 31 March 1961, she sent a telegram to her husband, saying that he had a son. Right away Stashinsky put in a request to be allowed to travel to see her and the baby. The request was refused. 'On the contrary,' the KGB controller told Bogdan, 'we have already extended your wife's stay on two occasions because of her health. It is now necessary that she should return to Moscow.'

This for the moment looked like the end of the road for any hopes Bogdan and his wife might have of escaping to the West. There now seemed to be no doubting the KGB's impatience. Then came a faint glimmer of hope through unexpected and tragic news. On 9 August 1961, Inge telephoned her husband in Moscow to say that the child had died. He also had a telegram from his father-in-law. This time, as an East German family was involved, the KGB relented. Stashinsky could go on a quick visit to his wife, they said, provided their inquiries showed that the child had died a natural death. They must ascertain all the facts. Their inquiries apparently proved satisfactory, as Stashinsky was later informed that he could attend the funeral of his son, but that he would have an escort who would fly with him to East Germany.

So on 10 August Stashinsky flew to East Berlin accompanied by one Juriy, a KGB agent, who knew both him and Inge. The war of nerves against Bogdan continued. First, having indicated that they were satisfied that the child had died naturally, the KGB men who met them in East Berlin insisted that they would need to keep Bogdan and his wife under close supervision as there was just a possibility that the child had been poisoned by the Americans in order to lure Stashinsky away from Moscow, as it seemed they had discovered he was a KGB agent.

Despite this, Bogdan was able to hint to Inge that he was ready to make a break for it, though with the KGB insisting even on following them to the funeral, the chances of success still seemed dim. 'We are being watched all the time,' whispered Bogdan, 'and it is obvious we shall be shadowed even more intensively after the funeral. If there is to be a break, it has got to come quickly. We have got to get away before the funeral.'

The funeral was fixed for 12 August. Just how right Stashinsky was to plan his escape for that very day can be assessed by the fact that this was literally the last day on which he could have got away whether under KGB surveillance or otherwise. For on 13 August 1961, the notorious Berlin Wall became a fact of life: on that day the Soviet sector of Berlin was sealed off from all other sectors and the barricades went up. The Cold War was being waged with renewed ferocity as, at the end of that month, no agreement was reached in the Geneva talks on the banning of nuclear tests and the USSR announced that they were actually resuming nuclear weapons testing.

So it had to be the day of the funeral even if this meant their missing the burial of their own child. Bogdan said '. . . on the day of my child's funeral, we laid our plans to get away . . . as afterwards it would have been too late and pressure would have been put on me to go back to Moscow at once. Even at that time we were being watched by three cars, all stationed at strategic points in nearby streets. We were ringed by observers. Once we were alone and with nobody within earshot, we had to examine very carefully how we could slip away unobserved. We did this partly by studying street maps and partly by knowledge of where the KGB cars were situated. Each of us made suggestions as to how we could best fool our observers.'

Dallgow, where the funeral was to take place, was as close to the border as anywhere could be. The KGB were fully aware that if the Stashinskys were going to make a break for it, this was the best chance they had. Only the previous day two thousand East Berliners had crossed to the West. All that week droves of refugees from the Soviet Zone had been growing with rumours of a new crisis.

One thing worried Bogdan: he feared that, when it came to the crunch, Inge would not be able to avoid attending the funeral. Her strong emotions would prevent her from escaping. Together they watched the wreaths arrive, picked them up and looked at the inscriptions. All this time the KGB car stood in the road near the Pohls' address. But Inge kept calm, even though there were tears in her eyes: she told her younger brother, sixteen-year-old Fritz, that he would have to take the wreaths to the grave himself.

There was just one single route for escape and even that required a degree of luck. At the back of the house at the end of the garden was a fence. By creeping cautiously alongside the fence they could keep out of sight of the KGB men and reach a very narrow stretch of land that was planted with trees and shrubs and so provided excellent cover. Followed by Fritz, carrying only light hand-luggage, Bogdan and Inge made it safely to the sanctuary of the tree-shrouded strip of land. Fritz kept looking back to make quite sure nobody had seen them. Then they slipped out into the side-roads away from their observers and made their way to Falkensee, a suburb to the north, where they hired a taxi.

Eventually they reached the centre of the Soviet Zone, but before they got there they were stopped by the East German police. Bogdan showed his papers and identity card under the name of Josef Lehmann and the police waved him on. In East Berlin they boarded an electric train at Schonhauser Allee station and travelled as far as Gesundbrunnen station in West Berlin. At last they had reached the freedom of the West.

The death of Stefan Bandera had been a severe blow to many Ukrainian Nationalists both inside the Ukraine and in exile in West Germany and elsewhere. According to the calculations of statisticians there are about forty-five million Ukrainians in the world, very many, of course, driven into exile. The Select Investigation Committee of the US House of Representatives under Charles J. Kersten's chairmanship, stated in its report in 1955 that the Ukrainians 'rank in Europe next after the Russians and the Germans in point of numbers. The greater part of them live in the Ukrainian Soviet Socialist Republic.' But a sizeable number are to be found elsewhere in Europe and in the USA and Britain. For many of these exiles Bandera was a folk hero.

Born in 1909 in Galicia, the son of a Greek Orthodox priest, Stefan

Bandera joined an organisation fighting for Ukrainian independence from Russia when he was an adolescent. It could be said that, far from being the fascist reactionary portrayed so glibly by Kim Philby, he was as much anti-Polish as anti-Russian. For after World War I the Ukraine was divided between Russia and Poland, the latter nation controlling the Western Ukraine and Lvov. Attacks on Polish officials were a daily occurrence and young Bandera was loud in his condemnation of what he regarded as 'Polish fascism'. In 1934 the Polish Minister of the Interior, Pieracki, was shot in Warsaw and investigations showed that the assassins belonged to the OUN, Bandera's own group. Bandera himself was arrested and sentenced to life imprisonment.

When the Germans invaded Poland in 1939 Bandera was released from prison and he at once returned to the OUN fold, the leader of which was then Colonel Andreas Melnyk. Bandera, however, disagreed with his policies and formed a splinter group which developed into the most radical and effective of the Ukrainian Nationalist groups. During 1944 Bandera got into trouble with the Gestapo and was put into Sachsenhausen concentration camp. Then, during the Soviet occupation of Berlin, he was freed and managed to flee to Bavaria where he reformed his organisation from the offices in the Zeppelinstrasse in Munich. Here he acquired a printing press on which he turned out the Ukrainian Nationalists' newspaper for exiles and the underground – *The Way to Victory*.

There were people in the British Secret Service who looked upon Bandera as one who might well serve their own cause during the Cold War just as effectively as he provided a radical stimulus to Ukrainian nationalism. But Bandera was no compromiser. He opposed the supposedly democratically-inclined Ukrainian Government in Exile led by Liwycky, also from Munich, and was equally critical of the American-backed Committee for Liberation of the Ukraine from Bolshevism which ran 'Radio Liberation' in Munich. This no doubt was what caused the CIA to regard Bandera with some hostility and distrust. From this post-war period onwards it was difficult to ascertain the truth about all of Bandera's moves, or his views. Propaganda by Americans, Russians and rival Ukrainian nationalists all played a part in distorting accounts of his career.

For example, though Bandera may have been implacably opposed to the type of Ukrainians the CIA were proposing to back, he was certainly not anti-American. Indeed, there is evidence that he visited the USA with a view to establishing better relations in early 1950. At this time Kim Philby was British liaison officer with the CIA and it was possibly then that Bandera was smeared by the Soviet Union's agent inside British Intelligence. More important is that the Russians should have seen fit to plan his assassination. This can be taken as adequate measure of Bandera's stature as a nationalist leader.

It is worth noting that the USSR has consistently sought to kill Ukrainian

Independence leaders by political assassination. The first was Symon Petlura, who was murdered in the street in Paris in 1926. Then in 1938 Colonel Konovalec, founder and leader of the UVO, was killed in the street in Rotterdam by the explosion of a time-bomb. Both their murderers were caught and arrested. It was after this that the USSR started thinking about plotting the perfect murder, which, in the case of Rebet, would have succeeded but for Stashinsky's ultimate confession.

There is one interesting query about the escape of Bogdan Stashinsky and his wife to the West. As far as one can gather, reconstructing the evidence, after they reached Dallgow town centre without being seen, they walked for about three miles along small side roads to Falkensee where they took a taxi at six p.m. Why did they not seek transport earlier? Long before they had walked three miles some of those KGB observers must have realised they had disappeared. If so, they would have been scouring the whole area by car, looking for them. But there is a second query: by what route did they take the taxi? The direct route would have taken them straight through West Berlin. If they took this route, why did they not simply get out of the taxi in West Berlin?

The evidence is confusing. Either they took a taxi on this very long route (it would have meant a journey of more than forty miles), or the story of the taxi was a cover for the fact that they met some accomplice they needed to protect. The latter theory seems a distinct possibility. Inge herself may even have arranged for outside help from a German sympathiser, or even an American, while she was waiting for the birth of her baby. All reports confirm the Stashinskys' story that they were stopped by the *Volkspolizei* at the East Berlin border and that Stashinsky produced his Josef Lehmann identity papers.

Their first call in the West was on some people named the Villvoks, friends of Inge. Herr Villvok escorted them to the West German police who, surprisingly, took them straight to the United States Security Offices in West Berlin. This certainly suggests that plans had been carefully laid for getting in touch with US Security before the escape was made. And in this fact one can see how Kim Philby was able to build up a story that Bandera had been killed by the CIA. Using the evidence of favourable treatment by the Americans, Philby could argue that they knew all along that Stashinsky had killed Bandera as he had done it on their orders and that it was the CIA who forced the West German police to hand Stashinsky on to them for questioning.

Having questioned Stashinsky at length, the Americans handed him back to the West German police and he was brought to trial in Karlsruhe on 8 October 1962, charged with killing Rebet and Bandera. Bogdan had confessed everything. There is no doubt, too, from the evidence given at the trial that everything that had happened inside Germany had been checked and double-checked, including hotel bookings and air flights. In this respect there was undoubted co-operation between the West German authorities and the Americans. One interesting new point that arose in the evidence given at the trial was that Inge Stashinsky had been offered a West Berlin hairdressing salon by the KGB, with false hairdressing certificates forged by them. This Inge indignantly rejected, saying she could qualify on her own.

On the fifth day of the trial the prosecution asked for life imprisonment for the two murders and the espionage. There was one unexpected yet pleasing gesture made in response to the prosecution's plea. The lawyers for Mrs Rebet and Mrs Bandera both stated that the two widows did not seek revenge; they felt pity for Stashinsky in his dilemma as a mere tool of the Kremlin. A cynic might have said that this plea for magnanimity was simply to help the German judge pass a light sentence after secret representations by the Americans that Stashinsky should not be punished too harshly. On that same afternoon a memorial service for the third anniversary of the murder of Bandera was held for Ukrainian exiles in the Karlsruhe St Stephen's Church.

The next day Stashinsky's lawyer put up an argument that his client should only be found guilty of manslaughter. At the same time two United States lawyers, including Congressman Kersten, made brief statements on the significance of the USSR government in all these matters. On 19 October 1962, Stashinsky was sentenced to six years for each murder and one year for espionage, this being commuted to eight years altogether. The President of the Court added that 'the sentence pronounced by this court is not intended to destroy the accused. It is to help him to atone.'

Inge Stashinsky did not give evidence at the trial. For her own safety from the KGB it was considered more important that she should be hidden away. Bogdan was released from jail somewhat earlier than scheduled. Officially this news was only given in Bonn on 18 February 1969. The West German Ministry of Justice announced that he had been secretly released two years previously, on New Year's Eve in 1966, and that he was now living in America.

So there can be no question that Stashinsky came in from the chill, frightening security of a career with the KGB to the freedom of the West, which must sometimes have seemed to Bogdan and his wife a beckoning beacon, and at others a mirage and illusion. Bogdan was taken out of Germany by a US military plane, while Inge, in fear of the KGB, had changed her name and gone to work in Stuttgart in a hairdressing salon. To complete her camouflage she was divorced from Bogdan on 23 June 1964, and she has now disappeared . . . to rejoin Bogdan? Who knows: both of them need protection from KGB killers.

Stashinsky was a genuine escaper and not a plant from the KGB. Indeed, some of Stashinsky's evidence that the Soviet Union had penetrated General Gehlen's West German Secret Service led to the arrest of Heinz Felfe, the very man who as a KGB agent inside the Gehlen organisation had protected the Ukrainian earlier on. Under the Nazis, Felfe had been a member of Heinrich Himmler's Gestapo and employed as such in the Ukraine. In this way he had become known to Gehlen who, during the war, had been head of German Army Intelligence in Russia. It had long been suspected that the Russians had cunningly infiltrated Gehlen's organisation: this arrest gave them proof.

This, however, was not the end of the Stashinsky story and it would be interesting to know just how much help he has since been able to give Western Intelligence, both American and German. Further inquiries into his early days suggest that he was genuinely frightened into giving information to the KGB and that in the beginning he was brought into the Russian Intelligence network by being made a probationary member of the Border Guard. This was an organisation designed to link that predecessor of the KGB, the Cheka, with the defence of the borders of the USSR. It has since been developed into three distinct types of Border Guards – Maritime, Land and Aviation. Its main duties were the prevention of illegal immigration to the USSR, keeping a watch on coastal movements and stamping out smuggling.

Once trapped into the role of killer, Stashinsky would have been closely watched at all times. From what one knows of Soviet techniques for political murders, the killer is shadowed before and after the murder by probably two or even more agents. Usually there is yet another agent whose job it is to remove incriminating evidence if necessary – a carelessly disposed of weapon, for example.

Whether Stashinsky would ever have plucked up courage to escape to the West without his having met Inge Pohl is doubtful. He might frequently have been tempted to do so, but the relentless probing and brainwashing of the KGB would have held him back. He would be wanted back in Moscow after each killing not merely for the Russians to question him and to provide a sanctuary, but to assess his attitude of mind. They would fully realise that the killings were repugnant to him and that his conscience troubled him. It is easy to say that even after the killing of Rebet he had a chance to escape when he was sent to kill Bandera. But the subtle mind-control which the KGB can operate from a distance proved too great an obstacle. How was this done in Stashinsky's case? Partly by flattery, by playing on his one great weakness – the fondness for being a 'big shot', which he had retained since his youth. In similar circumstances the KGB have used electro-convulsive therapy after a killer has returned from his mission: more than once this has damped down twinges of conscience.

At his trial Stashinsky made it clear that he had been told by Moscow that eventually he would be selected to kill a third Ukrainian exile leader, Yaroslav Stetskow, who had been Prime Minister of the Ukrainian Republic in 1941 and was then living in exile in Munich. He also gave the names of other victims of Soviet assassination tactics to the Americans as well as the West Germans. Such details were not given at the trial and, as they come secondhand from American, German and British sources, they are to some extent suspect and unconfirmed. However, as Britain, like the USA, has always had a sizeable number of Poles and Ukrainians in its population, this remarkable story published in the highly respected *Yorkshire Post* of 29 October 1962, is of special interest:

'A professional Soviet assassin has confessed to the murder of Father Henrik Borynski, a Polish-born Roman Catholic priest, who disappeared mysteriously from Bradford nine years ago. The killer says that he killed the priest with an injection of cyanide and buried the body on Ilkley Moor . . . Bogdan Stashinsky, a professional killer, who last year fled to West Berlin . . . and was sentenced to eight years hard labour for political murder . . . has now named Father Borynski as one of the victims. Scotland Yard has asked Bonn police if they can get more details from Stashinsky, particularly about the spot on Ilkley Moor where he saw the body hidden.'

Father Borynski did disappear mysteriously and his Polish congregation in Bradford believed he had been abducted by Soviet agents. They felt that his constant exhortations to his fellow-countrymen not to return to their native land had angered the Russians. He was a priest who had escaped from Poland to England during World War II. The priest he had succeeded, Father Bolesian Martynellis, had been found unconscious in his study; on his desk were thirty-two matches laid out so that they spelt in Polish '*milcz Klecho*' – 'be silent, priest'.

But it is certain that Bogdan Stashinsky was not in Britain at any time, let alone in 1951 when Father Borynski disappeared. The Russians may well have murdered Father Borynski, but this particular report was based on a misunderstanding of evidence Stashinsky had given. He had indicated that another Soviet killer had been involved in the killing of a priest whose name resembled that of Borynski. And the long arm of the KGB still reaches out into Britain even in the seventies, though not always in the form of assassination. There was the case of the British student Andy Klymchuk, who in January 1978 flew home to London after spending five months in a Russian jail, accused of anti-Soviet activities. In a statement made on his return Klymchuk said: 'I have to confess I was taking one hell of a risk when I entered Russia. As I walked past customs officers at Kiev airport my brown brogues pinched my feet with every step. No wonder. I was walking on 10,000 roubles worth of notes – about £7,000 – nailed into the soles and heels. And in my battered suitcase I had two rolls of undeveloped film, which turned out to be anti-Soviet propaganda.'

Klymchuk's story was that he had offered to act as a messenger to deliver the shoes and the film to a Ukrainian he knew only as Ivan. He had met a stranger with a Yorkshire accent while he was a student teacher in Hull. The teacher had introduced himself as James Dickson and represented himself as being strongly anti-communist. It was he who had asked Klymchuk to hand over the material and notes to 'Ivan' in Lvov when the student teacher went on holiday to his forefathers' country. It would seem that Ivan was a KGB agent.

So, despite everything, there are still Ukrainians prepared to take great risks to seek independence for their country and the KGB is as ruthless as ever in its desire to crush any semblance of nationalism among Ukrainians. There could be no way of taking a referendum for devolution in the Ukraine by Soviet standards. On the American side there was a rather strange sequel to the Stashinsky case in 1966 when Senator Thomas J. Dodd was criticised by the Senate Ethics Committee for his role in the Stashinsky affair. Dodd was accused of going to West Germany in 1964 to help a friend of his when, in fact, according to Dodd, he had gone to investigate the Stashinsky affair. It was confirmed by the then Director of the CIA, Richard Helms, that Dodd had 'been in contact' with the CIA both before and after the trip to obtain 'information on Soviet murders, assassinations and kidnappings, and on the Stashinsky case in particular,' but there was no indication given as to the real reason for Dodd's trip. Later, as chairman of the Senate Internal Security Sub-committee, Senator Dodd outlined all the events leading up to the Stashinsky inquiry with special reference to the overall question of 'Murder International, Inc., Murder and Kidnapping as an instrument of Soviet policy.'

Meanwhile Soviet policy has undoubtedly improved in finding answers to the eternal question of the perfect murder. The techniques for this are being developed all the time. What may have seemed reasonably safe when Stashinsky first killed Rebet in 1957 was thoroughly outdated long before the end of the fifties. A nerve gas called GB, which is colourless and tasteless, was developed from a formula which the Russians had been experimenting with in the last war. The vapour from as little as three drops could kill a human being in four minutes. When inhaled, it paralysed the nerve centres almost immediately. It was cheap to produce. This secret has since been discovered in the Western world.

Relatively recently developed 'nerve gases' include three nerve poisons – tabrun, sarin and soman. Such is the necessity for national security reasons, for nations to keep abreast of these developments in killer chemicals that the Western world has also experimented in seeking what might be the perfect killer drug. A few years ago some of Britain's leading specialists in this field explained how one could commit the perfect murder: 'All you need is a minute quantity of the gas called FEA.' This is a highly complex compound which can be made only in laboratories equipped for experiments in obscure poisons. The expert in question, Dr Bernard Saunders, toxicologist of Magdalene College, Cambridge, disclosed his secret formula to thirty scientific Intelligence officers at a meeting in Cambridge.

Bearing in mind all one knows about the thoroughness of Soviet examination of such new techniques, there can be little doubt that the USSR has already tested out FEA. An expert gives this view of the gas: 'From what we know the Russians must have full knowledge of how it can be used. There are some suggestions from cases not yet fully substantiated that they have already used it in some political murders. You could put this gas in a person's drink in liquid form and he wouldn't know the difference, as it is odourless, colourless and tasteless. There is a delayed action of twenty minutes and then, after a slight convulsion the person is dead. A post mortem would show no unusual chemicals present in the body. A doctor would suppose that the victim had died of respiratory failure. This is as near as you can get to the perfect murder.'

There have been numerous efforts in recent years both by the KGB and the CIA to improve on murder techniques. The CIA seem to have gone to the absolute limit in this respect by actually asking members to put forward plans for the perfect murder. It is in this way that for some years the Western world's major Intelligence service lamentably lost its scruples simply by trying to compete with the KGB. This particular CIA move was as stupid – farcical, if you like – as it was intended to be serious, and it led to its own questionnaire being picked up and infiltrated by the KGB. Discussion in recent years has centred around two obscure but deadly chemical substances which leave no forensic clues. Sodium fluoracetate, swallowed in sufficient quantities, leaves no characteristic pathological lesions which might be detected by quantitative methods. Tetraethyl lead was even more promising: 'Dropped on the skin in very small quantities, producing no local lesion, and after a quick death, no specific pathological evidence.'

Desperate attempts have been made to find the ideal solution for a replacement for the World War II pill for secret agents who were captured and faced with torture. The old cyanide version of this pill took up to fifteen minutes of agonising asphyxiation before death. A shell-fish toxin was discovered which killed in ten seconds with no more than a faint tingling sensation in the tips of the fingers. The first person to carry such a toxin pill was Gary Powers, the spy-plane pilot. But he never took advantage of this in his U 2 flight over Russia. A further development was to lure intended victims into a tightly-sealed room containing a block of Co ice (presumably ice impregnated with lethal carbon monoxide fumes). Once this was done, they would probably die fairly soon, leaving no clues as to what killed them.

And so the quest for the perfect murder continues long after Stashinsky has slipped out of the net in which he was trapped. In more recent years the KGB has struck at Bulgarians and Czechs as well as Ukrainians. There was the case of Georgi Markov, the Bulgarian defector who found work with the BBC in London, and was struck dead by a mysterious assassin who not only got away completely, but was never identified.

Markov suddenly felt very ill with a temperature of 104. His wife called the doctor who thought he was suffering from 'flu and advised that he should be kept 'as cool as possible'. But that night Markov told his wife, 'I have a horrible suspicion that it might be connected with something that happened today. I was waiting for a bus on the south side of Waterloo Bridge when I felt a jab in the back of my right thigh. I looked round and saw a man drop his umbrella. He said he was sorry and I got the impression that he was trying to cover his face as he rushed off and hailed a taxi.'

The inquest verdict on Markov was that he was killed by a metal pellet containing poison twice as deadly as cobra venom: the poison was ricin, derived from the seed of the castor oil plant. The pellet containing it was only fractionally larger than a pinhead. But perhaps the most sinister revelation was that not only Markov, but other dissident Bulgarians as well, had received anonymous threats that their lives were in danger if they continued to broadcast their anti-communist views to the world at large.

6
John Vassall

'The most absolute authority is that which penetrates into man's innermost being and concerns itself no less with his will than with his actions'

JEAN-JACQUES ROUSSEAU

It might be said – to parody a famous saying – that some people are born spies, some become spies and that others have spying thrust upon them. The tragic case of William John Christopher Vassall occurred entirely from the fact that the tasks of espionage were thrust upon him under the threat of blackmail.

The Vassall Case is important not so much because it is a sordid story of spying against the interests of one's own country, but much more in the historical context of the lesson that blackmail and espionage recruiting have inevitably been linked down the ages and will undoubtedly continue to be so. Such blackmail has been operated by a variety of means and it has usually paid off by reason of the fact that – at least in the past – the more highly placed and important a person is, the more easily he is vulnerable to blackmail. And the corollary was that such a person could therefore provide the most vital Intelligence. But in more recent times, the lowly-placed and insignificant person who finds himself in a position where he can betray secrets has become even more vulnerable to the blackmailing spy recruiter.

In this era of ciphers, code-rooms, computers, tapes, hidden micro-cameras and other paraphernalia of espionage, thousands, if not tens of thousands, of ordinary people have become targets for the spy recruiters to exploit if they can. Thus it is that even in a democracy the old practice of giving such people jobs involving national security demands something far more than personal references, or even the type of 'vetting' accepted as satisfactory twenty years ago. To ensure against blackmail and treachery today a system as drastic as 'positive vetting' every few years is highly necessary. That, indeed, is what national security is all about and it comprises one of the stark lessons of the Vassall Affair. Had such checks been carried out as rigorously, thirty or even twenty years ago, not only would several spies inside Britain have been stopped in their tracks long before

OPPOSITE John Vassall as a National Serviceman

they became dangerous, but the probability – indeed almost the certainty – is that Vassall would not have been sent to Russia and he would therefore never have been trapped into espionage.

He was born in London on 20 September, 1924, his father being a Church of England clergyman and his mother a former nurse. It was about as highly respectable an entourage into which anyone could be born. Yet it is often in such environments that the seeds of future aberrations are sown. The marriage of Vassall's parents was not a happy one from the very beginning and there were even differences of opinion on religious matters. Some few years after the marriage Mrs Vassall became a Roman Catholic. These things undoubtedly had a subconscious effect on the young Vassall to whom his mother was a much more sympathetic character than his father. A youth drawn too close emotionally to his mother and at the same time somewhat withdrawn from his father is frequently vulnerable in after life.

Like many other boys who are sent to boarding schools, Vassall had his first homosexual experience while in his teens. 'I lived in a secret world, one which I felt nobody could ever possibly know or understand,' he wrote in his autobiography. 'Knowing my own sex intimately never seemed strange or unusual. . . . Not that it made me happier. On the contrary, I think I was both lonely and unhappy.' This is not an abnormal characteristic of many boys in boarding schools, but most of them throw off these proclivities when they go out into the world. They adapt to the company of women and as often as not settle down happily as heterosexuals. Vassall's tragedy was that in his case the metamorphosis did not take place and subsequent events prevented any such development.

At the age of seventeen he volunteered for flying duties with the RAF, but was turned down. He was, however, called up into the RAF in January 1943, when he was trained as a photographer and served with 137 Wing in North-West Europe. While awaiting his call-up, Vassall worked at the Admiralty as a temporary clerk in a very minor position. When the war ended he had no intention originally of going back to the Admiralty; service in Europe and a certain amount of travel in the RAF after VE-Day had given him a yearning to see many other of the world's cities. It was suggested to him that, if he really wanted to travel, he ought to consider applying for one of the Admiralty clerical vacancies overseas. 'As it happened, the Washington post had just been filled, so with much trepidation I applied for the Moscow post' is how he describes the decision which led him back to the Admiralty.

Consequently he was duly interviewed by an Admiralty Board, the chairman of which was the Civil Assistant to the Director of Naval Intelligence. Out of forty applicants Vassall was the one selected for the post in 1954. It might well be said that on his education, parentage and general background, as well as his RAF record, he was a reasonable choice and indeed he appears to have satisfied the Board that he was smart, well-spoken and had 'a pleasing personality'. But in this period, as this author can himself testify from personal experience, questions put at Admiralty Board interviews, even for prospective officers shortly to be in command of ships, were often totally irrelevant. At such an interview in 1941, I was myself asked the astonishing question during wartime: 'Which way do you pass the port after dinner?' And they meant the wine, not some harbour!

When the Radcliffe Tribunal reported on the Vassall Case in 1963, they were critical of the system by which the Admiralty selected Vassall for the post of naval attaché's clerk in Moscow, saying that it was inadequate to the needs of the situation and only permitted a superficial check on his general reliability and character. Two questions remain unanswered: firstly, why were more searching inquiries not made concerning his conduct and character while in the RAF and secondly why, in any event, was an untried young man sent to Moscow before at least being groomed and watched either in London or some other Western capital?

One does not wish to labour the homosexual aspects of this story. It is perfectly true that a man can be blackmailed for certain heterosexual activities just as much as for homosexual pranks. But there is a difference and that difference was much greater in the fifties than it is today. It was much easier for anyone to resist blackmail for heterosexual misdemeanours than for the other kind. There was no permissive climate of opinion regarding such matters in the forties and fifties and homosexual conduct was still punished by quite severe prison sentences. All this made the homosexual much more vulnerable. Apart from this, British Security had been badly damaged by the defection of the two Foreign Office men, Guy Burgess and Donald Maclean, to Moscow. Both were homosexuals and the warning of how such people could be exploited was surely obvious some three years before Vassall was sent to Russia.

One other point seems to have been missed then and is still rarely touched on now: the Russians, more than any other nation, have for a whole century, if not longer, made a practice of using their Secret Service to blackmail and recruit homosexuals to spy for them. There was the classic case of Colonel Alfred Redl, chief of staff of the Eighth Army Corps of the Austro-Hungarian Empire, who supplied the Russians with a wealth of Intelligence in the years immediately preceding the First World War. It was not until 1913 that he was finally detected and then committed suicide by shooting himself. He left behind a note which stated: 'Levity and passion have destroyed me. Pray for me. I pay with my life for my sins.'

Redl had been a secret compulsive homosexual all his life and his blackmailing by the Russians was two-fold. First, because a scandal would have destroyed his career and, secondly, he was greedy for money so that he could indulge his bizarre tastes to an excessive degree. After his death his secret wardrobes revealed a huge collection of expensive women's dresses, perfumes, cosmetics of all kinds and a large assortment of whips. The extent of his treachery was appalling. He had even denounced personal friends and brother officers to the Russians, sending them a complete list of every Austrian spy on Russian territory and causing some of them to be summarily executed. He had passed on codes, secret documents, including the General Staff's 'Plan Three' for war against Serbia, and organised a network of spies for Russia.

Ever since the Redl Affair homosexuals in all walks of life have been singled out as targets for Russian exploitation, though much more systematically under the communist regimes than under the Czars. Under the KGB is a group of homosexuals strictly controlled for the purpose of trapping potential victims. They come from all manner of professions and trades and have been given the singularly sinister nickname of 'The Ravens'.

This is the background to the more ominous aspects of the kind of life in Moscow which faced the thirty-year-old Vassall. Had he arrived there a few years earlier, while Stalin was still alive, the rigidity of the communist governmental system towards all foreigners might have saved him from any untoward incidents. Then he would have been virtually a prisoner inside the British Embassy compound with hardly any opportunity of meeting Russians. But, unfortunately for him, he came to Moscow when the more optimistic of politicians and diplomats in the West were talking of a thaw in the Cold War. A modest degree of fraternisation was beginning to take place, though among those who had any experience of dealing with Russian officialdom and believed in the importance of security there was still a firm conviction that risks should not be taken.

But for Vassall Russia was, as he later said, 'captivating' and the turrets of the Kremlin were like 'something out of a fairy story'. And, when he began to come into contact with the Russians, he not only liked them, but in many instances found them more sympathetic and friendly than the upper-crust diplomats in the British Embassy. One of the major faults of British diplomatic conduct overseas in the past has been a tendency to divide the 'dips' and 'non-dips' in the bigger embassies into 'them' and 'us'. Such an attitude is particularly dangerous in an Embassy such as that at Moscow. Not only does it provide some excuses for the 'non-dips' being alienated from their superiors, but it prevents the 'dips' from being sufficiently knowledgeable about those serving under them. When Vassall was in Moscow this division between 'dips' and 'non-dips' was very marked, and inevitably meant that some of the latter were forced to lead very lonely lives indeed, unless they set out to mingle with Russians and people from other embassies and missions.

This kind of situation was one which the Russians were able to exploit, if not frequently, at least often enough to prove worthwhile. Attempts were made by the British government of the day to minimise the effectiveness of Soviet espionage, but Sir Charles Orr-Ewing, a former Civil Lord of the

Admiralty, declared in 1962 that there were 'thousands of Russians . . . all trained to detect weakness in character, weakness for drink, blondes, drugs and homosexuality.'

Vassall was at first very lonely in Moscow and found the social atmosphere of the Embassy inhibiting and depressing. Slowly he sought company outside the Embassy confines: 'In restaurants I would meet worldly-wise Russians – civilians, servicemen on leave, or just casual travellers. . . . I was the centre of attraction; I felt honoured.' While most people in the British Embassy were restricted in their movements, Vassall found out-of-Moscow travel relatively easy. Yet it never seems to have occurred to him that this was unusual. No doubt the KGB kept a close watch through the Russian servants at the British Embassy on all newcomers and had reports on their duties and weaknesses. To have been allowed to travel as far afield as Vassall did (once he flew down to the Black Sea Riviera), the Russians must already have earmarked him as a potential informant. From the evidence presented at his subsequent trial and from further probing by the Radcliffe Tribunal it was evident that one of the observer-spies was Sigmund Mikhailski, who was in the employ of the Soviet Secret Service at the same time as he was working inside the British Embassy as an interpreter and general factotum. But this part of the Moscow story is best told in Vassall's own words:

'When I was in the Embassy in Moscow my work took me to the administrative section where an official who was employed locally was very helpful. He was known as Mokosi [Mikhailski]. He was a Pole. He invited me to dinner at restaurants. In the course of the social contacts other people were introduced to me. I met a number of educated Russians.

'These normal social contacts lasted for about three months. One evening the Pole introduced me to three of his friends whom I had not met before. One suggested I should have dinner at another restaurant near the Bolshoi Theatre. I was taken to the first floor which I at first thought was a dining-room, but in fact was a private room.

'We had drinks, a large dinner and I was plied with very strong brandy. After half an hour I remember everybody taking off their jackets. Somebody assisted me to take off mine. I remember the lighting being very strong. More of my clothes were removed. There was a divan in the corner. I remember two or three getting on the bed with me in a state of undress.

'Then several compromising sexual actions took place. I remember someone of the party taking photographs.'

The KGB had played the trick practised so often that it is now known in the jargon of espionage as '*son et lumière*' – a rather satirical description of the sordid act of obtaining evidence from a setting-up. It means that the seduction of the victim is recorded by hidden cameras and microphones. From then on Vassall was at their mercy. They did not strike at once, but waited until Mikhailski lured him to another flat in central Moscow. There he was confronted by two officials in plain clothes who started to question him. Suddenly they produced photographs of Vassall taken at the compromising party. Then they went on to say that this constituted a very serious offence for which there were penalties and could even result in detention. They told him that if he mentioned the matter to anybody at the Embassy, he would not be allowed to leave Russia and they would make an international incident of the matter.

It was a cat-and-mouse game for some time to come. The Russians finally took him home to his flat, but he was told to meet them again the following night outside a railway station. They took him to the Sovietskaya Hotel where there was further questioning. More warnings followed and yet another meeting was arranged. By this time the Russians must have been fairly sure that they had frightened their prospective victim into acquiescent silence. From then on it was all too easy.

As Vassall himself put it, '. . . I could have talked with one of several male friends about my secret world. But not in our Embassy. Not only would they have been shocked and horrified, they would have scorned me. Presumably the Russians kept a watch over our movements through staff who worked in the main building of the Embassy. . . . Throughout this period I don't think anyone who was responsible for our welfare came near us. There is no record in the diary I kept of such visits.'

Anyone as vulnerable as Vassall was doomed in such circumstances. Ultimately he was told that unless he was prepared to give them some Intelligence on naval and other matters, he would be taken into custody. Before he went to Rome in 1955 he was informed by the KGB that he would be under surveillance all the time he was there and that unless he returned to Russia, they would 'deal with him'. Now Vassall had become a Roman Catholic largely to please his mother in 1951, but, he added, 'the fact that I was a Catholic was as close a secret as my spying. My father did not know.' He had written to the Vatican for an audience and had been placed on the list of people who would be given a semi-private meeting with the Pope. Perhaps – who knows? – he even had the idea of confessing all to the Pope and hoping that this way he might not only find forgiveness, but be shown what best to do. But as he drew near the Vatican Vassall noticed that there was someone shadowing him: 'In a sweat I turned my back on the Vatican and hurried away. . . . My faith did not desert me. I deserted it.'

When he returned to Moscow he continued to meet his Soviet contact men. Then in June 1956, he was introduced to a third man named Gregory. The Russians knew he was returning to London in June and they informed him that Gregory would contact him there. Vassall had hoped that on his return to Britain he might at last be left alone. It was a naïve hope. Gregory and he met in Finchley Road and Vassall was immediately asked exactly what work he was doing at the Admiralty and what access he had to secret documents.

At first the demands made upon him in London, where he was working as an Admiralty clerk, were not too great. His work was then almost exclusively concerned with highly-classified material, yet there appear to have been no serious new attempts to screen him, or even to seek reports on his many contacts with Russians while in Moscow. The Radcliffe Tribunal seemed to go out of its way to exonerate the Admiralty for any blame on these counts, despite the fact that for the previous three years there had been suspicions of leakages of naval Intelligence to the Russians. In the mid-fifties the ace Soviet spy, Konon Molody, masquerading as a US naval commander named Alec Johnson, had contacted another Admiralty clerk, Petty Officer Henry Houghton, who had previously worked in Poland. Houghton was at that time employed in the Admiralty Underwater Weapons Establishment at Portland in Dorset. Not until January, 1961, were Houghton and his girl friend, Ethel Gee, arrested just as Gee was handing over to Molody no less than 212 pages of technical details about British warships. Nor should it be forgotten that George Blake at one time served in Naval Intelligence in Germany.

The Radcliffe Report, in fact, was little better than a white-washing job for the Government and the Admiralty. In some ways, surprisingly for a judicial inquiry, the report tended on occasions to contradict its own findings. For example, while claiming that no blame should be attached to the Admiralty for Vassall's appointment to Naval Intelligence on his return from Moscow, the Tribunal found fault with the failure to follow up a report by a member of the Embassy staff that Vassall had been cultivated by Mikhailski. Quite rightly, the Tribunal Report felt that initial responsibility for this should be shared between senior members of the Embassy. But why did not the Admiralty insist on a close questioning of all Embassy personnel? The Radcliffe Report stated: 'It seems clear that the warning circular about Mikhailski, which had been issued on the 3rd December [1955], produced results, for by 16th December, Miss Wynne, a typist in the office of the military attaché, who was herself a friend of and much cultivated by Mikhailski, reported several invitations passing between them and was warned to be on her guard and to report further from time to time. She reported again on the 8th January to the effect that he had said something to her indicating positively that he was under Russian control.'

A later minute stated that Miss Wynne had volunteered the information that Mikhailski's recent 'targets' had been five members of the Embassy staff in different offices. They included Vassall in the naval attaché's office. Then came the Radcliffe Report's most devastating comment: 'The result is that no one approached Vassall on the matter to try to find out how far his contacts with Mikhailski had gone or whether anything untoward had come of them. It seems certain that the minute, which pointed clearly to attempted penetration of the Service attachés' offices along with the other sensitive parts of the Embassy, was never discussed at any of the weekly meetings which the Service attachés held with the Ambassador.'

Yet all the Tribunal could find to say on this quite astonishing revelation was that they had found it 'not easy' to account for the inaction over the minute, and that it must remain a matter of speculation whether anything useful would come out of an interview with Vassall who had then been working for the Russians for six months.

Back in London, Vassall would on occasions make a rendezvous with the Russians and hand over secret documents for photographing. 'I handed them to Gregory at our meeting. He went round a corner and I presume handed them to someone in a car. We would then walk around for an hour or two and then return to the original rendezvous. He would then leave me briefly and return with the documents.'

The quality of documents which Vassall eventually passed to the Russians must have been considerable. His work at that time brought him into touch with such categories of Intelligence as radar, communications, torpedo and anti-submarine techniques, gunnery trials, Allied tactical and NATO exercise publications, Fleet operational and tactical instructions as well as general matters such as details of naval liaison with Commonwealth countries.

When the arrests were made in connection with the Portland Spy trial in January, 1961, Vassall was at once told by his Russian controller that though he was not himself compromised, he was to stop all espionage work until further notice, as it was not safe to resume. The all-clear was not given to him until early in 1962, but from that time until his own arrest he was actively at work for the Russians. Meanwhile he was given a new contact, one Nikolai, who turned up for a rendezvous instead of Gregory, announcing himself thus: 'I know you because I recognise your face from photographs.'

The very mention of photographs must have given Vassall an involuntary shudder at the thought of those taken in Moscow. But, to indicate that he was a trusted contact, Nikolai added 'Can you show me the way to Belsize Park?' This was a prearranged code with Gregory.

'Do nothing again until you receive a motor car catalogue,' said Nikolai.

Various sums of money were paid to Vassall by the Russians during this period. 'The first time I received any money from them was before Christmas, 1955, as a gift. I was handed 2,000 roubles – about £50. About every fourth meeting in Moscow the Russians used to give me 2,000 roubles and I used this money for food and holidays in Russia.

'After I returned to England Gregory or Nikolai used to give me money in sums ranging from £50 to £200, but not on every occasion we met. The sums handed to me ranged from £500 to £700 a year.'

Every precaution was taken by the Russians to ensure that Vassall was not being followed. His instructions were that every three weeks he was to report at a certain place in Golders Green at seven-thirty p.m. If he could not keep the appointment on the scheduled night in question, he was to do so the next evening. Sometimes nobody would turn up, but the Russians would be making sure he was there all right and checking as to whether he had been followed. For emergencies, or any unexpected contingency, he was told he could go to the Duchess of Bedford Walk in Kensington and mark the plane tree at Plane Tree House near Holland House with a pink chalk cross. He was also given a Kensington telephone number to dial and ask for 'Miss Mary'.

Other meeting places were at Worcester Park, Southfields, Wembley, Edgware and, somewhat surprisingly, Mount Pleasant, a site dangerously close to national newspaper offices and hostelries patronised by journalists. This does perhaps show how the longer a single highly productive agent is kept operative the greater the risk of some slight slip-up in the arrangements. Months later scores of newspapermen were scouring London for background information on Vassall and any one of them might have recalled seeing him with his contact in that area.

The Russians showed great skill and psychological understanding in handling this agent and their talents in this direction must have gone a long way to stifling Vassall's conscience. Through their contact inside the British Embassy in Moscow they would have been made fully aware that Vassall was unhappy in his environment there. So they set out to be friendly and again and again he has stressed that he tremendously liked the Russians as individuals and as a people. Inevitably he must have compared their friendliness, especially when he returned to London, with the indifference and coldness of the British Embassy hierarchy in Moscow. They studied his likes and dislikes, played on his love of good food and wines, of the arts and ballet, even making the kind of jokes which they knew would appeal to him.

This skill in handling agents of another nationality is one which the Russians have developed better than perhaps any other power and their success can be assessed by the achievements of such agents as Alger Hiss, Donald Maclean and Kim Philby. They also possess a subtle talent for making such people feel highly important and that the service they render to Russia is really on behalf of the noble cause of humanity as a whole. The Russians, especially Gregory, even tried to convince Vassall that what he was doing was not espionage, but merely providing 'information needed to brief a possible future Summit Conference' and therefore would be useful in the cause of peace. The aim was always to try to show that the Soviet Union desperately wanted peace, but that it was so difficult to deal with the suspicious and deceitful capitalist West. This was, of course, completely misleading, but in the late fifties it was not difficult to persuade many intelligent Britons that *détente* was something worth seeking and that the nuclear weapons of the Western powers were something to be deprecated. These were the years of the Nuclear Disarmament Campaign at its zenith, of the bonhomie of Nikita Khrushchev and, to those who preferred to wear blinkers, the belief that the Cold War was beginning to thaw.

ABOVE The Minox camera used by Vassall

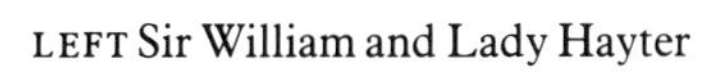

LEFT Sir William and Lady Hayter

RIGHT The plane tree outside Plane Tree House, Duchess of Bedford's Walk, Kensington, where Vassall is alleged to have drawn a circle of pink chalk – a code which indicated he wished to get in touch with the KGB

Vassall in his flat in Dolphin Square, aged 38

1959: a CND 'Ban the Bomb' Rally in Trafalgar Square

ABOVE Vassall leaves Wormwood Scrubs to attend the Radcliffe Tribunal

RIGHT Vassall leaves Maidstone Prison on 24 October 1972, after serving 10 years out of his 18-year sentence

Such arguments were fallible even then, but there was not as much evidence to counter them as exists today. It would not be surprising if Vassall, under the threat of blackmail, even managed to convince himself that what he was doing was in the cause of peace and would in the long run help and not harm his country.

As Somerset Maugham showed in *Ashenden*, that most realistic of spy novels based on his own espionage experiences in World War I, the life of the small-time secret agent is often boring and lonely. 'Ashenden's official existence,' he wrote, 'was as orderly and monotonous as a City clerk's . . . he waited for the information that came through and dispatched it; he went into France once a week to confer with his colleague over the frontier and to receive his orders from London . . . he kept his eyes and ears open.' Increasingly, such an agent leads an unreal life and becomes more and more isolated and conscious of loneliness. In a desperate effort to compensate for this deeply-felt inner loneliness he tries to make more friends, but in reality they are only casual acquaintances. He dares not have really close friends and the only person he can confide in is his controller.

This is undoubtedly the kind of trauma through which Vassall must have passed. He could only talk freely of his problems to his Russian controllers, people like Gregory who used to take him out to dinner occasionally. For a long time he had lived with his parents, but the Russians persuaded him that he needed to have a place on his own. It was for this reason that he took a flat in Dolphin Square, a major mistake as the rent charged (£500 a year) was much too high for an Admiralty clerk of his relatively lowly status at that date. It is surprising that the Russians allowed him to choose such a place.

Though Vassall was a trained photographer in the RAF, he came up against problems when the Russians asked him in 1957 to photograph documents for them. The idea was that he should take documents back to his flat in Dolphin Square at night and return them to the Admiralty the following day. He was not to develop the films himself, but to give them to Gregory, or another specific agent.

Vassall was told to go abroad and buy a certain type of camera. This seems to have been a singularly curious and clumsy procedure, as the Russians could very well have provided him with the right kind of camera in London, which in the end was what they had to do. Maybe this was a psychological ploy; in other words, 'if you will undertake the photographing of documents for us, we will pay for your holiday abroad.' But the jaunts abroad constituted further mistakes on Vassall's part, for they only drew attention to the fact that a young Admiralty clerk was tending to live beyond his means. Apart from going to Germany, where he bought the camera, Vassall visited Corsica, Cannes, Nice, Brussels and St Tropez.

When he returned to London with the camera, he was instructed to practise by photographing newspapers. But the results, he was informed, were a total failure and his contact told him to go to a telephone kiosk in Grosvenor Road, Pimlico, to pick up a parcel which would be left there. This contained an Exakta camera. Again, one begins to see how desperation can turn to clumsiness and lead to errors when there is a crisis. Clearly at this period Moscow must have been applying acute pressure on their KGB officers in London, who, in turn, thought up this singularly unprofessional method of providing a camera. If Vassall had been shadowed by MI 5 at that time, his emerging from a telephone kiosk with a parcel could have aroused considerable suspicion.

Then, after a year spent in the Naval Intelligence Division of the Admiralty, Vassall was transferred to the post of assistant private secretary to the new Civil Lord of the Admiralty, the Hon. Thomas Galbraith, MP for the Hillhead division of Glasgow. This was later to prove to be a disastrous move from the point of view of the Civil Lord. Because Galbraith showed to Vassall the consideration, friendliness and hospitality which he had never experienced in the British Embassy in Moscow, he was most unfairly criticised long afterwards. Tragically, in political terms, he paid the penalty for having treated Vassall as a human being as well as an employee. Yet the blame lay, as it still does today, on the whole security system in general and that of the Admiralty in particular.

During the autumn of 1959, Vassall was off on foreign travel again, visiting Capri, Naples, and towards the end of the year, Egypt. Did the Russians not realise that, however much foreign travel might delight their agent, it was leading to the destruction of their plans? Not only did these jaunts draw attention to Vassall's overspending for a man in his position, but they laid him open to all manner of other influences. To allow so vulnerable an agent such freedom of travel was in itself courting trouble. On one occasion, Vassall himself relates, he met a Frenchman in St Tropez who knew he had been to Russia, that he had worked in a defence department and was also a homosexual. 'Little did he know how deeply involved I actually was. In fact, he said that he thought I had been very unwise to accept the post in the circumstances. Apart from an Australian diplomat I had known in Moscow, I don't think there was anyone so aware of the dangers I was letting myself in for then. This Australian friend was confined to his Embassy during the Petrov case in 1954.'

When he returned to London, Vassall found himself transferred to the Military Branch of the Admiralty, a posting which was not at all to his liking, though it seemed to please the Russians. It was at this time that he was reactivated by his controllers after the period of lying low following the Portland Spy trial. Shortly afterwards he began to have that instinctive feeling that things are going wrong which sooner or later most spies experience. At first there is nothing the spy can pin down, just a feeling of apprehension. Then there are strange incidents, such as the early morning caller at Vassall's flat who inquired whether there was a leak of water from the flat above. 'I had a strong premonition that something was wrong. It was a most unpleasant sensation, feeling that time might be running out.'

His instincts were right. Slowly but surely, the carefully spun web of the various branches of the Security Service was being thrown around him. The Americans had long been convinced that there was a spy inside the Admiralty who was betraying NATO secrets to the Russians. One defector had hinted as much to them. Then CIA agents promised another Soviet defector, Major Anatoli Dolnytsin, sanctuary in England, if he would let them have a list of Soviet espionage contacts in the West. Among those he named was 'someone working in the British Admiralty'. He knew the code-name, but not the identity of the spy. The Americans immediately alerted the British, pointing out that this simply confirmed their previous suspicions of two years earlier.

This time the Security Service conducted a thorough search of Admiralty offices at night as well as investigating the private lives of staff discreetly by day. At that time there were 1,500 people employed in the Admiralty, and it took two specially selected men three weeks to conduct their secret night search of the premises. They found a couple of clues and then came a report from a private informant of the curiously free-spending social life of John Vassall. From that moment it was only a question of systematically checking up on his movements and his background and trying to fill in the gaps on reports on his previous screening. By August the Security Services were certain that Vassall was the spy in Whitehall. On 12 September 1962, he was arrested shortly after leaving the Admiralty buildings.

Taken to Scotland Yard and interviewed there, Vassall was immediately asked for the keys to his flat. There the detectives found two cameras and a hundred and forty exposures on film. Later Royal Marines Colonel John Macafee, Director of Naval Security at the Admiralty, testified that he had seen the 'hundred and forty enlargements and compared them with original documents. Seventeen of the documents related to between 24 July and 3 September, 1962, and all were secret documents the disclosure of which to a potential enemy would be a grave danger to the state.'

Eventually John Vassall was sentenced at the Old Bailey to a total of eighteen years imprisonment after he had pleaded guilty to all the charges, and, from all accounts, co-operated fully with the police in trying to answer the many questions that still needed to be posed.

But that was very far from being the end of the Vassall Affair. In many respects it was only the beginning. For weeks to come the Government was constantly besieged by questions from MPs of all parties as to how this case of espionage had lasted so long and why Vassall had not been positively vetted. The Government made matters worse by stonewalling on the whole subject. It was then the turn of the Press and in article after article attempts were made to show that security arrangements were deplorable, that there was 'a Mr Big' protecting homosexuals inside the Civil Service and the

Admiralty in particular, and that Ministers and officials were also to blame for this state of affairs.

After Vassall was jailed the Cunningham Committee, consisting of three senior Civil Servants, was set up to review the situation. Then, angered by what he regarded as being often wild, unjustified and maliciously mischievous innuendoes, the Prime Minister, Harold Macmillan, announced the setting up of a new Tribunal of Inquiry, headed by Lord Radcliffe, a High Court judge. In doing this he disconcerted his critics because he had chosen the most powerful weapon in the Government's armoury for the purpose. The Tribunal not only had the powers to subpoena witnesses, including MPs and journalists, to justify their allegations, but, should they refuse, they could be sent to prison for contempt of court.

At the time this may have seemed a brilliant move to call the bluff of the critics. For the Vassall Affair had become the butt of cartoonists and music hall artists. Later it was wickedly satirised in the *That Was the Week That Was* programme on television, when Ministers were mercilessly lampooned. But the aftermath of the Radcliffe Tribunal was totally unexpected and eventually it boomeranged against the Conservative Government of the day. For on 7 March 1963, two newspaper reporters, Brendan Mulholland and Reginald Foster, were jailed for six months and three months respectively for refusing to disclose sources of information to the Tribunal. While the Tribunal had the right to insist on such evidence being given to them, it was hitherto unknown for a court to rule that a journalist had no immunity from answering questions on the sources of his information unless, say, the Official Secrets Act had been breached. Indeed, this had always been a recognised conscientious right of the journalist, just as much as it would be of a doctor or a priest. What angered the critics was that the Government's own Attorney-General, Sir John Hobson, had brought the journalists before the High Court.

Mullholland and Foster did not betray their sources and so became heroes in a cause. From that moment on Fleet Street's relations with the government of the day, regardless of whether the newspapers were Conservative, Labour or Liberal, were as bad as they could be. There were many who vowed they would get their revenge. Their chance for this came astonishingly soon afterwards when, in the early summer of 1963, the Vassall Affair was followed by the Profumo Scandal, which produced that ubiquitous character, a Soviet agent, this time a bibulous Lothario of a military attaché, Captain Eugene Ivanov. Coming so soon after the Vassall Affair, the case of a British War Minister, John Profumo's involvement with the attractive Miss Christine Keeler who was, at the same time, enjoying an affair with the Soviet military attaché, was manna for a vengeful press. The question came to be posed: did the Macmillan Government have any adequate control of national security? For in that same fatal year of 1963 'Kim' Philby had defected to Russia and thus proved that all the protestations of the Government about his innocence had been false. As to Miss Keeler, she had regaled the Press with the headline titbit that Ivanov was 'a wonderful huggy bear of a man'. Then in July, 1963, there was a flare-up between MI 6 and the CIA over Anatoli Dolnytsin, the Soviet defector who had indicated a spy in the Admiralty. Through official channels the British had sent out a D-notice saying that there was a Russian defector in Britain, but would newspapers refrain from saying that his name was Anatoli Dolnytsin.

Despite this – and it was a measure of the extremely bad relations between Press and Government – stories giving Dolnytsin's name appeared in London papers. This in its turn worsened relations between the American and British Intelligence Services which had already been exacerbated by the Philby case. One high CIA official in Washington blew his top in these words: 'First we have the scheduled ultimate chief of the British Secret Service defecting to Moscow [Philby] and now we have this deliberate leakage of a defector we had promised to protect. This goddam D-notice wasn't given out to suppress the news about Dolnytsin, but to publicise it, and divert attention from other scandals.'

Such criticism may have been grossly unfair and the actual allegation without any foundation. But the system of D-notices can only work when Press and Government work closely together and trust each other. Once one has a situation like that of 1963, D-notices might as well cease to exist. David Wise and Thomas D. Ross, two American scholars who have studied the world's espionage systems, have summed things up remarkably well in this comment on British Intelligence: 'Historically the British have been superbly discreet in keeping their secret Intelligence machinery, MI 5 and MI 6, out of view, partly through tradition and partly through the D-notice system and the law. But Britain has turned a nineteenth-century virtue into a twentieth century fault. Imperial England could, in a sense, afford to have hidden citadels of totally secret power within its government. Perhaps this was true even between the two World Wars. But in the modern era of high-speed communications and insistent news media – and in the light of the KGB's unpleasant activities – a clubby invisible sort of Intelligence that is somehow an extension of Oxbridge becomes a political liability. When a spy scandal does strike in England, it seems all the worse because there is no one to blame. The result is often the opposite of that desired.'

John Vassall may have been a relatively insignificant figure as regards his job. His salary was only £908 gross, which in 1962 meant a net income of around £700 after tax had been deducted. At a time when inflation was beginning to bite this was no money on which to lead his kind of social life, or to indulge in his foreign holidays. One of the arguments heard by the Radcliffe Tribunal was whether or not the Admiralty had been asked for a reference as to whether Vassall could afford the rent of a flat at Dolphin

Square. Surely the much more vital question was this: the Admiralty must have known his home address, so why was the fact that he was living in such a place not noted much earlier by the security people?

However, the Radcliffe Report, though it can be severely criticised in retrospect, at least pin-pointed this damning piece of evidence of slackness in high places: referring to Mikhailski, the Soviet agent installed in the embassy in Moscow, it stated that from December, 1955, onwards: 'Mikhailski may be said to have been officially under special rather than general suspicion: but he was not got rid of . . . After whatever discussions took place, it was decided, with the approval of the Ambassador, to retain him. The balance of argument was, apparently, in favour of the view that, if he was got rid of, he would only be followed in due course by a successor no less under Russian control.

'It had also to be said that experience suggests that there would be considerable delay in supplying that successor and they would be unlikely to get another man as useful and obliging as he had been in serving the needs of the staff. This was a matter of some importance, *having regard to the desirability of making local conditions as pleasant as possible* [author's italics]. No one now claims that the decision to retain Mikhailski was a right decision in the light of all that later became known about him.'

But this same Tribunal did not pose a much more vital question: how and through what channels was Mikhailski engaged and why, after it was known what he was, were not all personnel who had been in close contact with him thoroughly vetted and screened not only at the time, but for some few years afterwards? Mikhailski had in fact been hired through Burobin, a branch of the KGB which supplied foreign embassies with local employees.

Lord Carrington, the First Lord of the Admiralty, was interrogated by the Radcliffe Tribunal and his replies seemed to suggest a degree of complacency in high places. First of all he denied that he had any knowledge of any microdot film of a secret document circulating in the Admiralty being found in the course of investigation into the Portland Spy case, as had been reported in the *Daily Express*. Yet the American CIA had evidence of this two years earlier and they certainly informed someone in British Intelligence. Why did this information not reach the Admiralty, or did it stop short at someone's desk and was not brought to the attention of the First Lord? The Radcliffe Tribunal took the view that 'there was no such film of any Admiralty document' (surely the rashest of assertions on purely negative evidence). But Allen Dulles, the former head of the CIA, in an article in the 1963 *Britannica Book of the Year* stated of the Krogers (the man-and-wife team of Russian spies involved in the Portland case): 'Microfilms found in their apartment eventually led to the apprehension of John Vassall, another Admiralty employee.' Who was right – the Tribunal or the head of the CIA?

Lord Carrington declared that he was first told that a spy might be operating in the Admiralty on 4 April 1962.

'Might be?' asked his counsel. 'Was there any doubt about the existence of a spy, wherever he was operating?'

'Yes,' replied Lord Carrington, 'there was.'

Now one would have thought that an alert First Lord would have immediately pressed for an all-out investigation. But Lord Carrington's statement was bland to the point of complacency: 'I was told the Security Service was beginning an investigation and that we were helping them.' Asked whether this investigation was under his direction or control, Lord Carrington added, 'No, this was the business of the Security Service, but the Admiralty Security Service would give every assistance they could.'

In fact Lord Carrington admitted that the first he knew that the spy had been identified was immediately after Vassall's arrest.

Much of the criticism launched both by MPs and the Press concerning the Vassall Affair and the Government's handling of it had been based on gossip (some of it highly malicious and inaccurate), third-hand information and intelligent guesswork which was not always correct. Thus a great deal of the Tribunal's time was devoted to shooting down the critics rather than concentrating on the more vital points. When their report was presented, MPs of all parties expressed considerable disquiet about both its revelations and its omissions. Mr Philip Goodhart, MP, who had been in Moscow in 1954–5 and visited the British Embassy on a number of occasions, made the interesting observation that 'it seemed there was no doubt on the part of everyone concerned that they were under siege and that every Russian or national behind the Iron Curtain they met was a potential spy.' He found it perplexing that more attention was not paid in the Embassy to the close contacts which Vassall had clearly had with the Soviet nationals.

In the House of Lords, Lord Walston referred to what he called 'gross inefficiency revealed at the British Embassy in Moscow' and revealed that this also occurred at other foreign centres. He told of a visit to a British military office in Berlin. 'I was impressed to see that the senior Army officer had two wastepaper baskets – an ordinary basket and the other marked "secret waste". I remarked on the increase in security since my last visit, but during the conversation a German civilian walked in with a large dustbin, picked up both baskets in the dustbin and took it out.'

Nor was this all. Lord Walston told of another experience when in the Foreign Office. His pass had expired and a document was sent to him giving notice that 'in no circumstances must this pass be sent out of the country', The Foreign Office had, however, sent the pass to him in Bulgaria!

It was not until June 1965 that the Security Commission published its report on its findings on recent spy cases. It noted that five of the six British subjects convicted of espionage since 1951 had passed information to a foreign power because they were able to remove classified documents from the buildings in which they were working. It should be stated that such uncaught spies as Burgess, Maclean and Philby did not come within the Commission's scope, which in itself made the report somewhat less than thorough. Nonetheless the Commission's consequent recommendation was that further consideration should be given to a system of spot searches of Civil Servants with access to top secret documents.

'More precise procedures should be worked out for the recording of documents which needed to be taken out of Government offices overnight,' the report stressed, 'as well as meetings during the day. We have been unable to think of any effective sanction for this purpose short of a right to search persons leaving buildings where classified material is kept.' Such a practice had been rejected by the Radcliffe Tribunal because, its members argued, 'it could never be wholly effective against a determined person; because it would be intolerable to those concerned; and because it would be resented by the staff and have a bad effect on staff relations.'

The Radcliffe Tribunal were quite prepared to see journalists go to jail for refusing to reveal their sources, yet they were unwilling to upset the Civil Service unions.

Sir William Hayter, the Ambassador who was in control in Moscow when Vassall was stationed there, produced his own book, *The Kremlin and the Embassy* in 1966. In it he said of Vassall, 'I remember him dimly as an obliging little figure who was useful at tea-parties. There was no excuse for him. If he had come to me or to the naval attaché, and told us that he was being blackmailed he could have been sent home at once without any opposition from the Soviet authorities. . . . Vassall's timidity or folly amounted to a crime and though I have always doubted whether he was really a useful source of Intelligence to the Russians, he certainly caused a great many people a great deal of trouble in the end.'

Following the publication of his book, Sir William, then Warden of New College, Oxford, was interviewed by the Press and he admitted that the Soviet Secret Service made three known attempts to blackmail British Embassy officials in Moscow between 1953 and 1957, but only that of Vassall succeeded. One must assume from this that at least one of these cases occurred prior to Vassall's arrival in 1954, which makes the Embassy's failure to see the security system was tightened up even more surprising. For Sir William admitted that Embassy people were 'constantly persecuted by Soviet Intelligence' and that 'we were obliged to act on the assumption that all our rooms were microphoned. Our servants were all believed to be spies.'

How could he seriously think the Russians would take so much trouble for so many years over Vassall if he was not a useful source of Intelligence?

When Vassall was sentenced he was first sent to Wormwood Scrubs where he was interrogated by Security men for six months. Many of these interviews centred on Vassall's repeated allegations that vulnerable practising homosexuals were serving in senior government posts, many with access to classified information. He also gave the names of two MPs (one of whom is today in the House of Lords) who were not only homosexuals, but friendly with Iron curtain country diplomats and officials.

John Vassall was released on parole from jail in October, 1972, having served ten of his eighteen years sentence. He had been a model prisoner, working first in the prison library and later in the canteen shop and at weekends devoting his time to a small garden plot. One of the ironies of his prison life was that, while in Durham Jail, before being finally transferred to Maidstone, he was, along with two other convicted spies – Frank Bossard and Henry Houghton – given the job of examining microfilm of ancient documents and extracting information to add to local records. During this period he had followed through his conversion to Catholicism by being confirmed by the late Cardinal Heenan. Today he lives quietly under an assumed name. After a spell in a Catholic monastery, where he wrote his autobiography, he took on research work for a City company.

Bibliography

Barron, John, *KGB* (Hodder & Stoughton, London, 1975).
Best, Sigismund Payne, *The Venlo Incident* (Hutchinson, London, 1950).
Chalmers, Johnson, *An Instance of Treason: Ozaki Hotzumi and the Sorge Spy Ring* (Stanford University Press, USA, 1964).
Cookridge, E. H., *Inside SOE* (Arthur Barker, London, 1966).
Deakin, F. W. & Storry, G. R., *The Case of Richard Sorge* (Chatto & Windus, London, 1966).
De Jong, Dr Louis, *De Duitse Vijfde Colonne in de Tweede wereldoorlog* (Amsterdam, 1953).
Farago, Ladislas, *The Game of the Foxes* (Hodder & Stoughton, London, 1972).
Hagen, Louis, *The Secret War for Europe* (Macdonald, London, 1968).
Hayter, Sir William, *The Kremlin & the Embassy* (Hodder & Stoughton, London, 1966).
Hyde, H. Montgomery, *The Quiet Canadian: the Secret Service Story of Sir William Stephenson* (Hamish Hamilton, London, 1962). *Cynthia: the Spy who changed the course of the War* (Hamish Hamilton, London, 1966).
Kahn, David, *The Codebreakers* (Weidenfeld & Nicolson, London, 1968).
Kirkpatrick, Sir Ivone, *The Inner Circle* (Macmillan, London, 1959).
Lampe, David, *The Last Ditch* (Cassell, London, 1968).
Masterman, Sir John Cecil, *The Double-Cross System in the War of 1939–45* (Yale University Press, London, 1972).
Meissner, Hans-Otto, *The Man with Three Faces* (Evans Bros., London, 1955).
Peis, Gunter, *The Mirror of Deception* (Weidenfeld & Nicolson, London, 1976).
Philby, Kim (H.A.R.), *My Silent War* (Grove Press, New York, 1968).
Poretsky, Elizabeth, *Our Own People: A Memoir of Ignace Reiss & His Friends* (Oxford University Press, London, 1969).
Schellenberg, Walter, *The Schellenberg Memoirs* (André Deutsch, London, 1956).
Seth, Ronald, *The Executioners* (Cassell, London, 1967).
Stevenson, William, *A Man Called Intrepid: The Secret War 1939–45* (Macmillan, London, 1976).
Trevor-Roper, Hugh, *The Philby Affair* (William Kimber, London, 1968).
Vassall, John: *Vassall: the autobiography of a Spy* (Sidgwick & Jackson, London, 1975).
Willoughby, Maj.-Gen. Charles A., *Shanghai Conspiracy: the Sorge Spy Ring* (E. P. Dutton, New York, 1952).

ALSO CONSULTED

The Report of the Tribunal appointed to Inquire into the Vassall Case & Related Matters (Cmd. 2009) (HMSO, London, 1963).

War Diaries of Abwehr II (Munich Institute of Contemporary History). (N.B. these diaries are not complete).

US House of Representatives, 82nd Congress, First Session: Un-American Activities Committee. *Hearings on Un-American Aspects of the Richard Sorge Spy Case* (Washington Govt Printing Office, 1951).

Russian Oppression in Ukraine: Reports & Documents (Ukrainian Publishers, London, 1962).

Murder International, Inc.: Murder and Kidnapping as an Instrument of Soviet Policy: Hearing before the Subcommittee to investigate the Administration of the Internal Security Laws of the Committee of the Judiciary, United States Senate (89th Congress, 1st Session, 26 March 1965).

Ukrainian Correspondence, edited by Yaroslaw Bentzal (Ukrainian Publishers, Munich).

Information – Scheft Grossbritannien, published by the *Rechtsicherheitshauptamt*, Berlin, for limited circulation only within the ranks of the Gestapo, Abwehr executives, 1940.

Files of *The Times*, *New York Times*, *Der Spiegel*, *Die Weltwoche* and *Pravda*.

Acknowledgements

The publishers would like to acknowledge their use of copyright material from the following publications: *The Venlo Incident* by Captain S. Payne Best, the Hutchinson Publishing Group Ltd 1950; *The Double-Cross System in the War of 1939–45* by Sir J. C. Masterman, © 1972 by Yale University. Crown Copyright reserved; *The Shanghai Conspiracy* by Major General Charles A. Willoughby, Western Islands, Calif. 1965; *Our Own People* by Elisabeth Poretsky, Oxford University Press 1969; *The Man with Three Faces* by Hans-Otto Meissner, Evans Brothers Ltd 1955; *Cynthia* by H. Montgomery Hyde, Hamish Hamilton Ltd 1966; *Vassall: The Autobiography of a Spy* by W. J. C. Vassall, Sidgwick & Jackson Ltd 1975; *My Silent War* by Kim Philby, Granada Publishing Limited; *The Schellenberg Memoirs* by Walter Schellenberg, André Deutsch 1967; *The Codebreakers* by David Kahn, Weidenfeld & Nicolson 1968; *The Game of Foxes* by Ladislas Farago, Hodder & Stoughton Limited 1972; *The Kremlin and the Embassy* by William Hayter, Hodder & Stoughton Limited 1966 by permission of John Farquharson Ltd; *A Man Called Intrepid* by William Stevenson, Macmillan, London and Basingstoke, Ltd 1972.

Picture Credits

Brown Brothers 81 (bottom); Central Press Photos 169 (bottom); Mrs Harold Dearden 110 and 111; Forman Archive 112; Gemeente Archief 's -Gravenhage 52 (bottom right), 55 (top); H. Montgomery Hyde 83 (top), 84 (bottom); Keystone Press 28, 81 (top), 82 (bottom), 113 (bottom), 145 (bottom), 168, 170 (bottom); Bridget Payne Best 52 (bottom left); Popperfoto 170 (top), 171 (top); Radio Times Hulton Picture Library 83 (bottom); Rijksinstituut voor Oorlogsdocumentatie, Amsterdam 52 (top right), 54 (top right and bottom), 55 (bottom); Stern Archiv 126, 144 (top); Süddeutscher Verlag 40, 52 (top left), 53, 54 (top left), 113 (top), 142, 143 (top), 144 (bottom); Syndication International 158, 169 (top), 171 (bottom); Ukrainian Publishers Ltd 143 (bottom), 145 (top).

Index